# Beyond Four Walls

## *The Untold Stories*

## Nenad Popovic

"Find a job you love
and you will never have to
work a day in your life"

*Confucius*

This book is dedicated to the memory of former students

Gary Roberts
David Wooton
Andy Poole
Andy Thompson
Nick Bates
John Gormley
Joe Hunt
Simon Davidson
Ben Houghton
Oisin Sweeney
Liam Keeling
Lee Collins WWFC

whose tragic deaths at an early age left a void in the lives
of so many people

# Prologue

Standing at the side of the room I couldn't help but smile. Seated rows of male students in the common room cheering and jeering. Five female students sitting at the back of the room not quite as engaged. This was my final presentation as entertainment's officer at the college … a 'gentleman's evening'.

The cheering and applause increased as Angel Starr approached a large Yorkshire lad known to all as Fives, removed his thick plastic spectacles and proceeded to refresh his pint of Worthington's with her left breast before gently placing his somewhat vacant face between her ample 'objects of desire'.

The smile was of relief. I had managed to turn around a proverbial cock-up with no financial liability to the college union.

I was less than forty-eight hours from the end of my three years at a College of Education, preparing for life as a teacher. For the past two years I served as the elected Entertainments Officer, catering for the different tastes of over a thousand students. I had turned a section of the Student Union previously haemorrhaging money into a self-sufficient unit, presenting iconic acts such as Status Quo, Slade and The Kinks at a minimal cost to students. I had organised internal events for both students and members of the local village, raising thousands of pounds for the long-running building fund.

This was not my finest hour… it was not how I had intended my tenure to end.

Earlier on that fateful Monday, a couple of days before the end my student life, I was enjoying a cheese toastie (a speciality of the adjoining café) in the sparsely populated common room when I was stopped mid-bite. A smug voice announced over the college Tannoy system "Pop to the union office, Angel Starr and Erotica await!" I ignored it. A wind-up, I thought. I continued eating. A second announcement a few minutes later assured me that they were *"still waiting"*.

The administrative assistant, Mrs E, an affable woman in her forties shook her head when I entered and cast her eyes towards the chairman's office with a wry smile. Paul, the chairman was sat on his desk, his eyes alive with humour behind his gold rimmed spectacles.

"These two lovely ladies are here to meet you Pop… I'll leave you to it, but I'll be back in fifteen minutes. Enjoy," his rolling Rochdale accent infused with the belly laugh that made him so popular.

Angel Starr was nearly six-foot tall with legs that were shaped like salad tongs. She was closer to forty than thirty with shoulder length hair and cheekbones that could cut you. She was wearing a long coat, worn open to reveal a leather mini-skirt and black boots with stacked heels. She was obviously in charge, standing over me to introduce herself and her colleague.

"I am Angel Starr and this is Erotica, we are your strippers for the night. The drag artist is on his way from Colchester and the comedian is coming from Norwich." A comedian from Norwich should have sent out the alarm bells. I looked across at Erotica, five feet tall, short hair and mid-twenties. Ribbed black polo top and silver hot-pants. Her face expressionless. I didn't ask her real name for fear of further disappointment. I was speechless.

Some months earlier I had been approached by some members of the rugby club about the possibility of a gentlemen's evening. I had explored various options but at £300 had decided that it was too expensive and had not returned a signed contract to the Agency. Angel produced a copy of the contract claiming that signed or not, it was a form of agreement. Should they perform or not, they would still be entitled to payment. There was no way out.

Leaving the ladies, assuring Mrs E that my pallor was due to surprise and not the need to vomit, I rushed to see Mr Challenor, the head of security to inform him that an unscheduled event was due to take place in the student common room that evening until 11.30 and that I would take responsibility for locking the two exit doors. Numerous late-night events had taken place previously without incident in this part of the building which was ideally situated at the very end of the college closest to the halls of residence. As a former officer in the Welsh Guards, I thought it best not to provide him with unnecessary details.

On my return to the office, I was informed that Angel and Erotica were now in my care! Being situated in a small village, I couldn't send them to the local inn as any word within the local community, many of whom were employed in various capacities at the college, would without doubt provide a major headache. They would have to stay with me at the halls of residence a short walk from the main buildings.

We descended the stairs to walk through the common room, which now amazingly, was heavily populated with smiling males throwing out the usual banter and a few perplexed females unsure who my "new friends" were. The jungle telegraph had been heavily in operation.

The walk along the path to the halls was no less eventful. My personal tutor (who fortunately I had helped to secure a job at my summer camp in the USA, and therefore owed me a favour or two) walked past me grinning... he didn't need to say anything. I tried to ignore the stare of a former girlfriend.

On arrival at the entrance to the halls, Jan the cleaner, who treated me like a son, was just leaving. In her early forties with a round and cheerful face she had lived in the nearby village all her life. Her two teenage children attended the school she herself had gone to. She was more village wise than street wise.

For the past year she had reminded me of important personal events such as birthdays and Mother's Day. Left reminders about meetings and early morning lectures on my desk and monitored the nights when I had not returned to read them. Jan was always available for a cup of tea and a chat. Sometimes she even brought biscuits. I exchanged college gossip for village gossip.

She looked at each of the women and then at me.

"I suppose these are friends visiting from Manchester," she said. "I've tidied your room." I didn't know if the look on her face was of disappointment or despair, but I had seen it once before.

When I was fourteen my Yugoslav mother, whose introduction to the English language was courtesy of the cotton mills of Stockport, had discovered a "packet of three" in my jacket pocket. She held them, between finger and thumb, in front of my face for an explanation. Disappointment in her eyes.

"Oh those," I said trying to hide my embarrassment, "...the barber gave them to me for a rainy day."

"So why he no give you an 'at?" she said before turning away in despair. Now Jan did the same. The halo was broken.

Word was passed around the College about the evening. No posters or flyers. £3.00 - pay on the door. It was a gamble. The only controversy was the five females who insisted as union members they were entitled to entry. To refuse could have resulted in a tense situation. I didn't want any protests or "sit-ins". If there was to be any repercussions they would arise by the end of the week, by which time I would be in the USA, enjoying my summer.

By 8.30 p.m., one hundred males had paid their dues. It was the appearance of the five females who made me smile. They ensured that the event returned a profit!

The few weeks leading up to the event had been hectic. The final teaching practice period of ten weeks had ended and the summer ball had been a great success. My attempts to return to Manchester to teach had all met with rejection, and my dreams of working in Cornwall had long been shelved, but I had secured a teaching contract for one year at a grammar school in Cannock, which was ideal as I hoped to eventually study in the United States.

Following a short interview at the school I was invited by Geoff the head of department to join the sixth-form outdoor activity session for the afternoon. The canoeing took place several miles away on the Shugborough Estate, home to the Earl of Lichfield. Without hesitation I changed into shorts and sweat-top and joined the group. Supervising fourteen responsible and capable youths with the sun beating down on the gentle flowing waters of the River Sow with the occasional sound of ducks was not far from paradise. My eyelids gently closed.

Big mistake.

When I "re-joined" the real world amidst total serenity I realised that my fellow kayakers had disappeared and so had my paddle. I scanned the immediate area but saw nothing and no one. The only option was to paddle by hand back to the base area. Twenty minutes later I reached the dock to muted applause and a smile from Geoff.

"What kept you?"

"I lost my paddle," I said, realising that he was holding it.

"You're lucky they wanted to tip you out, but I was concerned about Weils disease!"

"Oh, so you had my back then," I laughed. This was my kind of school.

****

Tuesday morning, my final day at teacher training college, began with a knock on the door at 8.45 a.m. followed by a motherly voice asking the all-important question... "Is it tea for one?" Jan had arrived early for work, with her first port of call being my top floor room to ensure I was "safe from harm". With a cup of tea and a chocolate digestive she listened as I explained everything, including Angel and Erotica leaving immediately after the show with the drag-artist. There was a hidden smile before she turned to leave.

"I'll give it three days before everyone in the village knows... and those that don't, I will tell 'em at the Pub!" she laughed.

It was the "get out of town" card, with a smile. Words of wisdom which were further endorsed in the main building of the college, where Mr. Challenor approached from behind his desk in reception as I tried to ghost into the dining room.

"How did the, uh-erm, *variety* show go last night?" he enquired, with a deliberate cough before expelling the word "Variety."

"Fine thanks... one of the breast we've ever had!" I replied with a smile.

Word was quickly spreading through the college. Time to leave. I sanctioned payment of the "artistes" and in between a meeting with my personal tutor and dinner I packed everything ready for a quick exit. I spent the night in the bar – a last drink with some of my friends, before a swift departure to Manchester early the following morning, leaving Jan with chocolates, a bottle of wine and assurances that there will be another student for her to mother next year.

# Chapter One

The eight weeks working in a summer camp in the Pocono region of Pennsylvania seemed to pass quickly with a growing reputation for my soccer expertise resulting in a significant bonus and an invitation to return the following year which fitted perfectly with my plans to study in the USA.

My final week in the United States was spent camping on Martha's Vineyard with Les, a close friend from college. With clear sunny skies and days on the beach my skin colour began to change from light tan to chestnut. So much so that on my return to Manchester my own mother walked past me on the street without recognising me!

A member of staff from the Grammar School had arranged accommodation in Rugeley, a short drive from the school for the sum of five pounds per week including bills so with few worldly goods, which included my Decca portable record player and a dozen LP's I moved again to Staffordshire.

Situated on the outskirts of the town, the bungalow was owned by a fellow PE teacher Ron, in his mid-thirties who was taking a year's sabbatical to study for a degree. I was provided with my own room and access to a spacious living area which had a sofa, a single armchair, coffee table, dining table and a television. Against one wall was a well-organised collection of books. Ron who was six foot three inches and a former County Rugby player, had amassed a collection of Timeform annuals for both flat and jump racing dating from 1960. To those uninitiated these books contained in alphabetical order, commentary on every horse to have raced on a track in the United Kingdom the previous year. It provided assessment of their performances with a numerical rating and information about their breeding and potential. They were Ron's pride and joy. No *real* racing enthusiast could exist without Phil Bull's articulate equine bible.

Adding to the mix was his father, Albert in his late sixties, who lived next door and who introduced himself the first Saturday morning at

7.30 a.m. with a delivery of newspapers. Once he discovered that I had an interest in horse-racing and greyhound racing he would burst into my bedroom every Saturday morning and throw a Sporting Life newspaper on the bed with the command – "get up Popski…time to study." This ritual would occur even when my girlfriend at the time was staying over. No filter for Albert. This was going to be an interesting year.

Jane the head of girls PE at the Grammar School lived in a nearby village with my bungalow on her route to school. She offered to provide me with a lift each day. On the first Monday in September, she arrived on time driving a racing green Austin Mini which made even my short legs feel cramped. The twenty - minute drive across Cannock Chase an area thick with forest was a delight, with little traffic and a terrain that reminded me of the summer camp I had just left. Following a short drive through civilisation with the pre-war detached houses giving way to post war council houses fronted by small, neat lawns, we turned left to see another sea of green, this time students in green blazers walking along the road and up the hill to the Grammar School a two-storey building which had looked out over the town centre since 1955.

The staff in the Physical Education department were both friendly and organised, which they had to be as the "office" was basically a boot/equipment room with a desk and phone at the far end next to a standard dark-green metal filing cabinet. Along one side was a large sink. I was unsure if this was for washing equipment or staff or both! There was only one electrical socket into which the kettle was permanently plugged resting like a trophy on top of the filing cabinet. Both sides of the room had wooden slatted shelves which held everything from cricket bags, hockey sticks and tennis rackets to footballs and rugby balls. Geoff welcomed me by my first name. Few people, including my mother, used my first name. It was often a sign that I was in trouble, hence the softer, shorter and more sociably acceptable Pop became the name of choice.

The male staff changing room, similar to many others at the time, comprised of a small space less than three square metres with a shower (rarely used) and a bench along a wall with pegs above. I was allocated two pegs. Several other pegs had a range of attire hanging from them. A couple of rugby shirts, a jock strap and some well-used baggy tracksuit bottoms. Below the bench was an array of footwear – a pair of huge muddy rugby boots which looked as though they had last been cleaned at the end of the sixties, some football boots and several pairs of trainers which appeared to have been abandoned or donated by former staff. In all it was a space limited to three people at any one time unless you were prepared to have someone's buttocks thrust into your face.

The school indoor sporting facilities were limited with a traditional gym twenty metres by twelve equipped with wall bars, beams, climbing ropes and two basketball rings. There was a small stand -alone twenty metre swimming pool. Outdoors, however, there was a vast playing field area shared with the local Secondary school which housed three rugby pitches and five football pitches with space to spare. To the side of the school were six tennis courts and a hockey pitch. The facilities were perfect for a Mediterranean climate, but this was Cannock. Plan for the best, be ready for the worst.

With all the students spending the first two hours with form teachers on that first day, Geoff, Jane and I sat down to go through the timetable. He removed a worn and faded piece of paper from the pin-board on the far wall of the "Office" and flattened it on the desk.

"This is last years, but it has been the same for the past five years so we can work off this for now."

From this opening comment by Geoff, I assumed all schools were the same. Organised, consistent and familiar. The discussion to decide who taught whom, when and where was concluded before my coffee was cold. No argument about facilities. The split was the same as the previous year and the year before that. Everybody was happy.

At the end of the meeting, I was handed the school fixtures for football, which I had agreed at interview to take overall responsibility for. Geoff then provided a list of staff who looked after the different age groups, two staff volunteers for every team except the incoming year. All I had to do was arrange the transport and ensure that all the equipment was ready and available on the Saturday mornings. Throughout the first twelve weeks there was a fixture every Saturday against schools from Wolverhampton, Rugeley and Stafford. I started at the bottom with the Under-12 team.

Before the end of the first week, Geoff and I were called into the head teacher's office. He had received a letter from the Director of Education regarding sporting fixtures.

"The Director has sent a letter to all schools stating that schools should seriously consider playing home fixtures only to reduce the costs incurred for transport. What do you think?"

"So, if teams are being advised against travel, who do we play?" I asked.

The head teacher looked at Geoff for a moment and then out of his window across the tennis courts contemplating a response, before turning swiftly and throwing the newly formed ball of paper into the nearby bin, at which time we both left. It was at this point that I first realised that those with their head in the clouds are often totally unaware of what is happening on the ground.

My first week was spent finding my feet, but what became increasingly obvious was that this was a "nice" school with pupils who were not only intelligent but cooperative and helpful. A thousand miles from the schools I had been placed in during my time at Madeley College.

Friday afternoon during that first week was a case in point. I had been told by Geoff that the head of English "always takes the football group" during the fifth-year games period and that I would take the hockey group.

"Don't worry they are mostly County players and will take care of themselves!" he said.

They did. Everything from an organised warm-up, short, structured practice to the game. I joined in - or at least, I ran up and down the pitch with a stick in my hand. My capabilities were exposed the first time I received a pass. However, they did humour me and tried to include me whenever possible. At least they didn't ask me to play in goal, the most brutal and damning of peer assessments.

It was a few weeks into my tenure that I met up with the sixth-form group who had been part of the induction at my interview. Every Wednesday afternoon during September and early October they would meet on the car park of a local tavern on the outskirts of the town which had several wooden benches on a grassed area with pathways leading directly from the car park onto Cannock Chase. The group would then engage in orienteering in the extensive woodland nearby. They would usually start arriving by 1.00 p.m. for a 1.30 start.

Roy was always one of the first to arrive, usually in a car with a couple of friends which he parked on the car park. They were always affable and would often come over to reveal all the local news from the past week. One day the topic was cars and the fact that I didn't have one. (I failed to tell them that I couldn't drive!)

"Show him your keys Roy," one of the group said, at which Roy took out a chain of keys. There was an array of differing keys, silver and brass, large and small.

"These will get into most cars on this car park," Roy said. "I use them at the weekend when I work at a garage."

I looked at him with a certain disbelief.

"So, I could have any car I wanted," I laughed, rising from my bench and walking into the Tavern to relieve myself before the start of the event.

When I came out and returned to the bench where the rest of the group had now gathered, I could see a few of them smiling. I looked around and did a double take. A car, which had been parked near to the bench, had moved from one side of the car park directly opposite to the other and was now parked next to Roy's car. I looked at him and he just smiled. It was time to leave.

The last of the runners was about to set off as a young couple exited from the Tavern and walked slowly over towards the now empty space before stopping short. Bemused. They stood in silence for a few moments. He rubbed the back of his head for inspiration, before using both hands in an animated discussion. It was at this point that they both simultaneously realised that the car had not been stolen but had "moved." I was unaware of what was being discussed but if the hand gestures were an indication, it would no doubt have been firstly, how the vehicle had moved and secondly how it had done so uphill. It was time for a rapid exit towards the finish of the course.

Wednesday was a good day on my timetable with a third-year class from 9.00 a.m. till 10.00 a.m. in the gym. Whenever you move to a school this year group are pivotal. At 13 and 14 years of age they are at the cross-roads with experience of the system and a desperate desire to be recognised. If you can relate to them the next three years is a dream. They will always be on time; they will always have their kit (or borrow some prior to the lesson); they will cooperate and will repay your enthusiasm many times over. They set the tone for the younger years. If you do not establish a connection, it can be a struggle.

My class had a mix of little and large. They had some talented individuals but most of all they were enthusiastic and would take to any sport I introduced and developed. They were the ones who attended the dinner time clubs in basketball and volleyball. They were the ones who would never fail to represent the school when selected or volunteer at short notice if a player was unavailable. Dependable and reliable. They also had the capacity to empathise.

Ron's younger brother was studying for a doctorate at Aston University in Birmingham but would pick me up on alternate Tuesdays to explore the bars and clubs of the City, returning usually sometime after midnight, though on a couple of occasions it extended to the early hours due to parties or events at the University. One Wednesday following a party I was feeling deflated. My head was sore and I felt knackered. The basketball lesson with my group of stars involved attacking play, and every time the basketball hit the wooden floor when they dribbled it had the effect of a small hammer striking my temples. One of the students, Sivvy, realised my distress and immediately stepped in to structure the game – no dribbling or calling for the ball, instead hand signals were used. It was the quietest lesson ever, and I think I may even have had a cheeky ten-minutes dozing.

Many years later I was able to recall the lesson with fellow PE teachers stating how the objective of the lesson *"the importance of eye contact in attacking play using the heuristic approach"* was achieved. Manure of the finest calibre.

Every teacher must undergo a probationary year before they are qualified, with an external assessor reviewing their competence to teach. My one and only visit coincided with my Wednesday morning class with the assessor impressed by the "class control, organisation and progress of students." Sometimes you just get lucky!

When I was at college the head of faculty Sam Heafield addressed the whole of the year group regarding the process of applying for positions in schools or colleges and expectations once employed. Part of the session included some unexpected advice.

"Gentleman! Once employed in any school there are two members of staff who will have a major impact on your performance and development. Not your long-term career, but the day-to-day work with children in your care. They are the caretaker and the cook! Engage with them immediately and your welfare is guaranteed. Disregard them at your peril."

It was an almost Churchillian statement, but one that was to prove one of the most useful and pertinent during my career. The caretakers, who lived on the school site, would throughout the course of any year be disturbed by the Physical Education teacher more than any other, either on Saturday morning or in the evening on returning late from a fixture. If they said no, even the headteacher would have difficulty changing a decision. The head cook is self-evident as all have a motherly instinct. With a little nurture they will treat you as part of their extended family.

The Grammar School had a caretaker, Gordon and an assistant Ted. Gordon was five feet tall and of stocky build and Ted was six feet four inches and thin as a pole. Visually they were comic book material. One could paint skirting boards and the other could change light bulbs! They did, however, have a dry sense of humour. One thing I had developed during my time at Madeley was the ability to enjoy banter without feeling offended. Be prepared to laugh at yourself before you laugh at others has always been my mantra.

Whenever the duo was together, they would go into their routine, always finding something to fix on about me or the department and have the craic. On one occasion I was a little late for my lunch and I ran down a short corridor and around a corner, leaping the five steps in athletic style. However, in doing so I hit my forehead on the sloping ceiling landing in a heap at the bottom of the steps. The group of sixth-form girls in the hallway were not impressed with several laughing and others looking on in amazement. Gordon and Ted seemed to appear from thin air. The would-be Hobbit had the broadest of smiles

"Christ Gordon that's dangerous." I said still sat on the floor.

He looked up at Ted and with a hint of self-satisfaction and amusement before looking down at me.

"Well, it's never happened to me," he said, before offering a helping hand.

The small egg-shape on my forehead kept them amused for several days. The plus side was that the kitchen staff felt obliged to increase the portions to aid my recovery, and the school meals, which were free to the Physical Education Department were sensational. Often a roast meat with potatoes and vegetables plus a pudding…apple crumble a speciality.

From Monday to Friday, I delivered lunch-time clubs which would usually end 15 minutes before the afternoon session began and 55 minutes after the start of lunch. Very often I was one of the last in the queue for meals. Mary was one of the cooks, working alongside Irene, who in later life I learnt was the mother of Brian Horton who played over five hundred games in professional football and managed Manchester City. Mary was small and at times a stern looking individual who ran the kitchen with impeccable authority. However, as a new grandmother she had an obvious weakness, her granddaughter. On certain occasions when I over-ran the club and a stream of young lads arrived at the close of lunch, I would engage Mary in conversation about the new baby, much to her delight and mine as it saved me from a rollicking about timekeeping.

It was not just Mary I had conversations with. I had noticed other teachers just picking up their meals and breezing through not only without a word but with no eye contact with the canteen staff. Being young, single and active, this was my main meal of the day, and I was determined to make the ladies preparing and serving the meals feel valued. They were an essential part of my life. From throw-away comments to extended conversations I was always prepared to stop and talk.

They in turn would go the extra-mile by ensuring that I always had a substantial meal. Usually, towards the end of lunchtime the selection becomes limited, with the prime choices quickly disappearing. However, Mary would always reach under the counter to produce my plated meal covered by a metal dome with the widest selection of vegetables and choicest cut of meat or pie. Embarrassingly on more than one occasion the head-teacher glanced at my meal and then his with a mixture of curiosity and envy.

Six weeks into my teaching career, Geoff asked if I would like to earn some extra money. Having just received my first pay cheque of £120.00 I was all ears. It transpired that from October through to April, two of the local Secondary schools without a swimming pool would use ours on a Monday night from 5.30 through till 7.00 p.m. I would be paid £3.00 for the session. It was not an issue for me as there was a bus to Rugeley leaving at 7.15 from the nearby bus-station and the extra cash would be very welcome.

For several weeks it went well. One school would arrive at 5.20 accompanied by a member of staff for their forty-minute session and the second school would arrive at 6.10. I would specialise in teaching the swimmers with little ability. The groups were noisy but enthusiastic and they were certainly a different breed to the students I worked with. The Staff were also different. They seemed more student-centred; they would have the banter and were more down-to-earth. They seemed to be giving their time to ensure that their students were not missing out.

I would change out of my Fred Perry and shorts into my travel home attire at the change-over period, ready for my quick exit to the bus-station. A perfect arrangement. Complacency, as any sportsman will tell you is an ever-present threat. Ready to make you look a donkey without any warning.

Dave was a twelve-year old in my second group, who for the past few weeks had worked hard to overcome his fear of water and learn to swim. Now was his greatest test. With the pool cleared and the other participants changing Dave was going to attempt to swim across the pool without aids for the first time. He hesitantly let go of the side and with a flurry of action began to wave his arms and kick his legs. Go Dave go! Suddenly at half-way it all stopped.

"Just stand on the bottom Dave!" I shouted. It was then I realised that he was quite short and unable to touch the bottom with his feet. What was beginning to touch the bottom was the rest of his body. The rescue pole was at the far end to the pool so without hesitation I jumped into the water fully clothed, my watch flying off in a different direction, and scooped him up under my arm to carry him to the side.

He looked tearful, not because of the experience, but because of the failure to swim the width. He kept apologising.

"Dave, it's not your fault. I should have helped you more, and I will next time. You made a great effort and that's important so don't think you have failed. You only fail if you don't make the effort."

He went to change, seemingly with no ill effects and his ego intact. With the pool being detached from the school, I had no access to any other clothing other than my shorts and Fred Perry. Retrieving the coins from my trousers and with an Adidas wet top for protection from the developing rain I ran for the bus just in time to see it pull away into the distance. To make matters worse the next bus was in two hours.

Sometimes you just want to hide. Sat in a local pub in late January sockless, in shorts and a tennis shirt with half a pint of lager and a packet of crisps does not enhance your street credibility. I looked for the remotest table and some warmth. It was one of the longest two-hours of my life.

It was a lesson to be learned. Plan for the best, expect the worst.

There was pay back from Dave many times over. A few weeks later and without the aid of a pole which I held close to me for reassurance (his and mine) he completed his width swim, much to his delight. Several years later, still only counter-high, smart and well-groomed, he would often amble over in a bar whenever I was in the company of a female and recall the story.

"This is the man who saved my life!" was his opening line, giving me a broad smile which more or less said sit back and enjoy the adulation, before recapping the events of the night and leaving me to bask in the warm after-glow of admiration from my companion. The basic story never changed, only the depth of water.

My training to become a Physical Education teacher was comprehensive and delivered by experts in a variety of sports from boxing and fencing to volleyball and water polo. All aspects of child development and physiology were covered in depth. However, there was one issue that was never mentioned and would have a recurring impact during my career.

Gary was a member of my star third year group. He was compact but athletic and was always the first into the gym or out onto the field. Beneath his blonde fringe was a smile which seemed to be permanent. Even when a player got the better of him, which was not very often, he would smile with the confident assurance that it wouldn't happen again.

He was a bright, enthusiastic and intelligent games player who was a "dream" to teach. With any new sport he would listen and process information, adapting it to his strengths of coordination, quick feet and guile. He was a permanent fixture at every club and in every team. He was the go-to student if an older group suddenly found they were short of a player. He would never let anyone down.

On one occasion a first XI fixture against Royal Wolverhampton Grammar School was scheduled for Saturday afternoon. With only eleven players available I asked him to be a reserve and attend. A particularly brutal rugby match in the morning reduced the squad by three and it was suggested rather than postpone the game that I play to help reduce the imbalance. Forming a midfield partnership with Gary and an older student Neil, we managed to remain competitive for much of the game creating several chances before conceding two goals in the final ten minutes of the game. What was evident was the manner in which the fourteen-year-old breezed through the game with subtle touches and purposeful passes. Always in a position to receive the ball. Often demanding it.

On the Saturday morning in March when he failed to appear for a football fixture, I knew something was wrong. I didn't feel disappointment, I felt concern. Only on Monday morning was I made aware that Gary the boy with the smile and limitless enthusiasm had fallen at home and suffered a fatal head injury. For the first time in my life, I was faced with the death of someone I really cared for. This was not just a student but someone I had a special bond with, someone who made me feel good and someone who deserved the best of life. It was like losing a family member.

I was numb. Throughout that day I taught lessons but remembered little. Wednesday morning was even worse. A void which was obvious both before, during and after the 9.00 a.m. lesson. I had never considered the situation, and I didn't know how to deal with it. Had I become too attached? Should I leave some distance to reduce potential disappointment or hurt?

The answers were provided not by a colleague or a psychologist but by an electrician in Manchester. John Collins had been a football referee who then joined the very successful football team for which I played in during the mid-sixties. He had been a steadying influence during my turbulent school years. Whenever needed I would seek his counsel, knowing that the advice received would be simple and thoughtful. He was never judgemental but always honest.

"You are dealing with performers and if you want to succeed you have to invest time and energy. You must show them you care about them before they will care about you. And that is why you felt how you did. You cared."

Not perhaps a great philosophical statement, but one that gave me the re-assurance I needed and reminded me that the teachers I responded to most during my school days were those who cared.

"You cannot teach someone to swim without getting wet yourself. There will be many highs and a few disappointments. You cannot have one without the other."

John went on to enjoy over thirty years working with Manchester City in various support positions and was a mentor to many young players as they passed through their highly successful junior system. It did not prevent those disconsolate moments when I thought about Gary; stealing the ball from me in basketball; playing those delicate and inventive passes in football. The energy, the enthusiasm, the character. A life full of potential sadly ended.

What it did do was reassure me that my feelings were natural and of the inevitability that sometime in the future it would occur again.

****

Throughout the first year of teaching, I would often travel to Madeley College on Saturday afternoon to enjoy the rest of the weekend with my girlfriend at the time, Chris, who was in the year below me when I attended the College. This weekly journey started in mid-September when the students returned and continued throughout the year. Several of my friends had stayed for a fourth year and the security staff assumed I was in their cohort.

Colleges had a differing structure to universities with all meals provided free of charge to students and the meals at Madeley were exceptional. I enjoyed a three-course meal every Saturday night, followed by some great bands or a disco and subsidised beer. Breakfast on Sunday morning was five-star and the Sunday roast was to die for. It was worth the inconvenience of hitch-hiking from Rugeley to Madeley each week.

This was a time when all students without transport (probably the large majority), would hitch-hike around the country, with motorists and lorry-drivers often prepared to stop and give lifts in return for conversation. Once during my travels, I was given a lift by the legendary footballer Tom Finney for part of his homeward journey to Preston. The wait for a lift was rarely longer than thirty minutes.

Sometimes you hit the jackpot. The right place at the right time. One Saturday in October during the second stage of my journey to Madeley, a car stopped to give me a lift. Mike was a resident of the village near to the College. During the ensuing conversation he mentioned that the Sunday team he played football for at nearby Keele University was lacking a goalkeeper. I volunteered to play the following day providing he could give me a lift to and from the game and some boots.

Sunday 9.45 my lift arrived on the road outside halls, and I played my first game (under an assumed name). I saved a penalty, and the team won only their second game of the season. They asked me to sign for the season. Following a discussion with Mike I agreed and for his part he would transport me from the village to the A34 exit out of Newcastle each Sunday night for my return journey home to Rugeley. The team managed to win several more games and reach a semi-final during my time with them.

All good things must come to an end and for me it was in May 1974 when Mr. Challenor, a former officer in the Welsh Guards and now head of security at Madeley College approached me with a raised eyebrow.

"Pop, just the man. I happened to look at the list of fourth year students yesterday and failed to see your name on it. Expediate?"

"I found the course demanding and difficult. I couldn't seem to find the right direction," I said with a smile.

"Now that's where I can help," he said putting his arm over my shoulder in a fatherly fashion. He raised his left hand and pointed down the hallway.

"That is the way to the dining hall for students; students registered at this college." Then he swiftly turned me to my right. "And that is the way to cheese toasties for non-students. So, I think that covers your concerns about your future direction."

At that, he walked away shaking his head, before turning with a wry smile and a salute.

My application to undertake a master's degree in education at Westchester College had been accepted and details of a full scholarship approved in return for soccer coaching and playing. With my girlfriend Chris having returned home for Easter, I was more than happy to spend a morning with Roy at the local car auction as he sorted through a collection of cars that would suit my needs for the final three months of my UK residency. He settled on a beige Mini van. When I opened the back door there were gaps in the floor and a couple of big holes by the wheel arch.

"It looks a wreck!" I said.

"Don't worry, the engine's fine and the tyres have got enough tread on them for six or seven thousand miles, so unless you're planning to transport house furniture to Cornwall it will be good."

We were one of two bidders for the van, and we were successful - the hammer came down at twenty-five pounds. Roy agreed to drive the van to his garage for some basic work and would drop it off at my house in Rugeley once completed. Just before leaving he told me about his uncle's horse, which was running later in a hurdles race at a northern track. The family had all been encouraged to back it.

When I returned to Rugeley, my housemate Ron was sitting motionless on the settee, studying the form as he had done for the previous twenty weeks.

"I've just bought a Mini van," I said. He remained unmoved and focused on the Sporting Life and the open pages of Timeform.

"Roy told me his uncle has a horse running this afternoon in a hurdle race and it's strongly fancied to win. He has told everyone to back it." Now Ron moved. He shuffled in his chair and looked across the room.

"Ronson Avenue. Martin Tate trains it." I said,

Ron looked in the newspaper and casually called out, "It's eight-to-one."

"I'm not bothered about the price; the horse can't read. Has it got a chance?"

Following some frantic activity over a five-minute period Ron looked up from the book and said with a smile, "Yes."

"In that case put a fiver each-way on for me on your account," and I handed him the remains of the money I had from the auction.

Later that afternoon you could hear my shouts in the town centre as the heavily backed Ronson Avenue pulled away to land one of the gambles of the season. Ron produced my sixty pounds return within minutes of the finish (almost like a professional bookmaker – no quibble). I am unsure how much he had bet on the horse, other than he let me have a rent-free month.

Sometimes things fall into your hands when you least expect. The key is to be ready and grateful.

The week before the May Bank holiday, I received notification from Westchester that following a review of the scholarships they could only cover forty per-cent of my fees, the remaining $5,000 would be my responsibility, though they could arrange for some paid work in a local restaurant and provide an allowance for me to mentor freshmen. I needed another sixty Ronson Avenues. My American dream was over. I needed to look for another job in the UK staring from September.

Every Thursday night, a group of teachers from the Rugeley area would meet for a drink at the Horns, a pub on the outskirts of the town. There was a small group of regulars, supplemented by the occasional appearances of other teachers all with an interest in sport. One of the teachers, Vic, had not attended for several weeks but was out on this particular evening - celebrating his appointment that afternoon at the High School nearby as Head of Physical Education. I discovered that Vic had once worked at a summer camp close to the area I was familiar with in Pennsylvania and that he later worked at an Indian reservation in Canada teaching English for a year. I told him of my disappointment with the Masters.

"Why don't you apply for my job at the Catholic School in Cannock? You already know some of the staff," he said. "I am handing in my resignation tomorrow morning, which means that the job will not be advertised until after the holidays in early June and the only people eligible to apply would be those leaving university or college. They would be untried. You have experience and are qualified."

This was one of the schools where I taught swimming. The staff were friendly and the kids lively but enthusiastic. This could be the answer, I thought.

The following morning, I received a call from Vic. He had explained the situation to his headteacher who then contacted the Grammar School for a reference. I was released for the afternoon for an informal meeting. I decided to walk to the school rather than arrive in style in a battered Mini van with more rattles than Mothercare. I had a short meeting with the headteacher and a couple of staff. He showed me plans for the development of a sports hall (which was currently under construction), to be followed by a centre for performing arts. It all looked good.

Within an hour of my arrival, I had agreed to meet the Chair of Governors on Whit Monday for a formal interview. When you are on a roll you need to go with it.

My interview was conducted by a panel of two, the Monday being a bank holiday. The headteacher introduced me to Father Daly an elderly parish priest. Following the initial introductions and formalities he noticed that I was from Manchester. He had spent a significant amount of time in the city as an engineer before entering the priesthood. Things then began to fall into place. He had worked for many years at B&S Massey a huge engineering works which supplied a major train building facility nearby. A significant part of his life had been spent in the very district in which I grew up and where my family home had been since 1951 and where many of his former co-workers lived.

We spent much of the time ignoring the attempts of the headteacher to ask educational questions, with me providing Father Daly with developments in the area over the past twenty-five years. A past with enduring memories. The terraced houses, pubs on every corner, street parties.

Eventually, the headteacher managed to interrupt and offered me the job as Head of Department starting in September. He then began to refer to salary.

"What are your expectations?" he said.

They needed me, so taking a calculated risk and in a quietly confident manner I replied,

"If I am doing the same job as the outgoing member of staff, then I would expect to be placed on his salary scale."

The headteacher almost choked. I could see the look of disbelief. Before he had a chance to think of any reason not to award me the pay scale I jumped in with a compromise.

"Why don't you give me six months trial and then if you are happy promote me to the pay scale."

They both agreed and I signed on the dotted line to begin a new chapter in September 1974.

# Chapter Two

Three hours west of New York city is the town of Honesdale. Situated close to the Pocono region of Pennsylvania with its hills, forest, rivers and over a hundred and fifty lakes, the largest being the man-made thirteen-mile-long Lake Wallenpaupack.

The town itself, with a population just over three-thousand relied heavily on the numerous summer camps that surrounded the area and in winter months for visitors to the region to ski. It had two parallel streets about a half-mile in length. Main Street housed stores and small shops on both sides of the road, with the Hotel Wayne at the northern end of town at the junction with Route 6, the site of the only traffic signals in the town. Church Street had a mix of residential dwellings with manicured frontages alongside both offices and notable historic buildings including the Allen House, the Courtrooms and Central Park.

Like many of the small towns in the United States they were proud of their history, being the home of the Stourbridge Lion, the first steam locomotive in the United States. Built in 1826, the great engine hauled coal from the region to Honesdale, before onward transportation, by canal, to New York. In many ways, the area of Honesdale mirrored Cannock Chase – outstanding natural beauty and the embers of a once extensive coal industry.

Camp Towanda was situated eight miles north on Niles Pond Road, surrounded by forest with a secluded lake. For eight weeks every summer it was home to nearly two hundred children aged 5 to 15 years, mainly from New York, Long Island or New Jersey. They migrated from the cities to enjoy sport, the arts and "the simple things" in a safe and familiar environment.

I first arrived in the town on a Wednesday afternoon in June 1972, disembarking from a Trailways bus at Steve's Diner on Main Street with my two mates from College Les and Ian. Having departed from Port Authority in New York at midday with its frantic stream of people rushing to be some place five minutes ago and the yellow cabs darting through the lines of traffic like some choreographed dance routine, each with their own sonic fingerprint, we were now in a totally different world. A world where you could cross the street without fear of a collision with steel; a world where the sound of silence was as welcome as the warm sun, free of concrete obstruction; where people stopped to talk to others and the few vehicles or trucks cruised down Main Street at the speed of a Blackpool donkey.

We had been recruited to work at Camp Towanda for eight weeks during the summer through an organisation, Camp America, who placed students in various camps throughout the United States. The package included trans-Atlantic return flights and two nights of accommodation in New York. We received food, accommodation and laundry for the entire period, with a total of six days off and upon completion we would receive thirty-five dollars! At the time it was equivalent to about twenty pounds. It wasn't about money. It was about opportunity and adventure. The chance to see America.

I called the camp office from the phone at the entrance to Steve's Diner to tell them of our arrival and then sat down with Les and Ian at a booth with a glass of Coca Cola slowly digesting the songs available on the mini jukebox attached to the window whilst listening to John Denver singing "Take me Home Country Road". It seemed an appropriate introduction.

Within thirty minutes a gold and brown truck with the camp logo on the side door pulled up outside the Diner. No body exited the truck, just a lone figure behind the wheel growled:

"You t'ree limeys ger in the back." We did not wait for a formal introduction.

The driver we later discovered was called George and was the camp caretaker. In his early fifties he had a face lined with age, grey stubble, teeth set like gravestones and hair that looked as though it had been cut with a knife and fork. He had huge hands that had obviously worked extensively on the land for much of his life. He was a man of few words preferring to convey his emotions through his eyes. When he did talk it was through the side of his mouth. He rarely appeared happy. On the one occasion I met his wife I understood why. Millie had all the charm of liquid nitrogen. Though of medium height, George was not the type of person to upset or offend.

The final part of the journey was along a bumpy lane with trees on one side and cleared land and fields on the other with an occasional barn that had seen better days appearing without warning, usually accompanied by some abandoned farm machinery at various stages of decay.

The Camp was situated on a hill with the entrance to the right. A well- constructed drive climbed past a long two-storey building on the left facing the road, which in earlier days looked as though it may have been a large main house, towards the Office which was adjacent to the home of the owner. The Health Centre was directly opposite with rustic chairs and a table on the lawn to the front. Everywhere looked pristine, an impressive introduction for those arriving for the first time.

George threw our bags from the truck and then left without a word. We had obviously interrupted his day. One of the co-owners, Sam Norden, was more welcoming. Sat on a white rock he was one of those few people who appear smaller when they stand. He beckoned us over and introduced Bill Alexander, the camp chef. At six feet four inches and weighing two-hundred and thirty pounds, Bill had arms that could wrestle a bear, but he had a smile that could melt an iceberg. It was the start of a long and valued friendship with one of the most affable and genuine individuals I have ever known.

The camp itself was divided into an upper camp for boys and a lower camp for girls. The upper camp consisted of fifteen cabins built in a rectangle around a grass-area about sixty yards long and thirty yards wide and the lower camp twelve cabins built in an oval.

Each of the cabins had beds or bunks for up to twelve people, including two adult counsellors and bathroom facilities at the back of the building. There was no heating. Each camper was responsible for making their own bed each day after breakfast and a rota was established for various tasks from sweeping the bunk to cleaning the bathroom or outside patrol.

The indoor facilities included a large hall with wooden benches of various sizes and a stage. A smaller hall, used for religious services, roller hockey and gymnastics was situated next to an Arts and Craft block. Both halls had an upright piano. The canteen was impressive. A long and well-equipped facility to cater for more than two-hundred and eighty people in one sitting. The kitchen, Bill's pride and joy, was run with military precision.

Outdoor sporting areas included six tennis courts, three with floodlights, a large basketball court with lights and two smaller ones. There was a soccer pitch which was surrounded by a dirt running track which had four 90 degree turns. There were three softball diamonds and a couple of volleyball courts, a nature shack, an archery and a shooting range.

Across the road from the main camp a pathway led down through the forest to the lakefront and the boathouse. The lake about a mile in length and half that in width was quiet and secluded. There were three docked swimming areas with a water-ski launch pad to the right. To the left of the dock in a large area was a fleet of small sailboats, mainly sunfish, some Canadian canoes, kayaks and a couple of rowboats.

The whole area looked organised and ready for the eight-week invasion.

In that first year the eight-week session seemed to start slowly, but once inter-camp competitions began and visiting day was over it seemed to fly by. With only a handful of Brits in the camp we were a novelty and all the American counsellors and staff seemed to go out of their way to make us feel at home with lifts into town and organised events for our days off.

Sam Ettinger was a co-owner of the camp. A former distinguished head teacher nearing his eightieth birthday he was always approachable and friendly. However, his memory was in decline. He would put his arm across a camper's shoulder whilst gently rolling back their collars to see the name tag displayed before speaking to them. A grand-father figure with over two-hundred children to remember. For the first four weeks he called me Michael, having rolled back the collar of my Marks and Spencer tennis shirt on one occasion and seen that name. It was only after Visiting Day that he called me over to his porch.

"Why do they call you Pop and not Michael?" he enquired.

It was only then that I had the heart to tell him the truth.

"The tag on my tennis shirts is St. Michael and is the brand of the shirt, not my name. Pop is short for my surname."

He smiled, shook his head and walked away towards the office.

It was on visiting day that my celebrity status was cemented. This was the one day, usually after four weeks that parents and grandparents were allowed to visit for the day, often bringing gifts galore for their children. Arriving from 10.00 a.m. in a cavalcade of expensive and elegant vehicles from Rolls Royce to Cadillacs, dressed more for Royal Ascot than a rustic camp setting they took residence at various points around the grassed areas. They occasionally ventured to meet people deemed as "significant" by the camper. These would often be a prime specialist coach or their counsellor. During the day I was introduced to dozens of mothers and grandmothers, some accompanied by campers who I had no connection with, either through soccer or age group activities. Some returning for a second visit. It was a sweet Jewish lady in her sixties who took me gently by the elbow:

"Just keep talking," she said, "They are blowing a fuse over your accent." She then stood back. A crooked smile and a knowing wink of the eye, admiring the show. Before the end of the day, I had received multiple invites to stay at various homes in New York and New Jersey at the end of camp before flying back to England.

The weeks after visiting day seemed to pass quickly with inter-camp soccer tournaments for various age groups. Through a little organisation and some tailored practice sessions we managed to win three tournaments for boys and girls, with the campers responding well to the "guided approach" against the highly charged competitive drive that appeared to be in the DNA of the American counsellors and coaches.

On the penultimate day of camp, myself, Les and Ian were asked to meet with Lynne and Sam, the active co-owners responsible for all aspects of finance and maintenance. It was agreed that I should talk on our behalf regarding our return the following year. We already knew that a couple of other British girls had been paid $125 for the same work as they had been placed through a non-profit organisation called BUNAC. We agreed to organise our own travel and visa arrangements and it was suggested that I ask for $400 plus travel, but $300 would be acceptable. We also held an ace in that a camp director at a rival had made an approach for our services during a visit to his camp for a counsellor basketball game.

The first few minutes laid the foundation. Lynne spoke, Sam said nothing. They were extremely impressed with our commitment and professionalism and the overall response of the campers; the feedback from the Head Counsellor and parents plus the progress made by the campers in soccer. With each sentence there was a tariff.

"We would love to have all three of you back next year if that's possible," said Lynne.

"We've really enjoyed our time here," I said. "However, as you know the three of us have all worked at a significant loss this year and to return, we would need $1,600 each which will cover salary and travel." Les looked pale, Ian looked astounded, both were speechless.

With minimal hesitation Lynne nodded her head and agreed, commenting that it was a "fair request."

On that note we shook hands and I turned to my smiling buddies having negotiated a near five thousand percent rise!

By the summer of 1974 I was an established figure at the camp, recruiting Eddie Robinson (Athletic Director from my college) and a couple of other counsellors from the United Kingdom. I was not only the head soccer coach but also the counsellor for a second year to a group of nine-year olds, some of whom had been at camp longer than me. In the previous year one of the lads, Glenn, had been encouraged by his parents to lose some weight. Through a little discipline, some morning jogs together and continual engagement in sporting activity, he managed to lose fourteen pounds by the end of camp. Unfortunately, his reward on his return home was unlimited pizza and an accumulation of weight. Asked to repeat the regime for a second year I declined. It was unfair on Glenn, though he did take far more personal responsibility for his well-being, no mean feat for a nine-year old.

This group were a dream, with three or four in my soccer team which won the Wayne County soccer tournament. Richie, then aged nine but in his fourth year at Camp had a greater understanding of camp rules than most and would often keep me informed of anything about to happen that I should be aware of. He was to be the first of many, both at camp and in school who would remind me of events, procedures and in many cases initiate tasks for me to complete. They had my back. Their contribution was priceless.

Being an established counsellor also enabled me to borrow a car from the owners which gave me access not only to the local town and its three watering holes, but also Monticello Raceway. The Raceway was about an hour from camp across the New York State line. It was a large and popular venue for nightly harness racing with superb viewing facilities. With numbers attending the racing dwindling, the owners decided to add other attractions A new night-club facility with a state-of-the art disco was opened for post-racing entertainment and during the summer months a series of concerts before racing were presented to attract a younger audience. Along with eight other counsellors we attended the first of the concerts on our day off, seeing Frankie Valli and the Four Seasons for a couple of dollars entry fee.

Counsellors were on duty until 9.00 p.m. every night, after which they were free until a curfew at midnight. Some would venture into town where there was a couple of bars, a bowling alley and a Diner, whilst others would remain on camp to play basketball, table tennis or just chill.

Occasionally a counsellor was given the night off, which relieved him or her of all duties after dinner. Usually this was from 6.30 p.m. At those times it was possible to get to see the concerts at Monticello which usually started at 7.30 p.m. Having been given the night off, I found a couple of other British counsellors who were free and keen to see Chubby Checker at the Raceway. One included a friend from College, Tony who was at camp for the first time.

Using the owner's Buik I drove to the raceway, only slowing to explain and point out Yasgur's Farm as we passed through Bethel. In August 1969, the farm had secured a place in music history as the site for the Woodstock Music Festival. Originally expected to attract 15,000 people, the three-day event attracted almost half a million people, with cars abandoned at the side of the road up to ten miles from the venue.

After Bethel, the highway begins to widen and at the turn for the raceway is an eight-lane carriageway. I signalled to turn left into the entrance, but for a split second I seemed to forget that we were in the USA and turned left without a thought. It was only the scream from Tony, my front seat passenger which made me swing the steering wheel to straighten the car as two oncoming vehicles split either side of us. It was like an episode of Keystone Kops.

I must admit Chubby Checker was not a disappointment, though Tony appeared to be unusually quiet and still for the hour's concert. A "near death experience" affects people in different ways, I guess. He was not very talkative on the way home either.

Another newcomer was Henrich Van der Wettering, a six-feet four-inch Dutchman with a mass of curly straw-coloured hair. He was a counsellor with the youngest group of boys aged six and they adored him. He was enthusiastic, approachable and caring. He was also gullible.

At the entrance to the boy's camp was a small shed which served as the Head Counsellors Office and the store for games equipment. This was also the location of a Tannoy system which was used to communicate with staff and campers. One morning just after 11.00 a.m. when all the groups were getting ready for the session known as general swim, and a trip down to the lake, I summoned Hank, as he was known, to the HC shack. Alongside me was my great friend Murray, then the Boy's Head Counsellor. As usual Hank arrived without delay from his nearby bunk.

"Hank, I believe you have come to work at the camp through the BUNAC programme," I said.

"Yes," he replied.

"Have you read both the Camp and BUNAC contract?"

"Yes. Some of it," at which point he started to look anxious. At this time, several other long-time counsellors had gathered at the hut.

"The thing is Hank, when you signed the contract, it states that you are willing to adhere and follow the religious beliefs of the camp."

"Yes, I know, and I go to Services every Friday and sing..."

"I know. I have heard you," I said remaining serious. "The issue is Hank that I have noticed during general swim down at the Boat House you have not been circumcised and in the Jewish faith all men have to be circumcised." He looked at the others with quiet desperation in his eyes.

I urged him to go back to the bunk and find the contract. Open mouthed and horrified he turned and disappeared for few minutes into his cabin before returning with contracts in hand.

"Where is this about circumcise?" he asked.

I found the section in Conditions of Employment which stated that *"Staff are required to engage and support the religious beliefs at Camp without objection or obstruction."*

"It happened to me when I first came to camp," I said trying to reassure him. "It's just a minor procedure which the nurse will perform down at the Infirmary today and you will have the afternoon off." Murray nodded to support my comment.

"But what about my girlfriend in Holland? I must call her."

"She won't even notice," I said with a smile. "Get yourself changed and head down to the Infirmary, the nurse is expecting you before lunch."

Several minutes later Hank appeared, looking concerned and carrying a small toiletry bag. He walked down the path towards the Infirmary to be greeted by a mass of male Counsellors who had gathered to cheer him before a rousing rendition of "Why were you born so beautiful..." Only then did he realise it was a joke, laughing and with giant leaps he charged back up the hill to his bunk before any decision could be reversed.

That night we all travelled into town to Danny's Bar and Grill on Route 6 with its dance floor and music with the pitchers of beer on my tab. We were always well received at the two main bars primarily because the British counsellors not only seemed to drink the most beer but also lifted the atmosphere of the place. The closest bar to Camp was the Fireside, about fifteen minutes away. With good food and a couple of pool tables it was a convenient place to chill out.

Unfortunately, the age for legal drinking in Pennsylvania was twenty-one and some younger counsellors could not always join in the festivities. With the curfew time extended to 1.00 a.m. on Saturdays we would often arrange for several cars to travel the forty minutes across into New York State where the legal age was eighteen frequenting a couple of bars called Memory Lane and My Place.

The penultimate Saturday of camp was the final night off for any counsellor staff, the older specialist counsellors traditionally took over supervisory duties, freeing everyone else. I approached Lynne about providing a bus for everyone to travel to Memory Lane at Cochecton to enable everyone to be together. She agreed and for the first time in the history of the camp a school bus drove the staff to their favourite bar.

It was a night of great fun. Several drinking games ensued, including boat races, a team relay event which involved drinking glasses of beer at speed. The only rule was the first drinker would consume a glass of beer before inverting it on their heads to release the next drinker. It was a concept which the Americans could not seem to grasp, often resulting in a Budweiser shampoo.

The journey home featured rousing editions of various songs, punctuated by a relief stop in the middle of nowhere. The sound of music must have alerted all at Camp as the bus travelled along the approach road. I tried my best to reduce the volume to what appeared a gentle babble. With forty staff happily climbing the hill from the road, some more boisterous than others, Lynne appeared in her night gown. She did not look pleased, but before she could admonish anyone, she noticed that the most inebriated person being supported by Eddie Robinson and myself at the head of the group, was in fact her thirty-year old son, Josh.

"Please all go to your bunks quietly. And Joshua, I will see you in the morning!"

I resisted saying good night as I felt it would only add to the anger she was feeling as she trudged back to her house and Sam, who was probably still asleep.

The final ten days of camp are often the most exciting for campers and counsellors with an event that is unique to American Summer Camps – Colour War. With great precision the whole camp, including counsellors is split into two teams, red and blue. Two male and two female 'generals' are selected for each team with their identity a secret. On this occasion I was chosen as a general for the Blue Athenians, but the identity of the others was only revealed at a late-night meeting at the boathouse with the organisers Murray and Bobby. Ian was a red Spartan

The meeting was to decide the members of each team, including four camper 'captains'. This was the most prestigious position for older campers to attain. Chosen by the organisers and camp owners it was often awarded to the four girls and four boys who were long-time campers with good leadership and sporting qualities. The four differing age groups, which had previously been divided into two equal teams by the counsellors, were carefully studied before the toss of the coin decided which general would have the first choice from the various age groups, camper captains and counsellors.

The event was always announced (or "broken") in spectacular form – and this always occurred when the whole camp was gathered together, typically for line dancing, or a visiting sports group, or a campfire, or a flag raising or an event in the theatre. Only a few select people knew when it was going to break, with a couple of false alarms (fake-outs) increasing the tension and anticipation.

Once it was broken, the team lists were announced, with each team sent to their headquarters to be whipped into a five-day frenzy. The counsellors were given a schedule of events. It was their task to decide which of their team members competed in a designated activity. It was very inclusive, with no camper allowed to compete in two events before every team member from that age group had competed in one. No camper could compete in all three time periods until all squad members had competed in two. The skill was in placing the less obvious sports performers to gain the best advantage, the foot soldiers essential to any team. I had yet to finish on the losing side in the Olympics, with this strategy proving key.

For the next five days wearing either red or blue, there were points up for grabs in everything, including bunk inspection. With a track-meet, swim meet and many sporting challenges it was non-stop activity. Songs were written and learned in double quick time, with lunch and dinner being an ideal opportunity to be vocal with your team song.

On the penultimate evening, an event called 'rope burning' was staged on the soccer field, with a rope tethered between two poles about nine feet in height and four feet apart. Each team was made up of campers of differing ages all with specific roles. The camper captains would often be the ones to build the fire. They only had one stick of firelighter, a newspaper and one box containing fifteen matches. Within each team there were many differing roles. The foragers who would dive into the wood pile situated about fifty yards from the rope in search of various identified branches or kindling before passing it to the runners who would then run to pass the wood to the sorters who would then pass wood to the fire builders. Their task was to build a fire which would burn through the rope. At no point could contact be made with the rope by a branch, for which there would be a time penalty. Some teams would aim for a strong box- base taking the slower option to build a fire which would burn with greater heat for a longer period once established, whilst others would go for the quicker option of a tepee that would flare much quicker but for a shorter period. This was the gamble because if the rope did not catch light or burn through at the first attempt there was little opportunity to add to the weaker frame. Time was the main factor, but on some occasions so too was the wind. A sudden change could divert the searing flame causing it to dance seductively below the taught hessian whilst two hundred campers urged it to reach out and embrace their rope before its power slowly died.

The whole event culminated on day five with the Apache Relay in the morning and an evening sing-song. The Apache Relay was a fascinating event with over eighty tasks taking place across the whole camp. Each camper was given a designated task with a baton passed once completed. The tasks were random and varied from shooting a basketball free-throw to sailing around a designated buoy to serving three consecutive serves in tennis and so many more. My favourite was the task of whistling Yankee Doodle whilst eating a cracker, always done by a younger camper who would practice for two or three days before the event, usually ending with a perfect delivery. However, on the day it was a different story with the participant sometimes choking (literally). The more they tried to blow a tune the more cracker was emitted through their lips as an anxious coach stood with his hands on his head in disbelief, seconds ticking away. No advice or reassurance just water and more crackers.

The final part of the relay took part on the ground near the dining hall and was termed the "Fire Brigade." Once the runner completing the 150-metre uphill run from the water-front passed the baton to one of his team at the steps of the hall, the ten people poised would fill up their shot glasses or flimsy plastic cups from the water trough and run the twenty yards to fill a large jar to overflowing. Some younger team members would get over excited and trip or squeeze their plastic cup so hard when running that the water spilled out. Some arrived at the table and in their haste missed the opening of the jar completely, much to the displeasure of their gathered team-mates cheering from the hill side.

Once battle had ended, all that remained was the evening sing-song where hastily composed songs were delivered by each team, often short and humorous with reference to a member of the opposition. The final song was always a lively rendition of the team theme tune followed by the presentation of the Olympic plaque. Designed by the art specialist it featured an image of each team in respective colours with the names of the generals and team-captains recorded. This was then displayed on the hall wall alongside the many others from previous years.

Whatever the purists may think, the Apache Relay, the Fire Brigade and the whole concept of Olympics provided several useful ideas for future consideration back in England.

For the record, the Blue Athenians beat the Red Spartans. Result!

# Chapter Three

My time at the Grammar School ended on July 1st, though officially I was on the payroll until August 31st. This was an agreement with the Headteacher when I took the position, allowing me to travel to the USA to work at Camp Towanda in Pennsylvania as a soccer coach.

It also marked the end of my time at Ron's. Once committed to the area I needed to make different plans. During the year I had met on a couple of occasions an old friend from College Joe Chivers who taught at the Secondary school adjacent to the Grammar. He was at the time in digs and was seeking alternative accommodation, so we agreed to look for a shared house rental.

Less than a mile from Ron's house, a three-bedroomed semi-detached house became available which was ideal. The only difficulty was the reluctance of the Estate agency to rent the property to two young males. It would have been a total "no go" if they had realised that it was to be eventually occupied by four males.

In my last days at the Grammar School, I had mentioned in conversation with some colleagues about the house hunt, with the intention of a heads-up if they spotted anything suitable. However, word got out and a woolly haired young science teacher at the school asked to be included in any deal.

Rick had lived a somewhat sheltered life in rural Shropshire but was a keen football fan. He had a round face which following any form of exercise rapidly turned rustic red. He was likeable and reliable without an ounce of controversy in his ample build.

Joe in the meantime had engaged in a similar conversation with a teacher at his school. Doug was a more worldly Yorkshireman. Built like a clothes-prop he was six feet tall with shoulder length hair and had immersed himself into every aspect of university life and survived. He also had a great taste in music and no opinion on sport. Four very differing personalities. To find a house with four bedrooms in the area was both rare and expensive, so a compromise was reached. We had to create an additional bedroom. Converting the separate dining room into a bedroom seemed the only option.

The deal for the house on Bracken Way, however, was dragging on. Something was needed to create momentum.

Joe was probably one of the most humble and modest athletes you could ever meet. A national record holder at three distances and a silver medal winner at the World Student Games. Just to add a little spice was an appearance in an All-Ireland final for Gaelic football before playing in the European Cup for Glentoran against eventual finalists Benfica in 1968.

I needed him to step out for just one day and use the power of celebrity.

During the six months previous he had competed as an athlete at the Commonwealth Games in Christchurch, New Zealand. He was currently a member of the GB team training regularly at Aldersley Stadium, Wolverhampton as a member of the local Athletics club, probably the top club team in the country at the time with a host of international performers.

I called Joe one evening.

"Joe, you need to call in a favour from one of your coaches. We need a letter of support stressing how important it is that you live in the locality for both your development and the future of British Athletics. With preparation for the Olympics in 1976 it is vital that you have stability. We need the Estate agent to understand that he is letting the house to a star athlete and his bag carrier!"

The letter did the trick. With three months advance payment the deal was sealed.

The only issue now was rooming. We all met one night in a local pub to draw lots. Joe drew number one, so obviously chose the master bedroom. This was ideal with a constant supply of Adidas running and training shoes as part of a sponsorship deal occupying one side of his wardrobe. Doug drew number two and Rick number three. I was left with the "dining room" next to the kitchen... not ideal but with direct access into the garden, close to the kettle and remote enough from the other rooms to allow me to play my array of albums without disturbing anyone it was home. With a couple of cars in the household, both travelling past my new school each day it was a win-win situation.

My new school was a three-storey building constructed in the early sixties with four classrooms on each of the three floors which looked out onto the entrance road, the construction of which appeared to have been abandoned thirty yards past the school gate. Much of the school was situated to the left of the reception. Three stair wells, two on the left and one on the right led off the ground floor corridor to classrooms on the upper floors.

The PE department was at the back of the school (where most are) next to woodwork and metal work. Almost ironic that all the non-academic subjects are grouped together, kept in isolation for fear of damaging the clever students. The Grammar School was no exception.

There was no real office just two changing rooms for staff and a storage room which was the former drying room used originally to house the vestments and other attire belonging to the priest. It had rows of slatted shelves and without any windows often resembled a sauna. There was a single light and no power point. With heat generated from the series of pipes snaking beneath the shelves it had all the features of a Turkish jail.

The staff changing rooms consisted of a shower, toilet and mirror. Each room had two small shelves and three hanging pegs. All were situated across the narrow passage from the student's changing rooms and at the entrance to the gymnasium.

The Staff room was situated as far away from the students as possible. With much of the school being to the left of reception, the Staff room was to the right at the end of a small passage which had male toilets, female toilets and a first-aid room all on the right. The Staff room entrance was straight ahead.

The wisdom of having a first-aid room next to the Staff area with an adjoining door was unclear other than for convenience. It did give "sick" students an opportunity to listen to all the conversations taking place in the staff room and pass on any gossip to the troops.

The staff room was the same size as a small classroom with an array of old armchairs along three sides interrupted only by a set of wooden lockers which seemed to house cigarettes, tea bags, coffee and a few other less important items such as books. Directly facing the door was a mini snooker table and a dartboard on the wall. This was obviously the sporting corner of the room. It had a large window which opened onto a rear carpark. On the wall separating the staff room from the first-aid room was a series of wooden pigeon-holes for staff mail.

In all it was small, chaotic but vibrant. It had a heart and I immediately felt comfortable and at home.

When I first walked into the room for the initial staff meeting, I looked around to see a melting pot of individuals. There was a nun with a multitude of freckles suggesting that her natural colour was ginger, a teacher with shoulder length hair who looked as if he had arrived straight from a leaving party which had taken up much of the previous night and a guy in a running vest with huge feet and eyebrow like wings. An older teacher who was smoking a pipe sat in the chair on the left and nearest the door and a chain-smoker diagonally opposite in the far corner with straight blonde hair and a rasping laugh. By the First Aid door a honey-monster with a couple of double chins was recalling an amusing story with a couple of colleagues, hands reaching out in all directions as if trying to catch several tennis balls at once. Five or six starry-eyed individuals which I assumed were new to the school, sat with their hands on their laps taking it all in. Rabbits in headlights

The meeting passed without any controversy, and I remained silent. It was probably one of the few occasions I did so in the years that followed, whether to make a critical comment or inject humour. Then at the close of the meeting, all staff were given their timetables for the year. This seemed a massive departure from my experience at the Grammar School. It was at this point that I was approached by four older female staff. Three of them informed me that I should be aware that they *"always"* managed the results hub at sports day. Another that she was *"always"* in charge of girl's toilets. A male member of staff close to the conversation made me aware that he was in charge of the PA system. What surprised me most was the event was ten months away!

What it did do was make me aware for the first time that in any school there are generals and there are foot soldiers. These were definitely not foot soldiers.

When I looked through various documents regarding procedure and timings I came to timetable. It was then that I noticed the initials CL. Unsure I approached the honey-monster who was still in the staff room. He introduced himself as Pete and then looked at the file.

"That will be Colin. He is teaching some maths and PE. He was appointed in July," he said and at that he swiftly left the area. I couldn't see anyone that looked like a PE teacher.

I returned at the first break having checked through an inventory of equipment in the cell, with beads of sweat evident. I could imagine someone doubting the levels of fitness of someone who was perspiring profusely having travelled less than twenty yards from their teaching area.

Teachers with coffee in one hand and a copy of their timetable in another surged into the staff room. With some more vocal than others the room transformed into a trading floor with staff frantically trying to change groups or rooms, or both. Some students seemed to be used as currency.

"I will take him in my group as long as you exchange rooms,"....."that pair need to be separated they're like Bonnie and Clyde!"......"the bottom groups all day Friday...pass me the pills now!"....."someone help me I have twenty nine in a box room." I watched in amusement blissfully unaware of what the timetable had thrown my way. Then I noticed my new partner enter the room.

Colin was a newly qualified teacher who lived over forty miles away in Cheshire. With a young family he was desperate for a job. He was six foot three, looked lean and fit and had a certain raw honesty. Within minutes of our conversation, I realised that this was someone I could work with. Someone who would be flexible and who would make a significant contribution to the department. Originally from Sunderland he would often address me as "youth" which always made me smile.

Along with Sue, the girls' physical education teacher we occupied the "sports corner" in the staffroom for our first departmental meeting. Following some general discussion Colin asked about lesson plans. My reply was the same then as the day I retired.

"If you feel more comfortable writing a lesson plan and working from it feel free. I am more interested in the progress made by the kids and their level of engagement. If it's a case of time for lesson plans or time for the kids, the kids win every time."

They both looked at me with suspicion. "If someone higher than me asks for them, then I will ask you," I said. They both seemed relieved. Most teachers will know that in-depth lesson plans are necessary for teachers unfamiliar with their subject or teachers who lack the personality to engage with the students and who are unable to travel off course during a lesson fearing that the outcomes will disappear into the ether. I wanted people to teach, to be flexible and enjoy the work. Paperwork could wait.

Unlike my previous school, the timetable was different from the previous year. The length of lessons had changed. Some were of forty-minute duration and some were thirty-five. Within a short period of time we had agreed on the use of space with the girls having majority use of the gymnasium, our only indoor area at the time, during the winter months.

The boys would have use of two soccer pitches and a hard-standing area which had been constructed hastily as a replacement for the space lost to the sports hall development. A "cost effective solution"" may have been a better term as it was a large area of tarmac laid on a simple stone base without any perimeter fencing.

Sue had been at the school for a year and was of a similar age. Popular with the girls, she was enthusiastic and positive. A dream to work with. Throughout the whole of her time in the department we never had a crossed word. Sadly, she left to work in Spain after two years, to be replaced by a specialist dancer who could contribute little to team games which had a strong reputation at the school. It was an appointment "forced" on the school by someone in authority.

Colin initially was quiet. Travelling eighty miles each day in an old banger along the M6 motorway was not something to look forward to, particularly with a young family. During that first term a couple of breakdowns resulted in him being late for school and he did seem anxious. I was not. The work he was doing in lessons was exceptional. The students always seemed engaged and he had a healthy discipline. After six months of travelling, he finally moved to a house less than twenty minutes from the school.

Though he was a keen footballer he had a strong interest in gymnastics. With my interest in games, it was an ideal combination. In many of his gymnastic lessons he would challenge the students to walk from one side of the gym to the door on their hands. In very little time, students were walking down steps on their hands and the gym club was vibrant with both boys and girls attending.

Between us we held lunchtime clubs every day of the week except Friday. On the last day of the week the whole department would go to a local tavern for lunch. Once a month I would pay for the food. Being without a car Colin would always give me a lift.

One Friday we were late leaving the Tavern and turned into the road leading to the school as the bell for the afternoon session sounded. As we turned through the gates, I noticed the headteacher standing at his window glaring down the drive. At this point I ducked down into the passenger seat, leaving a clear view of Colin as he turned right into the rear carpark totally unaware. It was only at the end of school when he was summoned to the head's office that he realised why I had reached into the footwell. To his credit he took it on the chin with a smile.

Karma was quite a while in coming. Several years later, with gymnastics firmly established at the school Colin organised a county junior school championship. With children aged from 6 - 10 years competing in the new sports hall. It was a fantastic occasion, attended by many parents, the chief education officer and the director of physical education.

At the conclusion of the event and following the presentation of the medals and trophies a small 6-year-old girl stepped up to deliver a thank you speech. She spoke in short, breathless sentences thanking Colin and all teachers for their hard work in both developing the skills and organising the teams. She then turned to face me and in the most angelic and innocent of voices said:

"We would all like to thank…. Mr Popout dick…for letting us use his sports hall." Even the chief education officer smiled. Colin looked across at me with a smug grin and just nodded.

The lack of a communal office was a positive with all the department often taking residence in the sports corner facing the entrance door. As in all staff-rooms departments tended to sit together. The English teachers sat diagonally opposite with history and geography next along.

The middle three chairs seemed to belong to the three women who were the power base of the school. I referred to them very quickly as the Father, Son and Holy Ghost. The head of science, a deputy head-teacher and the head of art. They never seemed to say anything but would often have their own meetings to discuss any aspect of change which could impact on their security or modus operandi. Between them they seemed to gather intelligence from a variety of sources both from within and outside of school

Then there were the bohemians who would sit anywhere or stand at meetings. One was Bill, a teacher for students with Special Educational needs. In his late fifties he appeared to be one of those for whom life had never been fair. I remember the annual staff versus the parent's cricket match. We were short and Bill came out of retirement. He was so excited. So much so he was demonstrating to me in the confines of the staff room his "slow left arm" technique when someone opened the door, smashing his knuckle and breaking two fingers. Bill was out first ball.

The final insult however, and perhaps something that summed up his life, was a few years later when he retired following thirty-five years in the profession. There was a big presentation which was covered by the local press. A photograph was taken of him receiving a long-service award from the Director of Education. There was a substantial article to accompany the photograph. The article appeared on page four with a final line ".... pictured above receiving his award from the Director of Education" but there was just a large black square. A lightening strike over pay by the lithographers at the newspaper resulted in an edition without any photographs.

The honey-monster, Pete always stood up at staff meetings. He was over six feet tall and weighed about sixteen stones. He was the enforcer, the teacher vital to every school for overseeing discipline. Though some may think otherwise it is not about size it is about certain qualities and skills that the individual possesses. At the Grammar school the role belonged to a five-foot grandmother who could grasp the attention of the meanest 15-year-old boy. She would listen to them; take their concerns and roll them like putty in her hands, taking time to eventually arrive at a solution or response which they both agreed would be in their best interests. Job done.

That was Pete. He would walk onto the stage before any assembly and the room would suddenly become quiet. Not out of fear but respect. He was firm but very fair and the students knew that. He would have the banter on the playground and not be afraid to laugh at himself. He always appeared to have a large diary or book under his arm regardless of the time of day, only putting it down to drink a coffee. He was also the lead driver of the school coach, a fifty-seater former service bus which had been painted white. Judging from its appearance it was not a professional job but more likely the task of three or four students in a school detention whose only previous artwork was likely to be found in the boys' toilets.

The head teacher, who I referred to as "The Duke," was a small and unassuming man and a great supporter of Wolverhampton Wanderers. He was a gentleman in every respect, always knocking on the staff room door before entering. When asked why in later years he merely commented that the space belonged to the staff and that he would expect the staff to knock on his office door before entering.

He was always approachable and supported me consistently in the first ten years allowing me to develop as a teacher and as an individual. Initiatives and new ideas were considered and often given approval. Pete and he lived close to each other and shared lifts to and from work. I am sure that some of my ideas were often discussed on their journey home, with Pete having a major input.

He demonstrated confidence in my ability and vision and acknowledged the unique contribution the subject offers to students by establishing Physical Education as a separate faculty within six-months of my start, which also resulted in my salary being raised to the level of other faculty heads.

The vibrancy of the staff room and the support more experienced teachers gave to those new to the profession made for a relaxed working environment. Personalities began to emerge, with humorous lines thrown across the room like a game show. I realised quickly that my chosen seat by the window was also the late arrival entry or the quick exit route. The latter was particularly popular with staff on a Friday who did not wish to be confronted by a student or worse a parent at the end of the school day. It was also my shop window for the second half of the year.

My mother in Manchester was employed as a quality controller at a manufacturer of men's clothing. Her role was to inspect trousers for any faults or defects and reject those not up to standard. The women were paid for the number of items they produced per hour, so short cuts were often taken. A missed button, one leg slightly longer than the other, a dodgy zip all rejected. Each Friday the workers were invited to buy the rejects at a nominal fee. My mother would often invite me home to pick up a supply of trousers which varied from flares, smart suit trousers, Oxford 'bags' and hipsters. At first, I shared them with my house mates, but then I started taking them to school for the staff, who were extremely grateful to receive quality trousers and jackets for as little as £1.50, with, in many cases, the Home Economic department fixing any fault. My arrival on some Monday mornings was eagerly awaited by several male and female staff. The staff suddenly started to look fashionable. No more tweed jackets with patches at the elbows, as such attire was now replaced by blazers and smart suits - and all for the price of a sandwich.

The year passed without any controversy. I was only reprimanded once. A parent had complained that my climbing on the roof to dispense a bucket of water over Colin on his birthday was childish. Probably was. I should have been more imaginative.

In the final weeks of the school year, Sports Day was held. The races were won by those expected to win. The throws seemed to take forever to reach an inevitable result and more kids were watching than participating.

An afternoon off lessons.

That also included the Holy Trinity who having informed me of their perpetual role as scorekeepers at the beginning of the year spent the afternoon in the comfort of their state-of-the-art caravan camped for the occasion thirty yards after the finish line with cold drinks and television throughout the afternoon.

Some things needed to change.

With three days remaining of the year Honey monster Pete collared me in the staff room. He had a look on his face that had a hint of amusement and excitement.

"Pop, now that you're 23 you qualify to drive the school bus."

I was motionless. Lost for words. The reply I tried to make to indicate I had only passed my driving test twelve months previously seemed to be churning around my mind unable to link together in a coherent manner. Instead, from somewhere I uttered "Great! When?"

"Now," he replied. "Colin is covering your lesson, so let's get going."

With a distinct swagger of optimism Pete ambled over to the white fifty-one-seater bus and jumped in the driver's seat.

*Thank fuck! I thought for a minute he was expecting me to drive.*

"I'll just reverse her out and then you can take over. Here we go," and smoothly the bus reversed around the corner and out of the school gates into the road leading to the school. Pete jumped out of the seat, opened the small door with the ticket machine attached and uttered the dreaded words "it's all yours...."

How was I expected to go from driving a mini-van and Volkswagen beetle to a thirty-foot sardine tin!

Trying not to look nervous I lowered myself onto the driver's seat, realising quickly that I couldn't reach the pedals and with a degree of subtleness I searched for the handle to lower it. Once I was in a comfortable position and able to touch all pedals, I went through the various controls with Pete. He explained about the process of double declutching and then sat down on the opposite side of the bus, close to the door. It was at this point on starting the engine that I realised in lowering my seat the long gear stick was now almost level with my chest.

I pulled away smoothly and turned left up a hill which lasted for about half a mile. On the downhill decent I decided to change into third gear. I lifted the gear stick and the frigging thing came out of the gear box.

"Stay calm and don't panic," said Pete.

Don't panic!!??

Don't panic? I was holding a thin metal pole, with no control over the fifty-one seats behind me that were pushing me down a hill. What was there *not* to panic about?

"It happens all the time. Just wiggle it about and it will go back in, as the bishop said to the actress...."

Christ, I thought, the story of my life. At a time of crisis, I get the comedian.

With beads of sweats descending slowly down both cheeks and Pete seeming calm and relaxed I did manage to slide the gear stick back into the box and regaining some composure drove on. The trick I later learned was to "caress" the stick rather than lift it. Perhaps that should have been explained before my potential heart attack. The next fifteen minutes was uneventful, and I quite enjoyed the elevated view from the cabin using my newfound aid of wing mirrors.

We arrived back at school and I opened the cabin door to leave the seat.

"Where are you going? You've got to park it now," he said with a smile. "Reverse her in, it's the easiest way."

The next ten minutes felt like an eternity. Visible to half the school I did my best to remove first one gate and then the other. Once I mastered the gates, I seemed to have a mental block remembering where the coach was parked. One thing for sure, it was not parked in the driveway, blocking in all the staff cars. At the tenth attempt I managed to reverse round the corner just missing the white street lamp as I bumped over a kerb. Eventually the coach was home.

"Well done," said Pete. "With a little practice you will be fine." I looked at him in disbelief as he jumped down the steps and walked away. I felt the need to change my shorts which appeared to be stuck to my buttocks for some reason.

Now I was a registered driver of the school bus...Holy shit!

# Chapter Four

Over forty per cent of the students were bused in from a wide area, some having to leave home at 7.00 a.m. The other sixty per cent lived within three miles of the school and were exempt from the free transport provided by the Education authority. Many were from large Catholic families, often with siblings in the school or in the feeder Primary schools. One family had at least one child at the school for twenty years, the first a girl and the rest boys. During those two decades the mother and father together attended more Parent evenings than some of the teachers.

A few students were dropped at school. Most walked. Some were forced to leave home when the last parent left for work. They would start populating the school from 7.40 a.m., an hour before the start of the school day. Others would arrive on or after the bell for the start of the day having dropped off their younger brother or sister at the distant Primary school. They were the ones seen running up the road or through the park attempting to "beat the bell." They were often the fittest. Then there were the very few who would saunter up the road. For these the need to be on time was viewed with the same importance as the need to learn Russian.

A significant number of parents were Irish, Italian or Polish, with many working in coal mining which employed approximately five-thousand people in the area. With the demise of the industry the number of families struggling to provide for their children increased but so did their efforts. The majority were always grateful for any help provided by the school and the opportunities provided for their children.

Many of the of students were cooperative and helpful. They enjoyed attention and the banter, in some cases making up for the lack of it in the home. Small tasks and responsibilities such as opening the gym doors and getting agility mats ready for the lesson or taking the bag of footballs and making sure they all returned were eagerly accepted and carried out with precision and pride. It made them feel valued, and they were.

The one thing evident in every year was the smattering of characters.

The Artful Dodgers, the comedians, the fighters, the leaders, the rebels and those who would never give up. There were those who would hang onto every word and those who would challenge them. They made going to work each day totally unpredictable and never mundane. An after-school football match with the Under-16 team was a case in point. The lads had been sent out with a ball and I locked the changing rooms, put on my football boots and started to walk up the hill to referee the game. At the back of the gym, I noticed one of the players smoking a fag.

"What are you doing Terry?" I asked.

"Just warming up Sir," was the jovial reply. It was not a battle to be fought, particularly as once out on the field he was a classic mid-field general and always one of the stand-out players.

The game itself was not one of my best either, as a coach or an official. The school providing the opposition for two games, one for the under sixteen age group and the other for under thirteen, had only one mini-bus available for transport. I suggested that their teacher drops off the oldest group first as their games are longer before travelling the short distance back to his school to pick up the younger team. I would start the Under-16 game whilst their teacher was in transit.

At half-time, leading by the odd goal but under pressure I questioned the right back.

"Sully, you need to tighten up, they are running riot down your side."

"But I seem to have two of them to mark all the time Sir," said the usually quiet defender.

"Then call for help," I said. "It's all about communication," and then blew the whistle ready for the start of the second half. Ten minutes into the second half the teacher who up to that point had watched the junior game came across to watch the game. Within a couple of minutes of his arrival I could see him waving at me. When the ball went out of play, I ran across to him.

"I am awfully sorry ref but it would appear that my team couldn't sort out which player was to be sub and have been playing with twelve players throughout the game."

I was gobsmacked. To give the teacher credit he let play re-start before discreetly hauling off one of their players, seemingly without any of my team noticing, saving me the embarrassment. The one player who did make a comment at the end of the game was Sully.

"Things seemed to get a lot easier in the second half. Must have been the communication," he said with a knowing smile. A lesson learnt, always count the players.

I had a lot of admiration for Sully and the discretion he displayed. He was an athletic, reliable and very capable defender. Quick to praise and slow to criticise. Over the next ten years I invited him to play alongside me in some of the adult teams both on Saturday and Sunday knowing that he would never rock the boat or cause any disruption. He did not disappoint.

The school had a good reputation in football, netball and cross-country. Football matches were arranged both after-school and on Saturday mornings. This was a time when there was little opportunity for junior football so providing as many games as possible for each age group was a key focus.

Cross-country was a recognised strength with both boys and girls. Helen a fifth-year student was the reigning Under-15 Girls' National Champion and remains to this day the only athlete in its long history to win three consecutive Under-15 Championships, winning the first when she was thirteen years of age in 1972. There were several county runners, all of whom attended the local Athletics club for training. The school was helped by its location on the edge of Cannock Chase. Within yards of the school gates runners were able to run into parkland and along a bridle path at the side of a field which eventually became a golf course with rolling hills and distant oak trees, before turning right following a long sandy path through the forest to a council owned sports field which led directly back into the school grounds. It was without doubt the best and most exhilarating course in the area and with a range of distances from 2,000 to 5,000 metres it was a useful resource for the school. It had been the venue for the National Schools' Cross-Country Championships in the early Seventies.

Sadly, in recent times with health and safety restrictions and the need for ponderous risk assessments at every turn the course is no longer used with cross-country running consisting of laps of the school field. No trees, no birdsong, no freedom, nothing.

The school had a strange timetable. It consisted of eight periods during the day with all the odd periods being thirty-five minutes and the even periods forty minutes. The older students in year four and five had a double period but the younger groups had two individual periods of thirty-five minutes and forty minutes. With five minutes at the start for changing and eight at the end (including a shower) there was a need for creativity.

From September to October half-term and from February to Easter, the first lesson of the day was cross-country. For the juniors, fourteen and under the short course of 2,000 yards was ideal with all runners being timed. Anyone with a time beyond twenty minutes would receive zero. All times were recorded and displayed on a notice board. Points were awarded for improvement and outstanding times which the performers accumulated towards a PE department award. Every third week I would introduce a speciality race. Handicap races, where the runners with the slower times received a start ahead of the more able. Team races, selected by the students and Mystery team races, where the teams had been pre-selected and sealed in an envelope. This was opened at the finish with the top ten times for each team counting. With all these events the winners received a large trophy to celebrate their success for the "unforgiving minute" before handing it back to be used in many different sports over many years.

On one occasion I was looking through the times for one group when I noticed a coincidence. Three of the less cooperative students had consistent times just outside the level which would include them in school teams, but ahead of the pack. If they were cheating, no one would dare tell for fear of getting thumped. Those who would stand up to them were often the first to finish so were oblivious to any happenings. I needed proof. If I were to hide in a location and someone else start the race they would suspect. I did not have time to be at the start and run to the far corner of the school fields to get an unrestricted view. Then by chance, waiting for a race to finish I spotted the solution.

The next time the group were ready to race I started them in the same way, but then with a pair of binoculars in hand ran up to the second floor, interrupting a Religious Education class (by arrangement) and gaining access to the flat roof by the steel ladder which was located in a small cupboard at the rear of the room and was used by contractors. Running to the far end of the roof I had a glorious view across the whole course. My efforts were not in vain. The three amigos, half-way along the bridle path cut directly across the field, missing a third of the course. These are the chancers, the students who want to do things their way. They push against conformity, in action and dress. With most of the runners wearing the official school PE tops (red) they were easily identifiable in their black, white and grey tops.

In the changing room after the completion of the race I always read out the times and a comparison with previous performance. If it was a personal best, there was a quick applause. The "three amigos" waited confidently for their applause. They seemed totally surprised when they were given "zero – disqualified" staring first at each other and then around the changing room, searching for the "grass," before fixing their gaze at me once more still in total disbelief. How could this be? Was there someone out there hidden from view?

Finally for the bemused class I explained how my roof-top adventure provided me with a perfect view of everyone right up until the furthest corner. Then I provided a further shock to the stunned threesome

"Of course, under IAAF rules all your previous times are to be expunged," I said, knowing that they would not understand the word, never mind question the punishment. They were made to complete a total of four races in all during their lunchtimes to qualify for a mark towards their end of year grade. Word was soon passed to others about the lonely figure on the roof top. The female teacher whose lesson I occasionally interrupted would often tell her students that it was part of the process of identifying those who were committing venial sins, not quite a mortal sin but still significant. Whenever I descended from the roof through the classroom the students and the teacher would always look at me with eyes wide in expectation. Waiting for a white smoke moment, which when it happened was always followed by a customary cheer. Another sinner uncovered.

The students seemed to respond well to the young and enthusiastic teachers, who introduced them to some new sports and activities. The lunchtime at the school was eighty minutes long and could accommodate a couple of differing activities over that period, either different age groups or different sports.

These were always well attended due to the need for some students to catch the school bus home, only prepared to stay for matches. Public transport in the area was poor and unreliable. With football, gymnastics, netball, basketball and volleyball on offer for differing years there was just not enough time or space.

My Mini van had long gone to the scrap yard to be replaced by a red Volkswagen Beetle. With just two button style knobs, a gearstick, handbrake and an indicator/wiper arm it was the most minimalistic of vehicles but extremely reliable. It enabled me to extend the range of clubs by having early morning sessions to ease the pressure from lunchtimes and increase opportunity. Basketball was introduced on Wednesday mornings from 7.45 a.m., with a lift into school provided for some of the Rugeley players. The club was well attended and results in basketball began to improve dramatically. We would also allow students into the gym at break-times three times per week to practice their shooting under the supervision of staff.

The Under-15 football team were not the most talented, but they did have the current District goalkeeper who had the size and ability to progress higher. Having played for Manchester Boys as a goalkeeper I was mindful of the lack of training I received, often spending time after school on my own throwing a ball against a gym wall to catch. No one shooting, no one coaching. Tony lived close to my home so every Thursday morning we would arrive at school for 7.30 a.m. and have sixty minutes of goalkeeping in the gym. It was evident that with the length of the session I could accommodate another keeper and so Martin, two years younger but from the same area was invited to attend.

They were determined and very reliable. They never missed a session and always made their pick-up at 7.15 a.m. Both went on to play for the County and both became apprentice professional players at Wolverhampton Wanderers and Walsall respectively. Over the years the school had several others who played for Staffordshire between the sticks. I would often smile when teachers from other schools made a comment that we seemed to be "lucky" with our goalkeepers

There was light on the horizon, with the sports hall development due to be completed by the end of May. The plans had shown a 34-metre x

20-metre sports area with changing rooms for girls on the ground floor and on the first floor, boys changing rooms, an office overlooking the hall and a small balcony running along a back wall. The flooring was soft and performer friendly. With cricket nets and electronic basketball hoops on a full-size court it was the dog's bo****ks.

We returned to school following the Easter break and I went to view the progress. I was assured it was all going to plan, even though there still seemed to be a lot of work to complete. The walls were only fifty percent built at twelve foot high and the construction of changing rooms had yet to commence.

Three days before the half-term break at the end of May the foreman gave me a bunch of keys.

"It's all yours," he said.

"Hang about. What about the changing rooms? What about the rest of the walls? When is it going to be finished?"

"It is finished," he said. "They have run out of money, so some cuts had to be made."

The foreman opened the two doors which led directly into the sports hall from an uncovered entrance, and we stepped inside. The floor was not the blue on the plans, nor was it cushioned. It was the thinnest green material available to mask the unforgiving concrete underneath.

To say there was disappointment in my voice was an understatement.

"It's a barn," I groaned.

"Not quite," said the foreman, with the quiet confidence and optimism of someone who is quite familiar with the situation. "It's a SPORTS barn," and at that he smiled, turned and left me alone with my shattered dreams.

The grey brick walls that now surrounded me ended just short of the three sets of basketball backboards which lined the length of the side walls. The rest up to the roof was made up of a series of heavy-duty corrugated opaque plastic sheets, vertically bolted together. They were the type used for industrial scale hot houses, able to withstand the wind and the occasional flying object. Enough light was provided in the mornings and early afternoon without a need to use the gas-filled ceiling lights which when used did provide excellent illumination.

However, the enigma was the heating design. A series of canopy covered pipes stretched from one end of the sports hall to the other level with the light fittings. Why in the roof when heat rises? A service engineer on a follow-up visit explained that the rationale was to ensure the sports hall did not get "uncomfortably warm" for performers. It seemed to work as the hall was often "uncomfortably cool" in the early hours of the day until the periphery of the heat managed to have any impact about lunchtime or later. The one exception was during the summer months when the opaque sheets guaranteed tropical temperatures, with both the entrance doors and the fire-doors being permanently open to encourage an air flow.

Half-way down the sports hall was a recess three metres deep and five metres long for the storage of large equipment and waiting area for students. It had a tongue and groove wooden flat roof, which was exposed not by design but by cost. It resembled a domestic garage. A couple of doors at the far end of the space provided access into a room for the storage of balls, nets, posts and other items for lessons. Ironically, some of the shelves were too high for me to access without a chair. Some workman's way of getting even with the little guy who continually asked how things were going?

I was disappointed but I could not let this be evident to either the staff or the headteacher. I adopted a glass half full mentality. On reflection we had another indoor space with three mini-basketball courts, four badminton courts and a volleyball court. It would allow the expansion of our current programme and provide all groups with respite from cold and wet winter days; days which are not conducive to teaching or learning. It would allow the staff to be imaginative.

The school year ended on a high. The staff team defeated the parents in the annual cricket match, with the new blood inspiring the captain to search for additional fixtures. I was asked to join the Parent Teachers Association and the mid-summer party at Bracken Way proved an outstanding success with a dozen staff being amongst the sixty plus people who crammed into the house and garden until the early hours of Sunday morning. All the furniture from the house was moved to the garden next door and covered with tarpaulin along with all doors except for the bathroom. Some invited neighbours eventually left at 12.30 a.m. only to return a couple of hours later to re-join the fun. There were no complaints, despite the line of abandoned cars that seemed to cover the length of the cul-de-sac.

For the first time in four years, I was not going to America to work at the Summer Camp. Instead, a mate from Stockport, Phil Stevenson suggested we hitch around Europe for five weeks, so on a July afternoon with a backpack, a map and no plan we set off in search of Athens.

If every journey is an education, then this was to be no different.

# Chapter Five

The final act before any serious traveller departs from our shores is to consume a full English breakfast. Regardless of the duration of travel, the meal is consumed with a passion as if a return to England's green and pleasant land is a distant dream.

The hospitality industry in Dover must sell more bacon, sausage, eggs, beans and tomatoes than any other single product. On a cool but dry Monday morning Phil and I contributed to the numbers with additional helpings of black pudding, mushrooms, toast and of course a mug of tea. Across a small table with a yellow floral plastic covering, we made our plans for the next five weeks of our expedition across Europe.

Phil was a friend I had met at Madeley who lived near Stockport and even though he was a chain-smoking United fan who did most of his physical activity at a working men's club retrieving his darts, we got on really well. We would often meet up when home from college, visiting pubs, clubs and parties in south Manchester.

The first thing that became obvious was the limited range of useful items that we both had included in our ruck sacks. We had the inventory of two refugees on the run who had been suddenly woken and given five minutes to grab what they could before fleeing.

We were going to warmer countries, where it never rained in July or August so why take a tent? We each had a lightweight sleeping bag and a pillow. Mine was a blow-up version which was a useful as an umbrella in a hurricane. Phil had packed a torch and I had purchased a Swiss Army knife from Millets along with two enamel mugs and plates. With an abundance of shorts, tee shirts, a towel and flip flops we were ready to go, if we only knew where. Neither of us had a map.

The AA shop at the entry to the ferry terminal provided us with a basic map of Southern Europe at a significant cost, before walking on board the early morning ferry bound for Ostend. The four-hour journey began with a brief look at the map to decide a general direction on day one followed by a kip, particularly necessary if you have consumed a large breakfast and the Channel is choppy.

Just before we arrived at the Belgian port Phil woke me with some good news. During his stroll around the vessel, he had struck up a conversation and doubtless shared a fag or two with an army guy who was driving to a base in Germany. He was willing to provide a lift to the outskirts of Frankfurt. A great start.

Though the journey took most of the day, it seemed to pass quickly with the American soldier keen to talk about all things sporting. Both Phil and I had spent summers in America and though neither had visited his hometown of Philadelphia we had enough basic knowledge to make conversation. In return he dropped us at a lay by on a major road heading south towards Switzerland. There were toilets nearby and a van selling drinks, bratwurst and French fries, with lashings of mayonnaise. Not quite Michelin star but just as appreciated.

We took twenty-minute turns to stand at the roadside to hitch a lift. During my second spell a Volkswagen van pulled in with the girl passenger waving in our direction. We gathered everything quickly before they had a chance to change their minds and ran to the vehicle. Frank, the driver was a student living in Heidelberg with Ida, and he offered a lift to the town a few hours south. They were both in their early twenties and had a good knowledge of the English music scene. The journey was not long enough to exhaust the conversation, and they offered us both a room (floor in reality) for the night, which we gratefully accepted.

By eight o clock, we were well established as part of Frank's gang in a local bar, downing the local lager and buying a few rounds. The size of the group seemed to increase as the night developed, and we did our best to cement Anglo-German relations. Having been successful in the 1974 World Cup they were on a high, but we did try to remind them of 1966. Mexico in 1970 was too painful to even mention. Every so often the conversation would return to music where a random group or artist would be thrown into the mix.

"What about Pink Floyd and Dark side of the Moon?" exclaimed Frank before a brief discussion on the merits of the group and album ensued until another name was uttered which was either greeted with jeers or applause and sometimes even a bar room version of a famous song. Some even had the audacity to claim that the Beatles success was due to their time in Hamburg!

Following a late awakening we took Frank and his partner Ida for a coffee and breakfast, enjoying the atmosphere of the picturesque town. I had noticed some children playing handball and Frank told me it was a major sport in Germany, played in all the schools. I told him I had recently completed a Coaching course and had introduced it to the boys at my school. Little did I know at the time the impact the game would have on my future career.

Eventually they dropped us at the major road south which led to Basle. Having thanked them for their hospitality and watched them disappear, we suddenly realised that we had spent a small fortune buying beers and breakfast. Hitch-hiking was supposed to be a cost-effective way to travel. But can you put a price on friendship or a hangover?

For a while we seemed to be invisible to the fast-passing traffic. We decided to move on to find a slower stretch of road. Having walked for over a mile with my left arm extended, fist clenched and thumb raised we decided to stop close to a pull-in.

Phil needed to recover from the walk and have a cigarette and I needed to change arms. During my school days when I became bored or disinterested another character took over my body. The thespian. This was now my stage.

From a friendly wave to the plea with open arms and then the more desperate praying action. The sad "puppy dog" eyes to the tap dancer I was going through the full repertoire. A performance for every potential lift.

Then I noticed the dream car approaching. Open topped with a couple of females, their blonde hair blowing in the breeze. This called for something special – the drop to my knees, my arms open wide, the tilt of the head. Call it begging if you want. They hit the horn, waved and began to slow down. I jumped to my feet, heart pounding with excitement taking over. Followed by disaster. Spinning around like the lead in Swan Lake to alert Phil, I fell over my rucksack and disappeared head-first into a ditch. The girls disappeared too.

With Phil in stitches, and me crawling out of the ditch and dusting the Loser tag from my vest a car travelling behind had witnessed the episode and stopped to ensure I was okay. Whether it was compassion or just a need for company, he offered to provide a lift to the outskirts of Zurich. Every cloud as they say....

We discovered he was a professor at the University in Bern and that his weekend was often spent hand-gliding in the Alps, whilst smoking a joint and listening to Neil Diamond on his headphones. The insight did not fill me with confidence, but I was glad that the vehicle appeared to be "fragrance free." Just over four hours later, on a warm Tuesday evening we arrived in Zurich.

The first stop was for food and coffee. We then realised how expensive it is to live in Switzerland and sausage and chips became a necessity rather than a choice. The city itself was beautiful, situated on the tip of the Lake with an amazing backdrop. We managed to locate the exit road in the direction of the St. Gothard tunnel, but as night closed in our chances of a lift diminished and we found a sheltered spot near a fire station, ready to spend the night there if all else failed. We took turns to stand at the side of the road with our arms getting lower and lower as the flow of traffic decreased.

A little after 10.30 p.m. a large silver Mercedes saloon pulled in and that is when we met Felix. In his mid-thirties he was an investment banker on his way home from work. He was tall, well-groomed, smart and affable. With Phil specializing in economics, it was a match made in heaven and I was able to sit back and relax for a while whilst they discussed the world economy.

With the road ascending into the Alps, I was beginning to think ahead and the need to find somewhere sheltered once this lift was over as the chance of getting another was zero. We had now been in the car for over an hour and seemed to be on a side road heading up a mountain.

"You will of course stay at my house for the night as it is too cold in the mountains. My wife will prepare some food when we arrive." To refuse would have offended him not to mention the probability of hypothermia for the beach-ready travellers.

His house, Im Latt, was situated on the side of a mountain near the small town of Hombrechitikon, with several floors overlooking the valley below. He explained that the house was separated vertically from his neighbour (we referred to it as semi-detached, but that didn't seem to do it justice). The living space was on the third floor which was accessed by a series of ladders through the various levels. His wife, Marta was both attractive and friendly with a baby son, Etal, who she had just put to sleep. Without any hesitation and a few minutes to midnight, she began to cook steak and frites for all with beer and wine. Phil and Felix continued to talk about money, politics and the stock markets, whilst I talked about America and Canada to his wife who quizzed me about the McGill University jacket I was wearing. I explained about the American Summer Camps, the different types, what they offered and where the best ones were situated.

The two designated sofas were so comfortable and were a major step up from the rugs of the previous night. So comfortable in fact that we were finally aroused at 10.30 by the smell of coffee and a table laid out for breakfast. Etal was awake and in his high-chair banging a spoon at irregular intervals with enthusiasm on the plastic table, occasionally landing in the bowl which contained some food.

The breakfast was five-star luxury with croissants, rolls and various cheeses and meats. Felix had left for work a few hours earlier and Marta assured us there was no need to rush. I think our company was appreciated. As beautiful as the house was it was somewhat isolated close to a small village. Just after midday we jumped in Marta's jeep, with Etal strapped in for the ride and set off towards the main road. Having enjoyed two meals, some wine and a good night's sleep nothing else was expected. However, Marta decided to drive to the major highway where we would have a much better chance of a lift through the mountains. Thanking her, I gave my contact details for England should the family ever visit Manchester.

It was several days later when I realised that I had left my treasured McGill University jacket at Felix's place. Resigned to the loss I travelled on. It was only when I returned to England and opened a parcel delivered in my absence that I was reunited with my jacket. It was such a considerate gesture. I often wonder how many other travellers over the years dined at Marta's table and experienced the hospitality and kindness of Felix. Or if Etal ever went to a Summer Camp in the USA?

The next part of our journey through the Alps into Italy should have been a highlight. Winding roads with spectacular scenery and visions of

Julie Andrews. When the small, sporty Fiat pulled in to offer a lift, the appearance of the driver should have provided a clue. He had thick black hair which seemed to have been last brushed at Easter and a thick black moustache, in later years made famous by the electronic hero Mario. His double-glazed spectacles sat on his nose like those of a surgeon performing the most delicate of operations. And then there were the eyes, bulging and slightly bloodshot. I jumped in the back with both the rucksacks, one at each side for protection.

Over the next two hours Phil tried desperately to make conversation. Whatever the topic the driver seemed to have a strong opinion often becoming agitated and animated which impacted on his driving. With drops of a few hundred feet to my right he would accelerate into bends. Sometimes he would take both hands off the wheel to remonstrate and when he was overtaking on the narrow mountain roads, I closed my eyes.

Phil's voice in the front seemed to raise an octave at certain times of the journey, particularly when fast approaching a bend with the view straight ahead of eternity. He was starting to look whiter than pale and he seemed to stutter occasionally.

"What is the speed limit?" Phil enquired hesitantly.

"Speed limit is shit. It is for those people who cannot drive!" was the definitive answer. It was at that point I decided the only thing to do was close my eyes and wake up either in Como or heaven. Como was both.

I exited the car quite refreshed and thanked him. Phil seemed to stumble out of the passenger door with the demeanour of someone who had consumed eight pints of Boddington's and just vomited in the glove compartment. During the next half-hour in "recovery" he smoked three or four cigarettes whilst we sat by the side of the lake.

The rest of our time in Italy was uneventful. We stayed in Rome for four days in a hostel before accepting a couple of lifts ending in Brindisi, where we were to take an onward ferry to Corfu. Obtaining the tickets from the Ferry office was an experience and provided a cultural insight into the Italian way of life. It would appear there is no comparable word in the Italian language for "Queue." The minute the window opened for the sale of ferry tickets there was mayhem. I was a little slow off the mark. Even more embarrassing was the women in her early fifties who straight-armed me out of the way as she barged through. With the crowd now swirling like the tide in a storm and me trying desperately to hold onto the lira in my hand I had to take a more assertive approach. Over the top of people seemed to be more effective until in range of the window and then a bit of ducking, diving, twisting and turning. My eventual reward was two tickets for the ferry, a vest soaked in sweat and marks on my arms and neck which suggested I had run through a holly bush. Phil was sat on the bags, pissed off because he had run out of fags!

We arrived in Corfu with nowhere to stay and flexible plans. On the ferry we spoke with some other English travellers about various options, and we decided to head over to the far side of the island from Corfu Town to Pelekas. The small village overlooked a long sandy beach where there were many like-minded people camping in both the shaded woodland on the hillside and on the beach itself, forming a lively community. Those who intended to stay for a longer duration had built small shelters with semi-domestic accessories such as drying lines, hammocks and a cooking area. We had two plates; two mugs; three spoons; a knife and fork; a Swiss army knife, a torch and two sleeping bags.

Sleeping on the beach was not our preferred option. Cool breeze at night but the heat would wake you within the first hour of sunrise. On the third morning we made a forced decision to move. I was awakened by a movement in my sleeping bag, which I unpeeled slowly to witness a scorpion on my thigh. In a state of paralysis, I watched it take four short steps towards my knee, pause then turn to head back towards my thigh and pause again. Was it line dancing or just looking for the best place to land its sting? It then started to move in the direction of my crotch at which point a swift and sudden sweep of my right hand dispatched it into the air. At the same instant I expertly rolled out of the sleeping bag for fear of retribution from any of his mates who may have been in the bag or in the vicinity. Sleeping on the beach was no longer an option.

Dave and Phil from Warrington offered us a lifeline. There was a small space next to their "des-res" which we could have with use of their small stove and utensils, with a view to moving into a *"soon to be vacated"* shelter nearby. We had met the lads at one of the beach Tavernas. They talked our language, had our sense of humour and shared fags with Phil.

There were three Tavernas in total along the beach, simple shaded areas serving basic meals and drinks. Each morning, we would visit for egg on toast or a crusty roll with cheese followed by a tea or coffee.

Dave had mentioned a Taverna in the Village that served really good food and was inexpensive. He recommended that we eat before 6pm and be back on the beach before sunset. As a teacher you always tell the students to listen to instructions or read the full question. Phil and I did neither. On the late afternoon of day four we set off up a winding path on the twenty-minute walk to the Taverna in the Village.

The Taverna was both welcoming and lively and was obviously a popular place. We ordered dolmades, which consisted of stuffed vine leaves with rice, mince and a tomato sauce. They were exquisite particularly when accompanied with a cold beer. The meal in its entirety, with enough bread to feed the five thousand, amounted to less than sixty pence. As the sun began to set behind the houses, we exited for the return journey down the hillside and through the forest back to our base.

For most people, the actual time of the sunset is inconsequential. However, in this part of the world the sun does not set, it dives. Within fifteen minutes the world is transformed from day to night and in our case pitch blackness.

The path down the hillside was hazardous in the light, with twists and turns and roots reaching across to challenge any unsuspecting individual. In the dark it was impossible particularly without the torch, which for some unknown reason we had decided not to carry. Using all my outdoor activity knowledge, which could be written on the back of a bus ticket, I took the lead down through the trees towards the beach using a large stick to determine the way ahead. A combination of Blind John and a latter-day Moses leading his flock towards the Promised Land.

Seeing the lights of the beach I dispensed with the services of my sturdy staff. This was the point where caution was displaced by complacency. Turning right towards the light and the gentle sound of the strumming guitar I made what can only be described as one small step for man one giant leap for the insane as the path disappeared and I dropped eight feet through the roof of a lean-to shelter whose occupants were sat several feet away on the edge of the beach by a campfire

I scrambled from the debris with my shoulder sore and a few minor cuts on my legs. Nothing seriously damaged but my pride. For the inhabitants, stopped in mid tune it was a disaster. They were homeless. They were devastated. I tried to clear a space for them to at least sleep, before apologising and heading off, knowing that day five would be spent on re-building their shelter.

Phil in the meantime had found his way successfully back to our sleeping area and was responding to the crisis in the best way he knew with a brew and a fag.

"What happened to you?" I said.

"Well, you went right and disappeared, so I went left and the rest is history. I've done you a drink."

The beach with its soft sand and gentle waves was a great place to chill. There seemed to be no restriction on clothing. Some people were topless and others naked. There is something liberating and exhilarating about skinny dipping and this beach, which was not over-crowded, provided an ideal environment to swim and sunbathe in the buff. I was in my element. That was until a few days into my routine a middle-aged police officer struck my dangling Johnson with his stick. He was making me aware that at the weekend, there is no nudity because the local villagers make use of the beach. Fair play, but Christ did it hurt.

The time on the beach was really relaxing, but there was nothing to do. We spent a couple of days exploring the island and seemed to be on the leader board for the consumption of beer at the Taverna. Twelve days into our stay we decided to move. At this point it is necessary to mention that during our time, the beach community which consisted of many people from differing nationalities, had no reported crime, no incidents of aggression and was without doubt one of the safest and most sociable places I have ever visited.

With funds running low, I had sent a letter to my mother asking for some money to be sent to my stepsister Radmila's apartment in Belgrade. With the knowledge of funds in transit we set off for Athens on another ferry.

Athens was very similar to Rome, but with higher pollution. There were some famous landmarks and some excellent restaurants. The days were very hot and uncomfortable and without transport we were inclined to spend the day in the bar watching sport. Whilst in Athens I managed to obtain a fake Student Identity Card, which would allow me to obtain discount rail travel in various countries during the homeward journey. Phil had enough funds for a direct passage home.

Five days after arriving in the Greek capital, I decided to travel to Belgrade alone. I headed to the outskirts of Athens in search of a lift in the direction of Macedonia. In less than an hour I was on the road again. A Turkish family heading for Germany stopped to give me a lift. There were two children, aged about eight or nine years of age in the back. They spoke very little English, but every so often the driver would utter a random sentence which I then tried to respond to.

"Always it is raining in England?" or the more amusing "Why does Queen not show crown?"

About an hour into the journey, I felt some movement by my legs. Looking down I saw not one but two infants crawling around. I was totally unaware that they were in the boot of the car resting when I had been given a lift. Now with a couple of toys they seemed quite happy to crawl about in the well of the car and into the boot. Eventually we arrived at Skopje, and I exited the car to catch a train to Belgrade. On the short walk to the station, I was surrounded by a group of children aged between five and nine years, some dressed in paper-thin tee shirts, unkept and shoeless. Reaching desperately, pleading from behind eyes dark with sorrow for money, chocolate, cigarettes or anything. I felt helpless.

Once in Belgrade, I quickly made my way to my Radmila's home. I had never actually met her but had spoken to her at length from college during her lightening visit to my parents in Manchester in 1973. The address was easy to find. I knocked the door, once, twice but no response. It was then that a neighbour appeared and in broken English told me she was away at the Black Sea for two weeks. I glanced into her mailbox to view the distinctive air mail envelope with MY money in it sitting nicely on top, but out of reach. Nobody had a key to the apartment or the mailbox.

There was only one course of action a student discount rail ticket to London. At the station I produced my student card and asked for a ticket to London.

"Innsbruck," the ticket clerk said abruptly.

"No sorry Lon – don," with the city broken into two syllables, as the English abroad often do.

"Only in Innsbruck can you use this card."

With absolutely no idea where I was heading, with Innsbruck definitely not on the radar, I purchased a rail ticket to the border. The train eventually terminated at a station in Austria sandwiched between two huge mountains in the early hours of the morning. I tried my luck once more at the ticket office, explaining that I only had limited funds and needed a student ticket to London.

The slow shake of the head and the pursed lips said it all. My eyes were pleading but the bastard wouldn't look at them. I went to a machine for a coffee and a chocolate bar, my supper, and sat down on the station bench not sure of what to do next. There was a road outside the station, but I had no idea where I was or where it would lead. With my head in my hands, I was clueless.

A huge figure appeared from behind me. The stationmaster was six feet- five inches and about seventeen stone. Fearing the worst I grabbed my rucksack and stood up.

"English, take the next train which is for Munchen and sit in toilet," he whispered before walking away briskly.

Was this a set-up? Was it really an option? There was no choice. When the next train arrived, I jumped on board and headed for the toilet. This experience went some way to dismissing my aspirations to be an astronaut. An hour in the toilet was doing little for my sanity not to mention my aching buttocks.

I emerged into the actual cabin and found a window seat. At the next stop the guard walked the length of the platform, stopping to scrutinize the sleeping passenger he had missed on his walk through the carriage checking tickets. A quick return to a toilet was required before the train commenced its journey.

Eventually the train pulled into the station at Munich and before it had ground to a halt I was off running across the tracks. Freedom at last. Freedom.

I went to a local supermarket to buy some breakfast. It was then that

I realised that half of my money was in Dinar, which was not accepted anywhere accept in Yugoslavia. They wouldn't even exchange it. With less than eleven pounds to get home to England I bought a baguette, some cheese and a large bottle of Coke.

A couple of lifts later I found myself at a service station on the autobahn. There were many trucks, but the cars seemed to ignore my flowing arm. In desperation I went into the café for a drink and began a conversation with a Welsh truck driver called Eddie. He explained that trucks were not allowed to travel on the autobahn from midday on Saturday until 6.00 p.m. on Sunday. He also added that if I was still at the service area on Sunday night, he would give me a lift back to London.

That was a no-brainer. Spending half my cash on a bratwurst sandwich I settled down on the grass verge at the side of the road for the next 24 hours. My Sunday lunch consisted of a baguette, some Gouda cheese and a fruit juice, the service area special deal.

Eddie was true to his word. Throughout the journey we discussed many differing things from sport to culture and the current situation in politics. Eddie's knowledge was immense and far reaching. He explained that his work allowed him time to read and in doing so he had gained a useful knowledge and understanding of many different areas. It was a lesson that stayed with me throughout my life – do not judge the intelligence, capabilities or personality of someone by their job or their appearance.

When we arrived at Ostende, Eddie booked me on the Ferry as his co-driver, providing me with a cabin and a meal. He assured me he was not unique in his generosity with many truckers providing lifts for hikers. However, in many cases they would just curl up and go to sleep, neglecting the driver whose primary need is conversation and companionship.

I finally left Eddie in London and headed to Phil's place. It transpired that he had arrived home two hours earlier having endured a third-class rail passage through Italy, sharing a compartment with some chickens and an oversized women with a body odour problem. No air conditioning and no opportunity to stretch or sleep. All for forty quid. I made a brew, threw him a fag and then said "Listen to this ..."

# Chapter Six

During my teenage years in Manchester one of the most significant influences on my overall development both socially and physically was Gorton Lads Club.

Situated in an old Methodist church hall the club opened for three nights each week to provide the youth of the area with an opportunity to meet. The hall which was about twenty-five yards long and fifteen yards wide had a draped net across its entire width a quarter of the way down from the entrance on the other side of which was an area for four-a-side football with five-minute games taking place continually from opening to close at 9.00 p.m. A full size and a junior snooker table placed end to end occupied the other side of the net which protected players from the barrage of shots during the evening. On the first floor was a small room with a table tennis table.

It was part of a network which included amongst others Ancoats, Ardwick, Collyhurst, Openshaw and the more famous Salford Lads Clubs all with differing activities. All providing opportunities for young people to meet in a purposeful, active and safe environment.

There was a football league competition for all the clubs from September to April at two age groups, Under-15 and Under-18 with games played every Saturday afternoon. The best players were selected for the Manchester Federation of Lad's Club team to play against other areas and Manchester Boys. There was even an International representative team for the Under-18 age group.

For many, in the days before televisions in every room and play-stations, it was a lifeline. A sanctuary. A time to escape for a few hours from the small, terraced houses and live a life with banter, action and noise. It was a place with a pulse. It made long winter nights shorter. It was our community, occasional conflict, regular competition but always cooperation.

There was an unwritten code of conduct. Equipment was treated with the utmost respect. Replacement was not expected. Table tennis balls seemed to last an age and bats a generation. There was no vandalism and no equipment stolen. At the end of each session the snooker tables would be covered, with the equipment returned to the office ready for the next evening.

The Griffin had a Youth Club which would meet every Monday night from 6.00 p.m. till 8.30 p.m. Students who had travelled home hours earlier, some five or six miles, would return eager to be part of the social event of the week.

The new Sports Hall provided a major expansion to the activities on offer which had previously been confined to a gymnasium, a small classroom and an outdoor playground. With badminton, five-a-side football, basketball and table tennis available in the sporting areas and snooker, albeit a junior table, and music in the small room, there was much to occupy the nomadic groups who would wander from activity to activity.

No pressure. Free to move and free to choose. Freedom of expression, freedom of spirit.

When asked if I would like to be one of the youth workers there was no hesitation. The payment was minimal but that was not a concern. It provided a great opportunity to get to know the kids.

For some children, school is a cage. They have difficulty staying in one area for a length of time. They are inquisitive and need to prowl the cage. Some have difficulty maintaining their focus for extended periods and sometimes they are disruptive within four walls. In the youth club environment, the cage is unlocked, and a different animal emerges.

The youth club animal will engage in casual conversation. They will ask if you would like a game of table tennis or if you would be on their team in the next game of football. No barriers. You are one of them. They will place cans and papers in the bins and help clear away equipment without being asked. They take ownership. They grow.

With regular attendance of between seventy and a hundred students, Monday night was vibrant and an essential part of the school community. When Colin came on board the choice of activities was extended even further with gymnastics and outdoor activities added to volleyball and street hockey.

At the end of each term there would be a Youth Club Disco on a

Friday night with a local DJ, Geoff Anderson, providing music from 7.30 p.m. until 10.00 p.m. The event was limited to members and a friend but were always sold out. It not only raised money for the Youth Club but provided a controlled and safe place for different age groups to meet and chill out.

For two decades the club provided a release. Then the Council's "Educational Visionaries" became involved. Every activity should have a structure and be progressive. Youth workers would need to provide a scheme of work, a formal plan. There was no place for spontaneity. They introduced the very aspects that the children were escaping from. They extended the school day further. It was the beginning of the end.

Through the progressive reduction of funding for youth clubs, the vital connection between teenagers and the adult world has been destroyed. The opportunity for young people to demonstrate the qualities of responsible ownership are no more. The concept of Play has been eradicated from the conversation which in turn removes the platform for young individuals to be themselves. It denies adults access to their world, to develop mutual respect and create a bond, not just for Monday night, but throughout the week.

When I read or hear that the youth of today do not have respect for older people, I often try to remind those making the claims that a root cause is the lack of respect those in power have shown to them over many years. A total disregard of their needs at a vital stage of their development.

Responsibility comes through ownership; respect through recognition; growth through opportunity.

With the veneer that sometimes (for many different reasons) exists from 8.45 a.m. removed, the kids will share their hopes and aspirations, their fears and concerns, their likes and dislikes. They will indulge you in their past and include you in their present. You discover where they have been and what they have done. What life is like for them beyond the school gates. Sometimes the narrative is saddening.

For many their experiences of life was limited to Cannock and its surrounding area. Family holidays, if they existed were mostly westward along the A5 to the Welsh coast or Holyhead where the ferry across to Dun Laoghaire would re-unite them with family in Ireland.

My increasingly regular coach driving to sporting fixtures combined with my recent exploits across Europe led me to reassess the landscape. I could change the mindset of students. Ignite the desire to explore and taste adventure. I could do it through sport.

I remembered my times as a fourteen-year-old schoolboy playing for Manchester Boys, particularly the away games. The team would meet on Wednesday afternoon and Saturday morning at Aytoun Street in the City centre and travel by coach across Lancashire and beyond. The excitement and the expectation never diminished.

I could re-create that excitement. I had the coach. I was the driver. I had the time.

The perfect partner was handball, a sport I had introduced to the school following the completion of the new sports hall. The sport had been adopted by a group of fourth year boys who regularly attended training each Thursday lunchtime. Having played and won their first game against the Royal Grammar School from Worcester the team were keen for more. They asked for a further training session but due to after-school fixtures and other sports it was impossible to find time. I suggested time after youth club on Monday.

All the players agreed without any need for canvassing. The session would begin at 8.15 p.m. and end at 9.15 p.m. This was soon extended to 9.45 p.m. With the Sports Hall detached from any part of the school it was my responsibility to turn off the lights, lock-up and close the school gates when the session had finished.

It was now time to get serious. A couple of the players agreed to help Clive, the woodwork teacher who constructed some standard handball goals from the four-inch square wooden beams that a friend had found "surplus to requirement" on his building site. Painted red and white they were to last for over twenty years.

In December 1975, I contacted John D Timmins, the enthusiastic and ebullient secretary of the British Handball Association, and with his help acquired contact details of several teams, mostly clubs, who were currently playing handball in England. John was passionate about the sport and would regularly update me with potential teams and general information.

Things were quickly falling into place and with the momentum building the future began to look interesting.

# Chapter Seven

The new year did not start particularly well. The weather did not help, often cold and miserable and this impacted on the general demeanour of many students who were still in hibernation mode following the Christmas break. The majority of sporting activities took place indoors and those outdoors were short and not so sweet.

Every Friday afternoon the fifth and sixth form would engage in a programme of Leisure pursuits. Several teachers were co-opted into the scheme to provide a range of activities from wine making (how they got away with that I don't know) and photography to swimming and ice-skating. The students had a choice of four or five activities to cover five six-week periods with two in the winter, two in the spring and one in the summer. The latter reduced because of examinations.

Now a regular coach driver I volunteered to take the ice-skating group the twenty-two mile journey to the Silver Blades Ice Rink in Birmingham. It was a time before the M6 motorway suffered from intolerable congestion which currently often makes it the longest carpark in England. The journey from Cannock to Birmingham was never more than forty minutes.

A group of approximately thirty enthusiasts would join me on the ice for an afternoon of hilarity and wonder. There were the adventurous newcomers with flaying arms and legs of rope, the Bambi on ice group. Throughout the afternoon there would be at least one spectacular fall or a car crash on the ice where several people were involuntarily grounded by a mass of bone and muscle sliding out of control on the wet, cold surface. The amazing thing was that those responsible were often the first to their feet for another attempt to emulate Birmingham born Olympic Gold medal winner John Curry.

There were others who moved across the ice at speed with poise occasionally demonstrating their ability to stop in an instant and then skate backwards. The majority, however, were just content to circle the large arena at a steady pace either solo or hand-in-hand with a friend, but never far from the security of the substantial side walls. This was my designated group during early visits, but I did improve as the year progressed.

The session would last about an hour with a return to school in time for the regular school transport which departed at 3.45 p.m.

On the third Monday morning of January, I was summoned to the headteachers office.

"It would appear that you left Steven in Birmingham after the ice-skating on Friday," he informed me.

"I can't understand how. The doors to the coach are closed until I have the register ready and mark every student as they enter one by one."

"Well, I did say that to his mother." he said in a wonderfully calm and understated manner. "What Steven was quite expecting once you had departed with the group I don't know, but he eventually decided to go the police station penniless, and they arranged for a lift home at 7.30 p.m."

I was perplexed. I went straight to the sixth form common room to both apologies and find out how this had happened. That is when the story unravelled. Eighteen-year-old Steven did embark on the bus, in fact he was one of the first, moving to the back seat (always dominated by the eldest students). He had the beginnings of a painful blister on his heel so decided to exit through the Emergency Door and re-enter the Ice Rink to get a plaster from the reception. He told no-one.

The coach was moving away and about fifty yards from the venue when he apparently re-appeared waving frantically to no avail. It was three hours later when he realised the coach was not returning that he decided to go to the Police Station.

A lesson to be learned – always make a visual check immediately before departing.

My dismay was short-lived. Peter K stopped me to take the p*** before telling me he was off to the "graveyard of buses" in Middlewich to purchase a replacement coach.

"This one will have a proper gear stick," he laughed "... and an Emergency Exit alarm that works!" It was the end of the road for the white sardine can.

The new bus was a magnificent beast. A former Crossville bus which had served the population of North Wales and Cheshire with distinction.

The driver's seat seemed to float and the gear lever was short with no need to double de-clutch, have a grip of steel or have a passenger nearby to help replace the long wand back into the gear housing whilst driving. Everything seemed to work perfectly. It was the real deal.

Within a few weeks I had organised a handball game against a club team on the Wirral. Before leaving the school, I adjusted the destination screen at the front of the bus to display *"Birkenhead."* A nice touch.

The nice touch subsequently provided an afternoon of amusement for the lads. As we travelled on the A51 in the direction of Birkenhead, people old and young waiting patiently at bus-stops put out their hands to stop the bus. The universal signal. When it coasted casually past them, they all reacted in different ways. Some stood with mouths and arms open wide, others, usually the older generation shook their raised fists. For one gentleman it was too much. He had appeared from a garage forecourt and seeing the bus sprinted forty yards carrying his sports bag in one hand and a pie in the other. Reaching the stop with seconds to spare having lost some of his pie, he could only stand in amazement as the bus cruised by at which he threw his bag down in frustration before kicking it towards the wall.

It became a regular feature at the beginning of our trips to Birkenhead, at the time a hotbed for handball. Simply guess the number of angry or bemused commuters we would pass en-route to the game. We even nominated a judge to verify if they qualified – a reaction or a hand signal in expectation. The winner receiving a Mars Bar. The kids loved it.

I was now driving the bus to all the sporting fixtures, often driving it home on a Friday evening and parking overnight on the road close to my house. On Saturday I would pick up several players from Rugeley town centre and pre-arranged places on the way into school for football fixtures. For the parents it saved either bus fare or the inconvenience of driving across the Chase early in the morning.

On one occasion the games were against a local school a few minutes away from my house. I arrived at the changing rooms to discover that my fourth-year captain was missing due to his sister getting married. Rob was essential to the midfield, a ball winner and a leader when play got physical.

Today could be one of those days when everyone needed to pitch in. His best mate Andy was just about to get changed.

"What time is the wedding?" I asked Andy, his best mate.

"One o'clock sir, at the Catholic Church."

"Does he live close by?"

"Yes, up the road by the Miners Arms."

"Right jump in the car and take me there. Let's see if we can get him to play for part of the game."

He lived on a housing estate where many of the mining community lived. A hot bed for footballers. I drove straight to his house, walked up the short path and knocked on the door. His young sister answered but was soon followed by Rob who pulled the door closed behind him. He could see Andy in the car, and I could see the disappointment in his eyes.

"I wanted to play Sir, but I've got the wedding later..."

"I know," I said. "How are things going?"

"Fine, I think. My mom's busy with the bridesmaids and she has told me to stay out of the way."

"That's why I'm here.... we've only got ten players and you will be out of the way for the next hour or so. I promise to have you back here by twelve." He smiled and I could see the glint in his eye.

"But I've got no boots and if I go back inside..."

"No problem, you can have my boots and I have some spare shin-pads in the car. The rest I'll get at the changing rooms." Before I had finished speaking, he was down the path and jumping into the car next to Andy who was laughing. Looking back to the house I saw the bride-to-be stood in the window, shaking her head but probably not surprised.

Playing in a pair of shorts that had seen better days, odd socks and top of the range Adidas boots he played a blinder, almost scoring from outside the area, but leading the lads to another win. At the final whistle he was rushed from the field like a celebrity, changed quicker than Clarke Kent and then was driven the two miles for his second starring role of the day. The wedding went without a hitch.

It was also a big day for my house-mate Joe. Scheduled to run six hundred metres at a televised indoor international meeting at Cosford later in the day. He was tucking into a breakfast of beans on toast earlier in the day before I left for the school game.

"I am going to go for a world record today," he casually said.

"Oh, really and I am going to ride the winner of the three o'clock at Haydock," I replied with a smile. But then, who was I to doubt the man who had played in football's elite European Competition; played in an All-Ireland Gaelic football Final and won a silver medal at the World Student games all before his 21st birthday.

Later in the afternoon I was able to watch the race as Joe stormed through to beat the American world record holder, Mike Winzenreid, comfortably - but 0.06 seconds outside the world best. A few weeks later, he did achieve television immortality when he won the National Indoor Championships. The finish of the race was featured as the final action on the closing sequence of BBC's Grandstand for the next ten years.

Word began to spread that the handball team were prepared to travel anywhere to play. John Timmins accelerated the process by sending my details to anyone who called him. In the early games we were sparing partners for the established teams. On one occasion we played against a team from the Technical College in Nuneaton. Not only were the team three years older but had a current GB Player, Chris Unett and several who had played in League competitions. We lost by fifty-five goals to five.

On the fifty-minute journey home I asked different players to describe the goals they had scored and what it felt like? What about that pass? I asked the keeper, Pedro about some of the saves he had made with both his hands and his feet. What about that penalty save? Did you enjoy playing the game? Would you want to play them again in the future?

I looked in the large mirror of the bus and not a single player looked despondent. All I could see was positivity and excitement. They may have lost on points, but they were ready for the next fight.

The following day the players approached me to ask for additional training time. They wanted more. I was struggling with time. Two age groups playing Basketball, five age groups playing football, three age groups in Cross-country and a District football team, in addition to the popular gymnastics group Colin had set-up. I wasn't prepared to sacrifice any group, but they had desire and enthusiasm. How could anyone disregard that? A solution had to be found.

At the time the new bus arrived Peter K put his arm over my shoulder and presented me with the key and then suggested I should join the Parent Teachers Association as they would be a future source of finance for kit and equipment. The meetings were once a month.

The first meeting went quite well with the group made up of older mothers, a couple of dominant males and a couple of males with their wives, instructed to attend but generally saying nothing. I managed to sit and listen to various plans for future events and requests for money from departments within the school. Having just purchased the bus their coffers were almost empty.

At the second meeting I was asked for my opinions on certain aspects of fund raising, including the annual gala day, which I mistakenly gave. If you are ever asked for an opinion at any organisation concerned with fund-raising, ensure that the answer does not involve any change of direction or modus operandi. If it does, you will be invited to lead from the front. I suddenly became the focus of the meeting, not only was my idea to hold the festival over a weekend accepted but I was asked to lead on the Sunday. The Committee had already discussed a Merrie England theme and decided to run with it, but a Festival of Activity on the Sunday would be a major bonus.

With less than five months to the event I had to move quickly to put things into place. I needed to have kids involved. It was a shop-window opportunity for some of the teams and individuals. A junior five-a-side tournament was a must. Colin and Sue could produce a gymnastic display. The handball team could play a game. An "It's A Knockout" tournament, with teams from various parishes and guest teams would be a fun event.

Within a few weeks I had secured an exhibition game of wheel-chair Basketball, followed by a demonstration game of volleyball by the National schools' champions from Ounsdale, near Wolverhampton in the Sports Hall. Nuneaton Handball Club agreed to play the school team outdoors and I had managed to persuade the Wings Sky-diving team from Halfpenny Green to demonstrate their skills in return for a small renumeration and a free stall to advertise their club.

An All-Star team from Wolverhampton and Bilston Athletic Club, featuring many International and Olympic athletes agreed to enter the

"It's a Knockout" along with a team from Nuneaton. This would without doubt swell the audience.

The day was perfect. Warm with a few pillow-like clouds breaking up the sky. The Wings team opened the event with five participants aiming to land on a cross by the cricket square. The first jumper and his red flare was greeted with applause with everyone looking at the sky. However, it did not all go according to plan as the chute opened and he appeared to be heading off course. Was it a trick to get everyone excited?

The look on the group's leaders face said otherwise as the chute continued on its west-bound course eventually ending uninvited in a garden on Shoal Hill, which now had a severely damaged green-house and an embarrassed skydiver. The rest hit the mark in quick succession.

In all the two-day event attracted over thirteen-hundred people and made over a thousand pounds profit for the school. The "It's a Knockout" was well received and was won by the visitors from Nuneaton. The Chairman of the handball Club was Jeff Rowland, generally accredited with introducing the sport into England. Born in Wednesfield, he was the current Chairman of the British Handball Association. With pipe in hand, he congratulated me on the day and then said "You've got some good lads there. I need you on the Executive Committee running handball in schools. Ring John Timmins on Monday and he will fill you in." At that he turned and ambled away.

On a warm Sunday afternoon, following two long days and too knackered to say "no" I became the Chairman and Secretary of the newly formed England School's Handball Association.

Throughout June and July, the weather in 1976 was fantastic, with the All-England Schools' Athletics Championships staged in Cannock. The high temperatures did have a negative effect on some performances with some athletes also suffering from food poisoning. The heat was not just confined to the days. The nights were warm and dry, and even with windows opened it was sometimes difficult to sleep. I would often give Joe a shout and together we would go for a thirty or forty minute run at 1.00am, crashing out on the back lawn on our return, much to the surprise of the milkman the following morning.

Our time in Rugeley, however, was coming to an end. With Rick moving out to live with his partner and Dougie going back to Yorkshire,

Joe and I decided to buy a house between us. My equipment room at school became the temporary storage area for my limited "worldly goods", which included an expanding collection of vinyl records, a turntable and my clothes during the school summer holidays, whilst I travelled across the Atlantic for six weeks to renew my connection with Camp Towanda.

# Chapter Eight

Some headteachers recognise the contribution of an active and lively Physical Education department towards the overall ethos of the school. They are appreciative of the time devoted to both clubs and fixtures in providing opportunities for all students. Others see it as a necessary evil, non-academic and sometimes creating more inconvenience than value.

Then there are the very few headteachers who recognise the many additional hours that some staff freely give. They are the ones willing to give something back, who will consider requests for time or resources. They offer unconditional support. Peter Bateson, aka the Duke, was such a headteacher. Following a discussion about my plans for the summer and my house move he called me in to his office a couple of weeks before the end of term.

"You have asked to leave early on the last day of term," he said.

"Yes, I need to be at the camp in Pennsylvania by the Saturday. If I could leave early on Friday, hopefully, I will be able to get a late afternoon or early evening flight to New York."

"Look," he said. "With all the time you have invested over the past months I am prepared to let you leave midday on Thursday if that will help. However, the arrangement must remain confidential."

I was temporarily stunned but not surprised. He did after all promote me quickly within the school and always took an interest in the sporting achievements of the school. He had bought into the department's efforts to raise the profile of the school in the local area through a variety of sporting activities.

With the opportunity to take the early morning flight to New York, courtesy of Freddie Laker, things would be perfect. I would arrive at Camp for dinner and then re-acquaint myself with staff before the Friday night party in town followed by Visiting Day on the Saturday. Fantastic.

I arrived at JFK in New York just after midday on the Friday. With the enthusiasm of a two-year old thoroughbred. I breezed past the dawdling passengers towards immigration to be at the head of the line, which can at times take up to an hour to clear.

Having travelled overnight to London and with a healthy tan from the hot English summer I did appear to be more Berber than Brit. The passport control officer viewed me with some suspicion.

"What is the purpose of your visit?" he asked.

"I am working at a Summer Camp in Pennsylvania," I replied, immediately detecting a change of facial expression.

"Yours is a one-way ticket. What funds do you have with you?"

"Just over a hundred dollars. Enough to get me into the city and for the onward journey to Honesdale, with some pizza on the way," I said with enthusiasm and a smile.

"But not enough to get you back to England!" he declared staring into the huge immigration book in front of him. Totally still.

"No but my salary will cover that..." at which point he raised his hand and turned to summon an Immigration officer to the booth. Obviously posing a significant threat, a pair swiftly arrived.

"This guy has come to work but does not have a J1 visa and has insufficient funds to support his stay and return journey," he informed them.

With the rest of the passengers watching and no doubt exchanging views as to why I was being detained, I was escorted away to retrieve my bags before being taken to a small room and searched. The couple of deflated handballs were taken away for examination and the whole of my case was emptied.

For the next two hours I sat alone in the room, with an occasional visit from an officer who would ask another question, write down an answer and then disappear. I was questioned about my job in England, my previous visits to the USA (with a work permit) and about my future plans. Was I intending to stay? Would I become one of the thousands who have entered the country but not exited? The fact that I had not booked a return flight did not help my case.

Almost three hours after landing a tall a thick-set Officer, who appeared to be the most senior entered the room and explained that a lawyer for the Camp had confirmed that they were expecting me.

"It would appear from my conversation that the money mentioned is owed to you by the Camp for recruitment work carried out in England.

You will be staying with them for the duration of your stay, in which case you do not need a visa, and you are free to go."

No apology. No welcome to America. No "have a nice day."

I quickly packed my bag again leaving the airport to be greeted by the heat, humidity and the prospect of rush-hour traffic that would double my journey time into the Port Authority, the central bus station of New York. In keeping with Murphy's law, I missed the last bus of the day to Honesdale. The only solution was to take a bus to Scranton, situated thirty miles from Honesdale, arriving fifteen minutes past midnight and then with my remaining cash take a cab.

My first night at Camp in 1976 was spent in the Head Counsellors shack and Equipment room with eight dollars in my pocket, sleeping on a bed of goal-nets and softball bases before being aroused by the blaring trumpets of reveille at 7.00 a.m. Welcome to Camp Towanda!

Following a quick explanation of events to Murray, the head counsellor, I was then directed to my bunk, with an apology. I had originally been placed with an older group, but due to need I was being redeployed to a group of six-year-old boys away from home for the first time. They had already "worn out" two other counsellors and I would be helped by Mike, a sixteen-year-old CIT (counsellor in training). This could turn out to be the most tiring and challenging Visiting Day ever.

During the clean-up after breakfast the organiser of the "Cadillac count" competition, Bobby Miller arrived in the bunk. The annual event involved members of staff paying a dollar to guess the total number of Cadillacs that would be parked on site at 1.00 p.m. during the Visiting Day. Both Mike and I paid our dollar, my shout 120, his 121.

The day went well. The parents of my small group seemed relieved that they were still in one piece and safe. They were grateful that an experienced teacher was taking care of them, unaware that I had no clue whatsoever about young children. I had not even had an opportunity to gain a degree of knowledge in the family home being the only child. Mike stayed around for the morning before his parents arrived to take him to Honesdale for lunch just after midday.

With all visitors long departed, dinner was noisy with most of the campers talking frantically about the visit of their parents and grandparents. The topic was either money, gifts or candy depending on their age. At the end of the meal the winner of the Cadillac competition was announced. The total number at 1.00 p.m. was 120!

I walked forward to a mixed reception to collect my $100.00 prize, with my faith in humanity restored. It was only on my return to the table that I noticed a distinct pallor in Mike's face. He had his hands on his head, always a sign of some despair.

The distress soon became clear. His parents had arrived at camp during the latter part of the morning and following conversations with friends had departed at about 12.40 for lunch in Honesdale, twenty minutes before the count. The car they were driving was a Cadillac. The meal at the Fireside had just cost Mike $100.00.

I did ensure that my new-found fortune was shared through the traditional pitchers of beer at Danny's during the Saturday night, which unfortunately, due to his age, Mike could not participate in. Pizza would have to suffice.

One of my designated tasks on my arrival was to ensure that six-year-old Aaron, who slept directly opposite me visit the bathroom as late as possible each night to prevent any accident during his sleep.

Just before 1.00 a.m. I learned my first lesson in child-care. Leaning over his bed I gently shook Aaron to wake him, quietly whispering that it was time for the bathroom. At this point a small appendage appeared through his pyjama bottom, gushing forth in the spirit of Ole Faithful. Still in a state of slumber I lifted him from the bed and ran towards the bathroom pointing him directly ahead, spraying the route with urine, before finally reaching the toilet, by which time the flow had subsided. At 1.20 a.m. having put dry underwear on Aaron and placed him in my bed with his comfort teddy, I cleaned the bunk floor before going to sleep on his plastic-covered mattress with no sheets and a couple of blankets for cover. Life has a way of spoiling the party.

Throughout the following weeks I would always gently lift Aaron into position in the cubicle before uttering the magic words. By the last week he was often awake, so I gambled. Three nights before the end of camp I gently awoke him and walked with him to the bathroom before he relived himself and returned to bed without any guidance. He repeated this on the final two nights with minimal help. A result, and definitely not, a "flash in the pan," so to speak.

With the Camp now employing an increasing number of British counsellors the four weeks seemed to pass quickly. Each had up to six weeks for travel at the end of camp and in the final days people who were complete strangers weeks before, made plans to explore the vast and varied landscape of America. Some would go solo, using an unlimited thirty-one-day Greyhound travel pass whilst some would hitch in pairs. I hooked up with Mark, Marty and Trevor to use a driveaway agency.

Driveaway Agencies in New York and New Jersey would arrange for drivers to deliver a domestic vehicle to a given location often several hours or days away for a small fee. This would allow the owner the opportunity to fly in comfort. The agencies relied heavily on people wishing to travel throughout the USA from city to city for the cost of fuel and tolls only. A deposit made by the driver when receiving the car would be returned on delivery if there is no damage to the vehicle. It was an easy and economical way to travel long distances.

Following several phone calls to three agencies we finally came up with a hit. A vehicle from New Jersey to Coral Gables, just south of Miami to be picked up two days after Camp closed. We had discovered through conversations with others that the Agencies would only allow a maximum of two drivers and no passengers. There was also a time allocated for delivery based on a maximum of 350 miles per day which equated to eight hours driving time. Taking turns to drive, with pit-stops, we could complete the twenty- hour journey in a day, with a set of wheels for the remaining three.

Mark and I registered with the company as the recipients, both having driven cars whilst at camp. We arranged to pick the vehicle up at 10.00 a.m. on the Monday morning at the office in New Jersey.

Leaving Marty and Trevor sat on their bags a few blocks away from the Office, Mark and I went to pick up the car. On completion of the forms and handing across $200 security deposit we were shown to the car, a Cadillac. All the necessary papers were inside, including the delivery address and contact. The car was expected in Coral Gables on Friday morning. The guy gave simple directions to the Turnpike and from there it was a straight run on 95 South for 1300 miles.

When I was adjusting the driver mirror, I noticed that one of the guys in the office walking to a car. I waited a short time, but he did not move.

He only moved as I started to pull away.

"We are being followed," I said to Mark. "We may have to be a little bit cute."

I drove towards the Turnpike slowly as if getting used to the car and not wishing to exceed a speed limit. It allowed the following car to overtake if necessary. It did not happen.

What did happen was that we cruised past a bemused Trevor and Marty without any eye contact or acknowledgement, before entering the toll booth at the Turnpike, at which point the following car did a U turn and disappeared.

We left at the next exit before returning in the direction of the office to pick up our now agitated duo who were still slumped outside the Diner without a plan B, looking hopefully for a cream-coloured Caddy to reappear. Apparently, there had been little conversation after the exclamation by Marty of "what the fuck...." when we had driven by thirty minutes earlier.

The car was a dream. Cruise control, plush leather seats and a great sound system. Marty and Trevor relaxed in the back seat and were soon asleep as I drove south towards Maryland. Following a brief stop Mark took over at the wheel for the evening stint, with the two passengers finally awake.

Having passed a huge sign just before midnight which declared "Welcome to South of the Border" we decided to have an extended stop. When the waitress arrived to take our food order, we understood more fully what the sign implied. She seemed to speak a different language with a southern drawl that was unlike anything we had previously heard. It was to be part of our induction into the culture of the South during the next twelve hours.

Three hours later driving south on Interstate 95 with minimal traffic and three lanes of highway I was coasting along in cruise-control at a steady seventy miles per hour. From the cover of trees in the central reservation a patrol car appeared, lights flashing and a quick blast of the siren. It wanted me to stop. The officer approached and asked for my license and the papers for the car. A couple of minutes later he returned to hand them back and inform me that I was exceeding the speed limit. On some parts of the Interstate the limit is sixty-five miles per hour, but he informed me that on this stretch it is fifty-five miles per hour. Then he gave me the alternatives, drive with him to the nearby town and appear before the circuit judge later in the day if I wished to dispute the charge or pay $50 immediately. It was a no-brainer, reluctantly and without any formal ticket issued I handed over the cash.

"Yawl have a nice day." he said, before trailing along behind us for the next five miles.

Having reset the cruise control, we entered Georgia at sunrise, driving to a Diner just north of Brunswick for breakfast. Unshaven, tanned with long hair and dressed in cut-offs and tee shirts we entered the Diner with its proud Confederate flags at the door.

There were several men sat at the counter and some in booths. No women. The men were dressed in manual-work clothes and their physical features looked alarmingly similar. They were all white, heavily built with necks that looked thicker than their heads. Most had a buzz cut. The hum of noise stopped as I approached the counter.

"Good morning," I said, to which there was no reply. The men all were staring with a certain contempt at the four of us as if we were a threat or had dared to interrupt their day.

"Could I have ham and eggs easy over with hash browns and a coffee please?" I said in my Eton English. No impact. Just the quiet, uncomfortable stare from a room full of men. Some had even stopped eating and downed tools. We sat down in a far booth to eat our breakfast in double quick time. Having seen the film Easy Rider a few years earlier I could understand more clearly the intimidation felt by outsiders in some areas of America. It also partly explained why certain New Yorkers were reluctant to drive down to Florida. The immense breakfast also partly explained why the local men were so large.

We arrived in muted silence and left in the same way, trying to act normally whilst moving at a significantly abnormal pace. There were no sad goodbyes to Georgia, and she was definitely not on my mind.

On the drive from Daytona Beach to Miami I was able to pick up a couple of local newspapers and travel magazines. In one of the magazines, I discovered an article which mentioned a deal at the Castaways Motel on Collins Avenue in Miami. To commemorate independence from the British two hundred years earlier they were offering rooms at $17.76 per night throughout the year. One room with two huge beds could accommodate all of us for less than $5 a night, cheaper than a hostel. Welcome to Miami.

The Castaways motel was iconic. Situated on one of America's most famous avenues, it was built on a man-made island across the street from the Ocean. It had over three hundred rooms, a swimming pool and a famous night club. We checked in for seven days and was given a room which opened directly onto the pool side. The room was large with two king-size beds. A bonus was a daily voucher for a free drink before 7.00 p.m. in the motel's night club which was situated directly below our room.

Following a quick swim and shower, a shave and a change of clothes, we were ready for our first night out in Miami, starting with the free drink. Winding stairs led down to the Wreck Bar which was built to resemble an old galleon with polished wood and portholes. It was sizeable with a stage in a corner directly facing the curved bar which had several portholes providing views into the subterranean world of the swimming pool. The bar which opened at 11 a.m. and closed at 5 a.m. with live entertainment most nights had featured artists such as the Beatles, The Monkees and Jimi Hendrix in the past.

This had the makings of a solid base. That was until I ordered a second round of drinks. With a charge of twenty dollars plus tip for four beers it was time to explore alternative drinking stations and maybe return for a nightcap.

A few hours later with several beers consumed at a fraction of the cost we returned to the bar which was by this time well populated with both young and old. There was a female singer performing classic songs from the charts and shows. I was game for some amusement. I told Mark to stay where he was close to the bar, whilst Marty, Trevor and I disappeared. He realised that something was about to happen.

A few minutes later three figures were seen swimming past the portholes in the pool. It was during a rendition from Jesus Christ Superstar that the singer screamed "Jesus Christ!" and glared over to the bar where three bare buttocks appeared pressed against each porthole to the amusement of the crowd. Within seconds they had disappeared and so had we, back to our rooms with all lights turned off waiting for Mark's return and his report on the response.

Having the Cadillac till Friday was a massive bonus. It provided the opportunity to travel to the University and visit some of the famous parts of the city. It also provided reconnaissance for our evening entertainment.

Eventually we had to drive to Coral Gables to deliver the car to the owner. Marty and Trevor stayed by the pool. The address was easy to find and the owner in his early forties was tall and friendly. He asked how the journey had been and if there was any problem.

"No, it was fine. We took things easy as we had four days to get down here," I said.

"Really," he smiled "Only on Wednesday morning I was parked right next to a Cadillac identical to this at a Diner just off Collins."

I was speechless. Grinning he shook his head before handing over the $200 dollar deposit, much to my relief.

Carless, the next few days were spent by the pool or on the beach and at a local bar enjoying some live music and a few beers, before hitting on the delivery of a Buik Le Sabre to 65th Street in New York on the Tuesday which fitted perfectly with our plans. The all-singing, all-dancing convertible was not only huge with more controls than an aircraft but was less than three months old.

The drive to New York was uneventful, with a stopover at Norfolk, Virginia. I was pulled over again for speeding but this time the sheriff from Maryland was far more approachable reminding me that the laws in the US have been different than those in the United Kingdom for two-hundred years.

We arrived near Newark just before 5.00 pm, at which point Mark who was driving suddenly stopped and refused to drive the car through the Holland Tunnel into New York City for fear of pranging it. I had to take over. For the first part of the journey I resembled a Sunday driver, not exceeding twenty-five miles per hour. Emerging from the tunnel into the city I had three near collisions within a couple of minutes. Following the third of these and the expected noise from the horns of the cars around me I decided to drive like the taxi-drivers. Trevor dived for cover as I crossed from one lane to another at speed, in and out of the traffic using my horn with the frequency expected from a "local" to communicate with other drivers. One loud prolonged blast "get out of the way, coming through" and two blasts "get a move on."

In no time at all I reached the parking lot on 65th Street safely and without any cause for concern. I collected my $200 and passed Go.

A day later I returned to England with a Floridian tan and the financial health to match. I had some great ideas for the school programme. I was homeless.

# Chapter Nine

The house I was buying with Joe in Penkridge was not available for occupancy until the end of October. I had a couple of days to find somewhere to stay before the new term started. Fortunately, a great friend and a local Physical Education teacher, Rod McAlpine, invited me to stay at his house. I had met his wife June in September 1970 - during my first day at College, where she was a mentor for arriving students. I was sorted.

The boys had returned to school with the usual banter, stories of the summer, some of it fantasy, but ready to hit the new football season running. Despite the difficulties with transport for some, their commitment was amazing. We had another County goalkeeper in Martin and strong teams in the older age groups.

Colin continued his work in gymnastics, with a growing number of male and female participants, reaching impressive performance levels. He had spent much of the summer rock-climbing. It was a real passion, and he was keen to introduce it to the students at the school. With funds from the PTA the department was able to buy some ropes, carabiners and helmets. The Youth Club also contributed with the climbing wall in the corner of the gym offering another Monday night activity.

The interest in handball had not waned. Groups of players reminding me of sessions after Youth Club. They also asked for more games. I called John Timmins for guidance. The number of schools or Colleges playing was limited. He suggested we join the newly formed Midlands Senior League which at the time had five teams registered. It was the only way I could get them games on a regular basis. It also opened up an opportunity for me to play. Without any kit or senior handballs and a sixty pounds from my summer exploits we entered the league.

A local sports shop, Olympia Sports, agreed to provide some kit in return for limited advertising. In October 1976, Olympia Handball Club was formed, playing their home games on Sunday afternoons at a local leisure centre in Cheslyn Hay, with minimal width and a punishing tile floor. There would be no place to hide.

On the first Sunday in November, we played our first game against Leicester. Wearing our new kit of white shirts with a red and black diagonal stripe we looked impressive. The only issue was the man-made material which was not only robust but had no absorption properties which the players soon discovered. It was the equivalent of wearing a rubber suit. The weight of the players at the beginning of the game was significantly different than that at the end.

The game itself proved a close affair, with only the England keeper Mark Noon denying a fairy-tale opening, with Olympia losing twelve goals to ten. With adrenalin running high after the game, I suggested a possible trip to mainland Europe to play against teams in the Under-16 age group. For some of the players the only journey they had made from England was to visit relatives in Ireland. Others had never travelled beyond the shores. It was an opportunity for adventure, to experience other cultures and develop their character.

On Monday morning I called John Timmins at the British Handball Association to discuss my idea. Passionate about the sport he was part car salesman, part concierge. I knew that John would make it a priority. Within a couple of days and a phone call to Denis Ledegen, a Belgian friend of John's, a trip was organised over seven nights, staying in Ghent, and playing three games against Belgian clubs.

A car hire company based across the road from the school agreed to the hire of a twelve-seater mini-bus. It took five minutes to sell the idea to the headteacher and less to the players. One of the great advantages of being single is the ability to be flexible with time. There is no one else to consider before making any arrangements or commitments. On Boxing Day, 1976 at 4.00 pm, I drove into school in a blue Peugeot minibus with roof rack fitted, to a waiting group of players and parents. Excited, unaware that it would be the first of many adventures.

Once loaded with the luggage the players scrambled into the bus, seemingly into pre-booked seats arranged whilst I was on the roof of the van securing the bags. I made only one change with Johnny B asked to sit in one of the front seats next to me. Firstly, he was a bright kid with a good sense of observational humour and Eddie (my saviour in Germany) had stated how important conversation was to a driver during a long journey. Secondly, and a significant bonus, was the cake tin he was holding. Being the first trip anyone from his large family had made his mother had baked a magnificent fruit cake for sustenance during the journey, and Johnny B being a caring, sharing individual was sat right where he needed to be.

Apart from a couple of wrong turns in London the journey to Dover was smooth and we boarded the night ferry to Ostend, where I found a suitable space to get some sleep during the five-hour crossing. The team could either sleep or explore the vessel.

I managed to sleep undisturbed for almost four hours. Following a quick walk around the deck to stretch my legs I met up with some of the lads in a café. During the chat I became aware that one of the players, Goggsy, six feet two inches of bone and no muscle had bought a bottle of Brandy from Duty Free for "his dad". It was evident when he appeared looking whiter than the cliffs we had left behind, that "dad" may be a somewhat disappointed with the Hennessey VSOP which appeared to be half-empty. With the bottle securely in my possession I advised him to deposit the half he had consumed in a nearby toilet and not the minibus. There was no need for the riot act. The consequences would be a powerful enough lesson.

We eventually arrived in Ghent during the early morning. Denis had arranged for the group to stay at a small hotel which had dormitory style accommodation for twelve and a separate twin room for myself. The building was on a quiet and narrow back street. With no immediate place to park the mini-bus Johnny B remained in the bus to help search for a suitable place to temporarily leave the vehicle.

Less than a hundred yards away was an underground carpark, which seemed ideal. Spacious and secure. Our decent into the bowels of the carpark was followed by an almighty crash of metal as the roof-rack was launched backwards. The roof itself was intact, with just a few scratches, so we parked the minibus. Retrieving various pieces of roof-rack, clips and screws, we walked back to the hotel resembling a couple of Belgian scrap dealers. It was day one, lesson one – always be aware of the actual height of your vehicle.

Our first game was the following day late in the afternoon against Avanti Lebbeke. Due to his physical condition Goggsy was not selected to play, which reduced our squad to ten. Even though they lost the boys performed well and there were many positives to take from the game.

With the evening meal at the hotel cancelled we decided to eat at a nearby Chinese restaurant on our return to Ghent. There was a warm welcome for our party and the food was both tasty and plentiful. As we were leaving, Goggsy suddenly pushed past me and out of the front door at which point he projectile vomited into the road, with a colourful display of reds, yellows and greens, a smattering of carrots and a hint of brandy.

A man and a female companion about to enter the restaurant looked stunned. I turned to them and in an understated manner said:

"The food is excellent, but I would stay away from the sweet and sour chicken."

With the aid of a stiff brush and a couple of buckets of water the area was cleaned by the culprit and once completed he took a deep breath and moved on as if nothing had happened. Day two, lesson two – your mess, your responsibility.

I met up with Denis the following day before our game with Mechelen and he informed me that a small tournament had been arranged for our last day in addition to those already in the schedule. It was not a problem and the players welcomed the news.

Having lost both games our final scheduled match was on the last day of the year. It was versus a strong O.L.S.E. Merksem team from an area north of Antwerp. The team played exceptionally well, and the game was close until mistakes in the closing minutes allowed the home team to win by six goals. We returned to Ghent in a buoyant mood ready to celebrate the New Year.

We found a large bar nearby with a mixed crowd and some good music. Each of the players was limited to a couple of small beers. For some shandy was the drink of choice. Twenty minutes after midnight having joined in the lively new year celebrations the group gathered and returned to our hotel.

Just after 2.30 am, I visited the bathroom and decided to take a quick look into the dormitory. All was quiet, except for a tapping noise from outside a window. I then realised that three boys were missing. I returned to my room quickly taking three blankets from the spare bed and the bus keys.

The boys outside obviously saw a shadow as I approached the window. "Quick let us in before Popo finds out!" at which point I opened the window.

"He already has! These are the mini-bus keys, these are your blankets, training is at 8.30 a.m." I closed the window. They stood there for a moment in disbelief, before realising that there was no appeal, no discussion. They trudged slowly towards the Minibus parked across the street in the hotel's delivery bay.

The following morning, I woke all the players at 7.45 a.m. and allowed the "stop-outs" back into the building. They had obviously not slept well. I then informed the team that we would be training from 8.30 a.m. until 9.30 a.m. in the park area across the road.

"There is four inches of snow Sir," one of them said expecting a reprieve.

"Not a problem, just don't drop the ball and there won't be an issue." I gathered some balls and bibs and marched across to the park. For the next hour we worked with a high intensity and few breaks. Anyone dropping the ball had a penalty which involved sprinting. Three players appeared to find the going tough with a couple taking time out to vomit in a nearby waste bin.

A shower and breakfast followed with a team meeting after the croissants and hot drinks. I explained that if we are to succeed, we need to work as a team. There is no place for players who want to do their own thing.

"You must take responsibility. Discipline yourselves and others will not need to. We have a tournament tomorrow and it would be great to win a game."

It was an important lesson for the whole team. The coach makes the rules and sets the boundaries. Every player must buy into the conditions or accept the consequences.

The following day, we travelled the one hundred and forty kilometres to Hasselt, avoiding the centre of Brussels. The tournament was well-organised with four teams playing against each other in games of twenty -minute halves. The quality of passing and movement had improved dramatically during the week and the games were evenly fought. In the second game we finally secured the victory we deserved ending the day in a thrilling game against the host team the outcome of which was only decided in the final minute. Losing to the hosts by a goal is never a bad result. They are more likely to invite you back and it lays the foundation for teams to follow.

In addition to improving the level of technical ability and understanding, the purpose of the trip was to provide an environment for character development, not only on the court but off it. Being one of the first teams from England to play in Europe there was a responsibility, an expectation of high standards of behaviour. They were ambassadors for the school and the country.

Using the experience gained at summer camps the players all had daily tasks, from clearing the dining room and wiping down tables to sweeping the dormitory. Every player would make their own bed and leave the room tidy whenever we went to play games. In public places they would ensure that any litter was put into bins and that the court was clear of any debris once a game was finished. A rota ensured that certain players had responsibility for balls and medical equipment. They did not let me down.

The journey back to England was smooth with the bus arriving back in Cannock on time. It was a feat rarely repeated on subsequent trips.

I was born in Gorton a district of Manchester famous for Belle Vue, which was opened in 1836 and featured gardens and a zoo, all on a ninety-seven acre site. Until the late seventies, it was a major attraction in the north of England, with in addition to the zoo, an amusement park, a speedway stadium and a large hall which held concerts, wrestling, world championship boxing matches and an annual circus. It was also the location of the first greyhound track in the UK which opened in 1926. Greyhound racing was my guilty pleasure. From an early age I was a regular visitor to racing on a Saturday night, where on summer nights crowds of ten-thousand or more gathered to watch the canine stars of the day.

Having moved into the new house at Penkridge, I occasionally visited some of the many greyhound tracks in the area. At Wolverhampton I met Alan Satchwell, a keen tennis player a couple of years older than me, whose father owned several greyhounds. He lived and worked in Cannock near to the school. He had suggested on a few occasions that we buy a greyhound in partnership and in January 1977 I took the plunge buying a fawn puppy from the legendary Tommy Chamberlain whose Sugarloaf kennels had nurtured and trained several classic winners. Alan decided to call her Seattle Girl. For the next twelve months she would remain with Tommy until she was old enough and strong enough to race. She was the start of a long, colourful, exciting and enjoyable involvement in the working man's sport.

****

The word quickly spread both in England and in Europe that there was a handball team willing to travel anywhere to play games. Within four weeks of our return, I had received a couple of invitations to enter tournaments in Europe, had played a visiting German team in Dunstable and had a request to play against a team from Sweden to be televised in Wakefield. With access to the school bus and the head's approval to leave after lunch on the Wednesday afternoon we made our way to Yorkshire.

On arrival we quickly realised that the Swedish players were not under sixteen but under eighteen years of age, and none were under six feet in height. We were in for a physical mauling. I requested that I be allowed to play, not that five feet and seven inches would nullify the height and strength, but it would help with organisation on court and provide damage limitation. The first quarter of the game was close, but the visitors were only in third gear. During one of their attacking phases I happened to tackle one of their players and knock the ball away. I then looked down to notice that my right middle finger was at a right angle at the joint. Whilst the rest of my fingers were pointing straight ahead this was pointing to the ceiling.

I made a quick substitution and asked for the scorekeeper to knock it back into place. With my hand placed flat on a table he swiftly ran his hand across the top of mine, chopping the joint back into place. I strapped it to my index finger and carried on playing. We lost the game. The finger throbbing during the game was not a problem, though it did impact on my ability to shoot, it was the drive home which was the challenge.

I found it difficult to hold the steering wheel of the coach with my right hand and every time I turned a corner it seemed to take an age, passing the wheel slowly through my thumb and index finger. For those behind me at the time, it must have appeared that I was having my first driving lesson. In pain, I set a course straight across the Pennines followed by a left turn, straight down the M6 motorway. I needed a route with minimal turns. Stopping at a chip shop in Manchester for sustenance, I made the players ring home to revise the return time by an hour. Finally, at 1.30 a.m. exactly twelve hours after our departure we returned to school. Credit to all the players who arrived at school the following morning on time. They appreciated that the only threat to future days out was their punctuality and demeanour on the day after and their ability to catch up with any classwork missed.

The spring term was always my favourite term. The nights would start to get longer and the days warmer. It was the time when all the local football cup competitions took place and leagues were concluded. Fixtures took place every day of the week, including some on Friday. When teams reached a final it was often an opportunity for parents to visit Cannock Stadium to watch games with kick-off times usually at 4.30 p.m. We won two of the finals, which always lifted the moral of the school with a presentation being made in the morning assembly the following day.

It was also a time when small holes and crevices started to appear in the wall of the gymnasium. They were different sizes, having been gouged out at random intervals. At first, I suspected it to be the work of a student side lined due to injury being bored. That was until one Tuesday morning I arrived at school quite early and noticed the gym door open. In the gym was Colin, seemingly stuck to the wall like Spiderman, attempting to traverse from one end of the gym to the other using the small indentations. He had made the adaptions to the wall to help prepare him for a season of climbing. He informed me they were crimps and chips. It was the start of a strict training regime where I would often find him hanging from a bar with a single arm, still as a bat. I followed the chalk-prints along the wall, often stopping to test the number of digits that would fit into the seemingly impossible crack. Some were just the size of a normal fingertip.

Once the handball season had finished in late May, I would drive Colin and a group of enthusiasts from the Youth Club to the Roaches every other Monday night. It was a great place to climb and I could walk and enjoy the scenery for a couple of hours. On one occasion I was encouraged to join the group. It was a warm and clear evening, ideal conditions to be involved.

The first part of the climb was relatively easy, with a rest on a wide ledge some forty feet above the starting point. The next part of the climb was more difficult, about seventy feet with challenging holds that varied in size and location.

Safely attached to my rope, which in turn was controlled by Goggsy (which should have been a warning) at the top of the climb, I began the ascent. With help and direction from some of the more experienced climbers below I meandered across the rock face slowly making progress. The more I stopped to assess the route the more physically drained I became, with my forearms beginning to feel the "burn". About ten feet from the summit, I was stuck for what seemed an age with my left leg extended and my right foot on a ledge at knee height. I could not re-trace to an alternative route. The only way was up. At this point my right leg began to shake a little. I was running out of time. Perhaps the best solution was just to drop off and let Goggsy pull me up to the ledge. With a final effort I did what I had been told not to do, using my right leg, I sprung for a couple of holds several inches above my reach, with both hands leaving the rock face at the same time. Using my arm strength, I was then able to pull myself into a new and secure position to complete the climb.

When I arrived at the top and was unclipping myself, I looked across at Goggsy but something was not right.

"Where were you anchored?" I asked. He then did a three-hundred and sixty-degree turn, before realising that the sling he had used to secure himself whilst holding the rope had slipped down the crack during my climb and was now just hanging by his side totally useless.

Should I have taken the "easy" option and flopped off the rock face I would have plummeted like a stone closely followed by my trusty co-climber, hitting the limestone below about three seconds later. I seemed to turn a shade of white unimaginable to someone with southern European genes. I wandered back to the coach in a semi-trance, with my legs feeling shaky. This became more evident as I manoeuvred the coach for the return home, failing to see a small post before demolishing it and causing £400 damage to the bus. It was the end of my climbing aspirations.

# Chapter Ten

I arrived back earlier than usual from my summer work in the United States packed with equipment for school. During a clean-up on the penultimate day of camp any unwanted items such as softball gloves and American footballs were gratefully received, particularly the former which was extremely expensive to buy in the United Kingdom.

Within the first few days of the return to school I succeeded in arousing concern with a small group of staff whilst providing amusement for others.

Whilst at Camp during a conversation with several friends on the issue of censorship, control and Big Brother I had mentioned the role and influence of the Trinity at my school and the way they would monitor staff and finesse their own thoughts into the general ethos. The all seeing, all hearing secret police of the staffroom.

The Father would have a daily responsibility to deliver the mail safely into the pigeon-hole of each member of staff. She would often make a remark to me if I received anything handwritten, particularly if it had the female cursive, reporting onwards to the others no doubt on the frequency, thickness or where possible, the content.

I was talking with a couple of younger colleagues when she approached one morning with a face heavy with contempt. Thrusting a postcard at me with the speed of a Marvin Hagler jab to the ribs she snarled: "This is for you," then turned and left the room quicker than I had ever seen her move. I was holding the reason.

The postcard was from the southern Caribbean Island of Aruba, with a message which read:

*"Dear Nen, I am lying here alone in my hammock on a beautiful beach thinking about those passionate nights we shared in New York. I cannot wait to fill your stocking at Christmas.*

*Love always, Robert."*

Bobby Miller, a friend from Camp had well and truly burst the bubble with his juicy card, which had the whole of my department in stitches.

For several weeks I was viewed with cool reservation from across the staff room. The observational comments on my mail disappeared overnight.

In a matter of weeks further demands were made on my time from different groups. The first PTA meeting of the year granted funds to purchase new playing kit for two school football teams and a basketball team. The action was swiftly followed with a request from a couple of women in their early fifties who thought that a weekly sports evening for the parents and staff would be a good idea. The husband of one member who, for the past eight meetings had hardly moved and said anything, agreed enthusiastically. I thought that maybe there was an ulterior motive, with his wife's attendance providing him with some respite or an opportunity to visit the Pub.

It was agreed to trial the evening for six weeks from 6.30 p.m. to 8.00 p.m. every Thursday night with Badminton for the first hour and then a "surprise" activity for the last half-hour. I was left to sort it out and arrange everything.

The evenings were well attended with a real mixed bunch of parents and teachers from age twenty- three to sixty. Badminton was a popular activity with everybody able to participate at their own level. The surprise activities included netball, short tennis, volleyball and trampolining. The number participating varied each week. The last named featured for one week only but was hilarious and scary. With two trampolines end-to-end and crash mats placed at each end and in the centre for safety the first participants were young and quite competent. Good control and poise, they made it look easy.

Step forward the two fifty plus women whose physique indicated a lack of athleticism. The last occasion they did anything as physically demanding was probably at school. Getting them onto the trampolines was a task in itself with a couple of shoulders and hands pushing in places with dignity not a concern. At first, they tried to bounce but their coordination was poor. With a little manual support and guidance, I was able to get them bouncing a few inches off the bed with control, before stepping down to give them some space and make sure that all the spotters were ready for any unexpected movement in their direction.

This departure seemed to be a cue for them to let loose. They both went a little higher and then higher again before losing control simultaneously, bouncing randomly around the beds in fits of laughter. Added to which was the uncontrollable flatulence every time they hit the canvas. They were a human version of a whoopee cushion. Eventually the bouncing subsided and they both lay on the trampoline like an unset blancmange, much to the relief of the spotters. A second attempt was almost as funny as the first, with the dismount from the trampolines reminiscent of a cliff-side rescue of a stranded seal. Following the session, the trampolines were moved back to the gym, never to appear again in the sports hall.

Derek and Betty, both in their mid-fifties, attended on a regular basis. Derek enjoyed a game of badminton and was extremely competitive. His pride and joy was a bamboo racquet, which had been in his possession for nearly twenty years. Secured in a quality press and re-strung every two years, it was released for action every Thursday night.

Following a singles game against Derek, which resulted in him sweating profusely, we both sat down on a bench at the back of the court to vacate it for a doubles match in which Colin and his wife Elaine were taking on another couple. Colin was a physically strong athlete but not the most nimble of characters. On a badminton court he had the locomotion skills of Baloo the bear with every stroke played with maximum vigour and enthusiasm. When he was on court he was in the zone.

Several minutes into the game a high clear sent "Baloo" retreating to the back of the court, eyes firmly on the shuttle, totally unaware of the surroundings. Oblivious to everything apart from the shuttle. He was in the zone.

The recovering bamboo racquet placed against the bench did not have a chance. With a crunching final backward step Colin removed its head from the shaft, shaking his leg to free himself of the strands of cane which appeared to cling to his sock, before continuing with the rally.

Derek froze for what seemed a minute. His eyes and mouth both wide in disbelief. He had just lost a member of the family. He was in shock. Only when the rally had ended did Elaine make Colin aware of what had just occurred. He was most apologetic, but his words seemed to fall silently to the floor. It was the end of Derek's night. He quietly packed his bags and left taking with him the remains of his racquet. He was never the same again.

Handball training followed the parents and staff nights, with a good attendance each week and the players completing a three-mile road run prior to the start of training. Games against adult teams took place on Sunday afternoon with teams from Birkenhead, Sheffield, Bristol, Leicester, Milton Keynes and Nuneaton taking part. With most games taking place late Sunday afternoon, I could play football in the morning, catch a bite to eat before turning out for the handball team – perfect.

Perfection should be admired with caution. This is the time when history has a habit of repeating itself with its sharpened teeth as I was to discover following a game at Bristol.

We travelled to all games in the school bus as most players were sixteen years of age. Our game at Whitchurch near Bristol, proved quite eventful. Having played our game, during which I was on the receiving end of a straight right which flattened my nose (retribution for some earlier physical play) I decided to have a sauna leaving the lads to watch a Premier League game at the venue. It was not a good idea resulting in a banging headache with a near three- hour drive back to Cannock.

The journey north on the M5 was slow with caravans returning home for the winter causing intermittent delays. We stopped at Frankley service station, about an hour from Cannock, for some food and drink. I checked everyone was on board before jumping off for a quick visit to the toilet which was close to the bus.

We arrived at Cannock just before 10.30 p.m. The players, some half-asleep, began to leave the bus when a voice from the back delivered a second blow to my aching head.

"Sir, it would appear that Nick is not on board. His bag and coat are here on the back seat ... but he isn't."

I could not understand it. I had checked everyone on board before leaving the service area. Then a second voice hesitantly offered an explanation.

"I think he went for a pee after you." Unbelievable.

I did not have the energy or desire to question anyone further. I parked the coach and drove south once more this time in my Beetle, to pick up Nick, hoping that he had remained at the service area.

On arrival I noticed him sat in the café area eating some chips.

"This is my third lot of chips," he said with a smile. "I saw you pull away and I waved. I thought it was a joke and I knew you would come back, just didn't expect it to be this long."

Eventually I managed four hours sleep before facing a full day of teaching on the Monday, followed by a Cross-country meeting, youth club and handball training – Perfection?

Our reputation in handball was growing. An invitation to an international tournament in Utrecht for schools and Colleges was received and plans made for another Christmas trip to Holland and Belgium.

To reduce the costs, families in the town of Nieuwegein agreed to act as hosts for the players for the four day stay. The players were all well received and well-cared for. The purpose of each trip was to extend and enhance individual experiences. To see life beyond Cannock. The people of the town excelled, but nothing impressed more than the huge domed building near the centre of the small town. Under this domed structure was a swimming pool, a large sports hall, a conditioning centre, a dance studio, a cinema/theatre, a library, a restaurant, cafeteria and bar. Everything you could need for relaxation and regeneration under one roof. Whole families would attend for the evening, with children engaged in activities which co-existed in the sports hall from hockey and volleyball to trampolining, gymnastics and badminton. The social facilities remained open till midnight and the sporting facilities till 1 a.m. to allow for adults working shifts to play in "midnight leagues".

They were years ahead of the time in both provision and accessibility.

The tournament was played in the market hall with five full sized handball courts and the atmosphere was electric. The Cannock boys reached the semi-final where a crowd of eight-hundred people, split by terraced seating on opposite sides of the court, created a cauldron of sound. One side cheering for the English and the other for our Dutch opponents.

With twelve seconds remaining on the clock and one side of the arena going wild, Griffin led by a single goal, but more importantly had possession of the ball. It was just about keeping the ball. Six passes would do it.

Then it happened. With the ball firmly in his hands, one of the "stop-out three" from the previous year tried to play a trick pass which no-one was expecting except the grateful Dutch lad who ran the length of the court to equalise with two seconds remaining. Sadly, there was no happy ending in the extra-time played, with the Dutch team winning by two goals. They went on to win the final by six goals and receive a trophy the size of the European Cup. We finished third and received commemorative tumblers. Forty years later I still see that pass and ask WHY?

Following our stay in Holland we moved south toward Ghent, stopping en-route to play against OLSE Merksem. The game was much closer this time than the previous year. After the game I was approached by a coach and the mayor of Tournhout a town fifty kilometres to the west.

The town had built a brand-new sports hall due to open the following week and they wanted the Griffin to play the local team Technico as part of the opening day bonanza of sport. The problem was that we were due to leave for England three days earlier. I obtained a contact number before leaving for our base in Ghent.

The next day, a rest day for the players, I spoke with the hotel who agreed to accept payment for the additional nights upon my return to England. I then called the headteacher at his home in Wolverhampton and explained the predicament.

"If it's possible then do it. It will be a good experience for the boys, just make sure the parents know," he said, sanctioning the stay. During the next seven years it would be a conversation we had on a regular basis.

Once our final planned game had concluded in Liege, I informed all the players that we would not be returning to England the following day but would be staying for an additional two nights. Each player was given a Belgian Franc to make a quick call home from the booth near the hotel to tell their parents about the extended stay.

The game in Tournhout was fast and enjoyable, with the home team winning by a nine-goal margin and the people of the town grateful for our efforts to play. A mini-feast was provided for the players before the journey to Ostend for the night ferry.

Our ferry tickets, however, were for three days earlier and I was questioned at the port.

"We had an injury and had to wait for attention," I lied. A quick scan of the sleeping passengers in the mini-bus by the official and we were waived ahead.

We arrived as expected back at school in the early afternoon. The players helped clean the mini-bus which was returned to its base at Walsall and I drove home to Penkridge for a few hours sleep.

Waking up hungry, I fancied a curry with the nearest place being in Cannock. I decided to make the four-mile journey in my newly acquired white Fiat 124 Sports car.

On leaving Cannock with the curry on the passenger seat I was "t-boned" at a small traffic island which not only demolished the passenger door and front near side but propelled my curry all over the dashboard and me. The other driver did not realise there was an island and thought it was a straight road so did not slow down.

With my car resting against a street- light and blocking a road the police soon arrived. With one officer directing traffic the other approached and opened my driver side door. He immediately turned to his colleague.

"We need you to take a breath test," he stated, more of a command than a request whilst staring at me.

"I have not had a drink for three days," I said. "The smell is from the curry." The test proved negative, as did the address provided by the other driver for my insurance company. The insurers would not provide a temporary vehicle as it was not a condition of my policy.

For the start of 1978 I was car-less. Only following the accident did I appreciate the wisdom of honey monster Pete who commented on "flash foreign cars" being ok until something goes wrong. The body shop carrying out repairs informed me that the parts from Italy could take several weeks.

Travelling to school was not a problem with a couple of colleagues living in the village and prepared to give me a lift. The problem was the return journey, particularly on a Monday and Thursday evening.

With the momentum rising for handball and the players really committed I could not cancel the training sessions. Instead, I decided run home after training, a simple thirty-five-minute jog. If the first occasion in continuous drizzle did not affect my resolve the second did.

Running along a country lane for two miles without street lighting or a path at 10.00 p.m. is not to be recommended. Three near misses with vehicles travelling between 30 and 60 miles per hour convinced me to reconsider. There was only one alternative solution.

The equipment storeroom to the sports hall was accessed by an outside door. It was also the location of the large heating pipes for the Sports Hall, and as such was always warm. With a gymnastics crash mat placed in one corner, topped with a sleeping bag and pillow it was to be my "temporary" accommodation on Monday and Thursday evening for the foreseeable future.

A couple of lads who arrived just after 8.00 a.m. at school were tasked with knocking on the storeroom door to wake me up, allowing me time to shower and be ready for the day ahead. On Friday's one of them, would bring me a sausage sandwich from the local café. This arrangement lasted for four months.

I have always believed that drama provides an outlet for some who may not enjoy sport. A platform to build self-confidence and assurance. An opportunity to demonstrate abilities that otherwise may lie dormant. When Pat, the eccentric head of Drama at the school, asked if I would participate in an end-of-year Music Hall production I agreed, on one condition. Due to my sporting commitments my time was limited, so whatever my contribution it would need to be a solo affair with flexible opportunities to rehearse.

Within a few days she had delivered the perfect act. Dressed in a pink-tutu I would present the wonderfully named song *"Nobody loves a Fairy when (s)he's Forty."* A swarthy, hairy-chested fairy with a thick moustache was ideal for the part. That was until the very first rehearsal.

The lively and animated head of Music, a long-haired southerner in his late twenties called Jon, hit the ivory keys of the grand piano and I sang the opening two lines at the end of which he seemed to eject from his stool with arms high.

"Christ he's tone deaf! He can't fuckin' sing…. this isn't going to work!"

Not to be discouraged I looked at Pat, stood there with her mouth open wide.

"It's not meant to be pitch perfect Jon. It's a send-up," she uttered.

"I don't care what it is. It's not music and I can't do it! We'll get someone to sing from back-stage and he can mime."

I looked at him a little deflated but suggested that the audience would be distracted from the tone by the antics on the stage.

"That's not the point," he remonstrated "I cannot accompany someone whose voice is frankly, bleedin' awful!"

This was the point where an RE teacher, Robin stepped in and offered to play the piano. Jon took out his pipe and sat at the back of the hall unamused.

Six rehearsals and two performances later the act proved a massive hit with the never to be forgotten line: *"You can tell your spell is ending, when your wand has started bending,"* initiating applause and laughter to coincide with my once erect wand dipping sadly at the conclusion of the song. I would imagine that the audience were less concerned with the voice than they were that the man in charge of their child's physical development was prancing around the stage in a pink tutu, wearing a tiara and seeming to enjoy it!

These productions bring life to the school and the community. Their impact is often under-valued. The generosity of time and spirit is evident not just by the adults but the many students who devote their time to a variety of roles. For them there is a feeling of being valued, working side-by-side with teachers and other adults and of engaging in casual conversation. They realise that teachers are human after all.

# Chapter Eleven

There had to be a change. For three years the traditional Sports Day had been an Athletics meeting with the outcome of many events known before the start and a participation rate of about 30 per cent. It was not a reflection or celebration of the work the department did throughout the year in a variety of sports.

Having introduced softball and some touch American football to the school it was time to introduce some further ideas from my time at summer camp. Olympics or Colour War as it was known in some camps, consisted of multiple activities over a number of days involving everybody and more importantly, providing a stage for unlikely heroes to emerge.

The whole department supported the concept and we agreed on events that could cater for both team players and individuals. I presented the idea to the headteacher with some radical requests. The final week of any school year is often low key. With the eldest year group having left school weeks earlier, the last five days are an anti-climax with unstructured lessons. What we needed was a celebration, excitement, something to look forward to.

To ensure that all the events could be delivered we needed more time, despite the lunch-hour being eighty minutes long. I proposed that the event take place on Monday, Tuesday and Wednesday of the final week with a presentation assembly after morning break on the Friday morning of the last day. The Monday and Wednesday schedule would start at 12.20 and conclude at 2.40 p.m., with the Tuesday session starting at 11.20 and concluding at 1.40 p.m.. In essence a one-hour period would be lost from the timetable each day. Thursday lunchtime would remain the normal length but would host a special concluding event.

The Duke liked the idea encouraged by support from Peter and Dave, the senior teacher and deputy head. Several staff volunteered their services to supplement the work of the department across all days. Others volunteered with supervision on a designated day. This task would be so much easier than past Sports Days as most students would be taking part.

This was to be a competition between the six forms in each year group from Year 1 to Year 4 (now Year 7 to Year 10). Each year group would take part in three designated sports. Completed entry forms from each team would be submitted on Wednesday prior to the last week listing the names of the various participants in their chosen activities. No pupil could participate in all three sports unless everyone had participated in two, and no participant could participate in two sports or events until everyone had participated in one.

For the nominated captains of each team it was a great challenge to place their members to the best advantage for their team. Some performers had to contribute within areas outside their comfort zone. The events were varied with a swimming gala off site.

The programme was as follows:

| Year One – Girls | Athletics | Swimming | Netball |
|---|---|---|---|
| Year One - Boys | Athletics | Swimming | Five-a-side Football |
| Year Two – Girls | Athletics | Swimming | Netball |
| Year Two - Boys | Athletics | Swimming | Volleyball |
| Year Three – Girls | Athletics | Swimming | Indoor Hockey |
| Year Three - Boys | Athletics | Swimming | Basketball |
| Year Four – Girls | Netball | Indoor Hockey | Badminton |
| Year Four - Boys | Five-a-side Football | Handball | Boxing |

The Athletics meet featured all the recognised skills of throwing and jumping but in addition there was a cumulative broad jump event with ten participants from each team. The first participant would make their two-footed jump from behind a line with their landing marked as in the long jump. The next participant would then jump from this mark. Any participant touching the line or shuffling had their jump voided and the next participant would jump from the same mark. It was an event where the lead could change at any stage through a faulty jump or a jumper falling back on landing.

On the track the distances were changed. The maximum distance was four-hundred metres and there was a handicap race with some participants receiving a start based on their performances during lessons. There was a forty and fifty metre sprint race. The relay race featured teams of eight, each running fifty yards.

The Swim meet took place at the local baths next to the school. The pool was thirty-three metres in length and twenty metres wide. The races included all strokes, with most across the pool either one or two widths. Events included a kick-board race, a brick retrieval race, an individual medley and an underwater swim (one performer managed a total of forty-four metres). The meeting concluded with a cannon relay featuring six swimmers. Every participant achieved points for their team, win or lose in every event throughout the week.

Within the immediate area there were a couple of notable boxing clubs and several students regularly attended, with some achieving recognition at Amateur Boxing Association events both locally and nationally. There were three divisions. Lightweight (to include the less aggressive or coordinated performer); Middleweight B (keen performers who lacked strength and with moderate coordination); Middleweight A (capable performers with little significant experience of boxing) and Heavyweights (aggressive and more capable performers and those with significant experience regardless of size). Each form was required to enter a total of three boxers, one for each of the three divisions, with the participant volunteering rather than being coerced. The heats for the boxing were held the Thursday before the Sports week, with the finals watched in the Sports Hall by a capacity crowd at 5p a head as a culmination of the whole event.

What was always noticeable with this event was the lack of "volunteering" by some of the more intimidating and aggressive pupils from the year. The individuals who often stand tall in their groups but are reluctant to stand alone in the ring.

The finals were always a great event. Local professional boxers Jimmy Burns, Cordwell Hylton, Tommy Taylor and Scott Murray contributed to the judging with each bout consisting of two rounds of two and a half minutes. Head guards and appropriate gloves were worn by all the competitors.

The first ever bout on finals day was a lightweight contest featuring Roman. A quiet and well-mannered student of Ukraine parentage. He was heavier than most competing but was placid and lacked refined motor skills. He had insisted on taking part, and his form were majestic in their support with banners and even supplying him with traditional boxing shorts. They applauded at every mention of his name. He entered the ring in a gown provided by one of his form colleagues from the local club, with his shorts seemingly reaching his sternum. Sadly, he did not win, but he did manage to land a glove on his opponent a few times before tiring towards the end of the bout.

What he did achieve was the admiration of the many watching for having the determination to step into the ring and see out the contest to the very end. Another to gain recognition for his resilience and skill was John, an experienced boxer who had reached the latter stages of the schoolboy ABA national competition. He weighed in at about 100lbs but because of his experience fought in the Heavyweight division. Facing an aggressive, taller and physically stronger individual in the final, he traded blows in the first round with his opponent on the front foot. Having received a couple of tasty swinging blows I checked if John was okay at the end of round one. He smiled and winked.

The next one hundred and fifty seconds was an exhibition of controlled and skilful boxing as John bobbed and weaved, throwing jabs for fun which seemed to hit the target with amazing regularity. At the conclusion of the bout as I stood with both boxers Martin turned to me, blowing hard and muttered through his thickening lips, "He's good int he sir." I looked at him and replied, "You done good son!" before declaring John the winner, raising his arm to the roar of the appreciative crowd.

John, like his brothers was a member of the Rugeley Police Boxing Club where Tony Bates gave much of his time to help many local youths channel their energies and develop self-control through the sport. In mining communities or those where there is a lack of social investment these clubs and their volunteers are a life-blood for so many young people in danger of being disengaged and disaffected.

Though the accumulated points tally was available at the end of each day, the final totals which included points for participation was not revealed until the Presentation assembly on the Friday morning. At this assembly the performances of the week were revealed, both team and individual, building up to the individual awards. The boxers received medals and the outstanding male and female were given a trophy.

The winning form for each year was given a wooden plaque, produced by Clive in woodwork and painted Gold, which had as a centre the Olympic torch with the year inscribed. Each participant was then required to sign the plaque, boys on the left of the torch, girls to the right, before it was finally screwed to the extensive wall between the two PE Offices for permanent display. Future years would be added providing a visual history and more importantly a record of those taking part. They would eventually become of significant interest to visiting parents at Open Evenings, searching for familiar names.

With ninety-five percent of all students taking part in at least one event, it was a great success. Supervising staff were not stressed as the participants had to manage themselves to be at designated areas at specific times. Mrs Morris and the kitchen staff were tremendous and extended the lunch period to allow everybody access to food and drink at appropriate times. The general feedback from the staff was that it made the week fly by. The attendance on the final day (which was always a half-day) was significantly higher than in previous years.

Successful as it was the event very nearly did not happen!

A couple of months earlier I was supervising and coaching students at a lunch-time athletics club. Some were practicing long-jump, others were on the running track, and I was at the far end of the playground area with Michael and Andrew two strong thirteen-year old's who were trying to improve their personal performance in the Shot Putt. The area we were using was away from any other students or hazards. Following several throws, I told them to rest whilst I shouted across to some runners ready to start a 200-metre race. With the timekeeper ready I blew the whistle to start the race, then darkness.

According to medical science two of the hardest bones in the adult body are located at the sternum and the cranium. Nature's way of protecting the heart and the brain. Andrew or Michael, and to this day I do not know which, decided to test the theory by launching a nine-pound cannonball skywards. The thinning circle of hair on my crown was a magnet for the object which hit the target with amazing precision, knocking me to the ground.

With the world spinning around me and aware of a trickle of blood running down my face I pulled myself up using the boys as support and told them to walk me down to the staff-room slowly and not stop. For once they did as instructed.

When I entered the staff-room those in the corner playing snooker began to laugh at the blood, with one commenting on how authentic it looked, until he realised it was real. They continued their game. John an Irishman who was the head of lower school then demonstrated his knowledge of first aid and how not to respond, rushing across and almost falling over a coffee table.

Flapping around he grabbed a paper towel which was as soft as sandpaper, dabbing the wound.

"Holy Mary will you look at this now - someone get me some Germolene and a plaster." A female member of staff returned with some dressings and antiseptic cream. At this point he disposed of the paper towel before looking up at the clock.

"Jaysus, is that the time. I have to get some lunch before my meeting," and he disappeared out of the door leaving a trio of women to deal with the injury. All three agreed I "should get it looked at!"

The school secretary, Mrs Wooley a surrogate grand-mother, told me in no uncertain terms to go to hospital immediately. You didn't argue with Mrs Wooley. The only issue was there was no-one to drive me the seven miles to the Infirmary. I would have to drive myself.

The journey to Stafford was not difficult even though my head appeared to be resting on my shoulders. My neck had been pushed down into my thorax and any movement to look right or left was made from the waist. I parked my car and entered reception at the hospital.

Within minutes I was called into a consultation room where a friendly Indian doctor asked me what had happened.

"A shot landed on my head," I said feeling drained and dizzy. He removed the large wound dressing which had been stuck on the antiseptic cream, cleaned the wound and examined it.

"There is no shot there now," he said confidently "but it will need three stitches." He attended to the wound and told me to keep the area dry for twelve days before returning to have the stitches removed and then he said I was free to leave. I was feeling tired at this stage so drove the four miles to my house in Penkridge to rest.

Despite my efforts the following day I was forced to leave school at midday with all the signs of concussion – dizzy, feeling sick with, forgive the pun, a splitting headache. For the first time in my career, I was away from school for three days as I recovered. It was only during that recovery period that I realised what the doctor had said. He thought I had been shot! He was looking for tiny pellets that may have been imbedded in my skull. He had not considered major trauma – fractured skull, brain damage or injury to the spine or neck.

Was there any point in returning to the hospital who had totally misunderstood the nature of the initial injury? Twelve days later I spoke with the assistant caretaker Bill, an ex-policeman.

"Have you ever taken stitches out Bill?"

"Yes, when I was in the army and in the police. Nothing to it," he said with the assurance of a battlefield medic.

"Could you take my three stitches out for me instead of me going back to Stafford?"

He beckoned me to the meter-room and I sat down while he put on his glasses, grabbed a pair of scissors and some tweezers. The task was completed in less than a minute.

With nearly an hour of lunch remaining I decided to go to town to have my hair washed and cut. On reflection it was probably not the most considered of actions.

The young assistant was not enthralled with the prospect of washing my hair, thick with dried blood. With the sink flowing with rose coloured water I looked in the mirror to notice her pallor changing by the minute. A couple of shampoos later the task was complete. Then disaster struck.

Having dried my hair, she then put a comb through it, pulling me out of the chair as the comb located a FOURTH stitch. She screamed and started to sob. I looked in the mirror to see a comb resting horizontally about an inch above my head. The owner was not amused. He asked me to leave, with no charge for the shampoo and not to return as it would be too distressing. I carefully removed the comb and handed it back to the hairdresser trying to console the poor girl, before walking back to school with wet hair for Bill to complete the initial task.

# Chapter Twelve

In May 1978, two years after the formation of Olympia Handball Club the young players became National League Division One champions with promotion to the Premier League. In the same month I organised a successful tournament at a local sports centre with Belgian team OLSE Merksem victorious, despite losing their final game to the host club when guest player Larry Beard scored with the final throw of the match from what looked an impossible position around a six-man wall.

During a meal organised for the visitors a concerned leader of the party approached me. The group, all from catholic families had been to 6.00 p.m. Mass at St. Mary's church in Cannock where the celebrant Father Ted had "appeared unwell".

"Did he seem to speak quickly towards the end of the Mass?" I asked.

"Yes, and everything he did seemed to be very fast," said the Belgian guest.

I smiled. "He must have been behind time. The bar in the social club opens at 7.00 p.m. and he doesn't like to be late."

Father Ted was a character. He insisted on taking part in the staff versus first XI football match, often using his ample frame to great advantage from shielding the ball to knocking some poor soul off it. The tap on his left-shoulder with his right hand an indication to the referee that it was "in his eyes" a fair shoulder charge. No one disagreed, though I did ask him once after a game how a man of the cloth could be so physical.

"Read your bible Pop.... It's better to give than receive!" he said, before walking away to re-fill his glass with another Guinness.

Peter C was the head of English at the school and a keen cricketer. I was surprised when he approached me in early November with a proposal for a handball trip to Spain. His brother-in-law was a Physical Training Instructor to young Navy recruits and handball was a major sport. He could organise all the accommodation and games. Peter volunteered to be a co-driver.

Having just returned from a week-end tournament at Waterloos in Belgium where it rained for most of the time, the prospect of sun at Easter appealed not only to me but to the lads. I should have, at that early stage, looked at a map, done some research and asked some questions. Enthusiasm and the prospect of a new horizon got the better of me and an eight-day trip during the Easter break was organised. The potential cost to each player was reduced when it was confirmed that the group would stay at the archbishop's house in La Coruna with meals included.

With only a twelve-seater mini-bus available a squad of ten players was assembled, including a guest player, Paul Gallear, known to all as "Eight-Foot" due to his six-feet, eight-inch frame. A major asset on the court, but in a small mini-bus a nightmare. Once he climbed aboard the bus it was the equivalent of opening an umbrella in a phone box. His arms and legs seemed to hit anyone within a two-seat radius. For the first three hours of the day-long journey he sat in the front seat, knees under his chin and arms digging into Peter who shared the seat whilst I drove to Portsmouth.

The ferry crossing provided some respite, with Peter almost pleading to be allowed to drive for the next segment through France. I made some adjustments to the seating plans with Eight-Foot housed by the side door so he could stretch his legs, albeit over the front seat with his size twelves placed either side of my ears.

Our journey along the west coast of France was pleasant and without incident. We stopped for lunch just after midday in a small village having seen a shop with several chickens being cooked on a rotisserie. The shop owner looked surprised when the group walked in and even more so when they bought not only his basket of baguettes but all the Chickens from the rotisserie. A few minutes later, on a grass verge at the edge of the village our carnivorous picnic commenced.

We eventually arrived at Bayonne at about 4.00 p.m. on the Sunday afternoon. A sky-blue tide of men, women and children, rolled through the streets, not for football but rugby. Local club Aviron Bayonnais were at home and the city stopped for a while. So did we. With the sun resting on a shelf of cloud and the temperature in the low twenties, at the end of a day travelling through some ancient villages, past vineyards and elegant chateaus it was time for a beer. Could life get any better?

The border crossing was relatively simple and quick, so we stopped for dinner at San Sebastian in the Basque region of Spain. Only then did things start to become more complicated.

Other than Peter and myself, the whole group had only French francs, British sterling or travellers' cheques. They all had decided to change their money on arrival in Spain, but it was Sunday and the banks were closed. We needed food. The only option was to remain in the town over-night until the banks opened and complete the ten-hour journey the following day.

I walked along the road until I found a café which was not busy but looked clean and welcoming. Peter and I went inside with a bag of coins and a handful of notes and began to count our available funds as the owner watched carefully. With nine thousand, five-hundred and eighty-seven pesetas presented on the table, Peter asked what meal he could provide for twelve people. Thirty minutes later we were eating a large pork chop crowned with an egg, French-fries, tomato and mushrooms accompanied by a glass of orange juice. There was no vegetarian option.

The van was parked nose to the pavement for the night, close to the café with a bank a few doors away. Following a walk around the town we retired to our "dormitory on wheels" for the night. I fell asleep in the driver's seat. Some hours later I was abruptly awoken with dawn breaking by a policeman banging frantically on my window. His car was parked at an angle and his colleague stood a few feet away. I opened the door to exit expecting some retribution for sleeping in the van over-night. Instead, he pointed down. From under the bus a pair of legs protruded. With a little help from my foot, they started to move and then a head appeared.

The policeman looked at his colleague and raised his hands in despair satisfied that I had not run over the body or had any intention to, and he departed. When Anthony got to his feet, he explained that someone had "farted" and it stunk so he left the bus to sleep on the nearby bench. All was well until a light shower of rain began to fall, at which time Anthony decided to sleep under the bus, leaving his feet protruding so I would see them.

"What if I had run over you? How could we play three games with only nine players and no left-hander?" I said with a smile.

I had left the route to La Coruna to Peter. He had travelled there many times and assured me that the quickest way was to travel inland in the direction of Valladolid across the hills and table land of Castille. Following the exchange of currency, we set off for our final destination, La Coruna.

With most of the lads asleep we rose to an altitude of about three-thousand feet through hills and onto a large expanse of desolate table land. It looked arid and dry with only random pockets of farming activity. The road was adequate for the volume of traffic, with ample opportunities to overtake any slower farm vehicles or trucks. There was however a drop at the sides, so not ideal to stop or leave the road for any reason. Four hours into the journey, crossing a wide-open expanse of arid land and just before a bend in the road, we heard an unhealthy noise from the engine. The clanging of metal indicated that something had broken. With speed now reduced to less than thirty miles per hour we cruised round the bend to see a small service station about a hundred yards away. Having seen little evidence of civilization for almost an hour I was unsure if it was a mirage or a miracle. It was the latter.

The bus gently rolled into the parking area and the passengers got out. I began to search through our documents for details of the AA rescue package which we always purchased but had never used. The team contributed by going into the café and relaxing with a coffee whilst Peter looked under the bonnet. He discovered that the mounting which held the alternator in place had snapped.

I began to walk to the café to make a phone call when I noticed a building a short distance away which had farm machinery outside in various stages of repair. I interrupted a couple of older men working on a tractor and beckoned them to the mini-bus. Peter used his limited linguistic skills to explain what had happened and how far further we had to travel. They smiled impressed with his Spanish and waved the bus over to their building before sending us away for an hour into the café.

They were our saviours, welding the alternator onto the mounting. They told Peter with careful driving we should get to La Coruna. They would not accept any money, but we did buy them both a bottle of wine from the café/shop. We eventually arrived at the archbishop's house at 9.00 p.m., twelve hours later than expected. Undeterred the Nuns provided meals for all before we unloaded the bus and showered for the first time in almost forty hours. There were no complaints.

The accommodation was fantastic with large bedrooms, some with en-suite bathrooms. The dining hall was large with high wooden beams and ornate carvings. The walls were covered with artwork of various sizes, all with a biblical theme. The three meals per day were not only substantial but of a restaurant quality as were the bottles of wine and brandy that the Nuns placed on each table at lunch and dinner and which I swiftly moved before any diner could take advantage of the hospitality.

By day three the rain had ceased. Having played a game the day before, it was time for some rest and relaxation. We did what all British males do when at the beach, organise a five-a-side football match. Peter was off to see his family and Eight-foot was chilling.

The beach wasn't the most expansive, but we appeared to form the majority of users. A short back pass from Hughesy set me up for a long-diagonal. A game winning pass until I kicked the partially hidden anchor which seemed to pop-up between my right foot and the ball. I fell over in pain as my team looked on in disbelief. The ball travelled about three feet, just far enough for the opposing forward to take possession and score.

"Christ Hughesy, what have I told you about playing the ball back. Always look forward man!" He looked bemused and deflated, but I had to blame someone. For the next five days my right foot was so swollen I could only wear a sandal. Not a great look in a night club!

Back at the house I asked about the weather.

"Are we likely to get a few days of sun now Pete?"

"Not really," he replied before informing me that this was the wettest part of Spain with a yearly rainfall of about forty inches. Instead of Marbella I had organised a trip to an area with the micro-climate of Manchester. This couldn't happen again.

The next couple of games were close, even though we lost both and Peter's brother-in-law asked if we could stay longer to play another game. He had approached the archbishop who agreed for the team to stay a further three nights. A splendid gesture which we readily accepted.

With the mini-bus fully repaired our journey home seemed to be swift and without any issue, other than the fact that we were four days late. I dropped the mini-bus at the garage, agreeing to pay an access charge of the extra days. I did not mention the mishap with the alternator.

About two weeks later, in almost synchronised fashion I received a letter from the archbishop with a bill for the three extra days. Another dip into my Summer Camp spoils. This was followed by a phone call from my anxious buddy at the car hire centre.

"I appear to have a bill from a Spanish Garage for a repair to the mini-bus. I thought you said you were going to Northern France."

"That's what I thought but I left all the organisation to another teacher, and it was more Southern France."

"But this bill is in pesetas. It's from Spain."

"Right, we did play a couple of games just over the border in a small town. You probably won't find it on the map."

"And what about the mileage, you must have driven the Tour de France route…"

"I wish, anyway you did get the bus back safely and I'll give the company a mention in newspaper reports. Local company supports local team!"

In 1979 I decided to buy my own house and moved to Cheslyn Hay, about three miles from the school just before Christmas. The property was a Victorian semi-detached with a long garden which backed onto the local cemetery. It was less than a mile from the Sports Centre where the handball home matches took place and a ten-minute drive from the home football pitch for my Sunday morning league games.

One Sunday lunchtime a few weeks into the new year I was having a drink with Harry Hunt following a Sunday morning league game. He told me of a racing tipster who had contacted him a couple of weeks earlier with a runner at Worcester which had hacked up. He hadn't backed it. He had received a further letter about a horse Corn Street running at Hereford in the middle of the following week. The tipster expected Harry to place money on his behalf, which of course Harry didn't. I placed money on my behalf and the horse won easily. It provided the deposit for the next handball trip. No mistakes this time. I had to pull something out of the bag. A run for the sun. A new horizon.

The Cote D'Azur at the end of May was perfect. Sun, sea, Monte Carlo, topless bathers and a few handball matches in the mix. For the lads it was hitting the jackpot. No "Eight-foot" this time, but Johnny B and his legendary fruit cake was back in the squad. Phil, a young English teacher whose mother Mrs. Wooley was the school secretary, was a keen follower of sport and offered to be the co-driver. Within twenty-four hours I had secured a six-bedroomed villa in a village close to Nice for seven nights. Unfortunately, I had to acquire a mini-bus from a new source as my previous contact had "left for pastures new" just a few weeks after our return from Spain. Each of the players was asked to contribute forty-five pounds. Any shortfall would have to be met from my Summer Camp fund.

Just before the Easter break, I managed to confirm a couple of games at the University of Nice and one at a town near Marseille. Things were looking good, but there was likely to be a significant over-spend, despite a reduction in the fee for the mini-bus.

Sometimes, without warning, things happen to help you in your endeavours when you least expect it. Being in the right place at the right time. A chance meeting. In my case it was running into Harry again. It had been several weeks since the last contact from the racing tipster, but he had a few days earlier received a letter from the tipster informing him that another gamble was due to take place "in the near future." The details, however, would only be revealed if he agreed to place fifty pounds on the horse in question. Harry was hesitant, but I convinced him to chip in a tenner and I would put in the rest. Phil, who enjoyed a flutter, was keen and contributed a tenner and so did Joe my handball captain. Harry contacted the tipster agreeing to the terms.

On the 13th May 1980, Harry received a letter with the information. It contained the name of not one horse but two, one on the flat and one over jumps. Both were trained in the north of England. The final paragraph asked for complete discretion and integrity when placing the bets to ensure a reasonable starting price. If a bookmaker suspected that a gamble was taking place, they would immediately contact their colleagues on the course to shorten the starting price thus reducing any potential pay-out.

The first of the horses was French Touch. Trained by Arthur Balding in Yorkshire it was declared to run in a race at Ayr and was to be ridden by John, the trainer's son. However, also in the race was another Balding trained horse, Montazem, for which the astute trainer had engaged the service of champion jockey Steve Cauthen. The jockey booking was a very significant indication to the public at large that it was the most fancied of the two runners. A limited few knew otherwise.

The second horse Cap Too, was trained by Gordon Richards one of the North's leading jump trainers and was running in a handicap chase later in the afternoon. According to the newspapers it would be favourite in the betting.

On the evening before Phil and I travelled around the area to locate bookmakers between Cannock and Walsall devising a route which could be completed during the eighty-minute lunchbreak. In order not to arouse suspicion small bets would be placed. Across the road from the school was a small betting office. It was owned and operated by a gentleman in his mid-sixties, and I would occasionally have some small bets during Cheltenham or Ascot week. We did not include him in our list because a win could impact on him financially, but his shop did play another important role.

During the morning coffee break at the school, I walked across to the bookies to check that everything was in place. I also noted the name of a horse which had been withdrawn. When the lunch bell sounded Phil was already at the wheel of his car and I jumped in, dressed in an athletics vest, running shorts and trainers with a boot bag full of cash.

The first three shops I went in I placed ten pounds on each horse and a five-pound double. No alarm bells sound. The fourth shop was closed for some reason which put us behind time. I had to increase the stakes without arousing suspicion.

In the remaining shops I wrote a betting slip which had Cap Too and the non-runner, increasing the size of the bet to fifty pounds. On handing in the written slip, I asked the clerk to check the bet to "make sure it was ok." As expected, I was informed that one of the horses was a non-runner, with the slip returned to me to amend.

Following a quick scan of the Sporting Chronicle for dramatic effect I added French Touch in place of the non-runner. Bet accepted without hesitation. A mug punter.

We returned to school minutes before the afternoon bell with the adrenalin pumping having invested just short of £250. By 2.45 p.m. we would know our fate.

Phil was teaching an English class to sixth form students when I popped into the room with a smile and uttered three words "Thirteen to Two," and left. The students were bemused, particularly as Phil seemed visibly shocked. We were ahead. In Scotland French Touch had won easily, with a significant and well-orchestrated gamble landed by connections. Later in the afternoon Cap Too duly obliged for an eight-fold return on our outlay. How appropriate that the shortfall for the trip to Nice should be settled by a horse called French Touch.

Two weeks later we were travelling down the Autoroute in the direction of Provence with not a care in the world. Johnny B was sat, as always in the front with his cake tin secure on his lap and the rest were either asleep or engaged in meaningless banter. Having travelled through the night we arrived at our first destination thirty miles from Marseille by late morning a couple of hours before our intended game against Paris Police. Considering the length of the journey the lads played remarkably well to win by four goals. We celebrated with a meal at which I informed the group that it had been paid for courtesy of one Arthur Balding. Only Joe and Phil understood.

We arrived at the village near Nice early evening. I reached down for the black brief case which carried all documents and information for every trip. Travel documents, insurance, details for every player, contact details of opponents, pennants to give to teams and souvenir stickers. It was adorned with stickers from every team we had played on numerous journeys and was unmistakable. It was always in the front of the coach in plain sight.

Before leaving for France, Johnny B was dropped off at my house, sometime before others arrived. He asked to look at the brochure with details of the villa. Being the most reliable, sensible and intelligent of them all I directed him to the briefcase. The problem was that the brochure was no longer in the case. I looked at John.

"Any ideas about the file with the details of the villa John?"

Open-mouthed and rapidly turning milk-white he stared at the windscreen.

"Shit! I think I left them on top of the TV at your house."

With the mini-bus parked in the small village square I took a handful of francs into a nearby bar to phone my next-door neighbour who had a key to the house. Despite numerous attempts there was no reply. For the second year in succession the first night was spent sleeping in the mini-bus. It was a mistake and as such there had to be a consequence. I ate the last piece of John's the fruit cake.

The following morning my neighbour answered, went into the house and obtained the address and code to access the villa. It transpired that the Villa was on the hill over-looking the square where the team had slept some fifty yards below.

The rest of the trip went without any hitch. Despite losing to the University team, the lads enjoyed the sun, the beach at Menton and the spectacle that is Monte Carlo. The villa with numerous balconies was a great place to relax with Phil and I often walking down to the bar in the village for a night cap.

On that Tuesday night in May when euphoria and champagne over-flowed in equal measure under the smiling face of Fortune, we were blissfully unaware of how fickle and savage she could be.

Three months later Phil, the sports-loving friend and young teacher at the start of a promising career; the cherished son who always made time for others was tragically killed whilst a passenger in a stationary car, struck by a reckless young driver.

# Chapter Thirteen

My summer trips across the "Pond" were now a regular occurrence, so much so that my bank manager would arrange a meeting in late April or early May to confirm that I was indeed taking up residency in the Land of Hope and Dreams for the summer with an anticipated injection of funds into my account in September. As always, his nod of approval granted carte blanche on my spending.

The renumeration for my time at Camp was increasing year on year, faster than the rate of inflation, with an increment for every soccer tournament won. My arrival often coincided with visiting day and allowed me to catch up with parents who I had a long association with. It was some of those parents who insisted on my re-instatement years earlier following a decision by the camp to terminate my contract following an unofficial end of camp party which I organised at the Waterfront for overseas staff after normal curfew. The parents had significant power. The parents held the chequebook.

Usually, the first Wednesday following my arrival was a party night. Not only was I required to drive the camp transport, an Air Bus which carried up to fourteen people in style, but I was also expected to provide a couple of pitchers of beer to start off the night.

Being a nominated bus driver had major advantages of which taking part in the Senior trip was by far the greatest. Each year towards the latter part of camp and before the break of Olympics (Colour War) the two oldest groups on camp would have the opportunity (at a significant additional cost) to visit a major city over a period of five days. Included would be visits to some Universities giving everybody an opportunity to see the facilities and sample the atmosphere of the campus, which could impact on their future educational decisions. In 1978, the numbers wishing to travel to Niagara Falls and Toronto exceeded the space available on the coach. I was asked to drive the Air Bus for the additional campers supported by a fellow counsellor, Barry Mittelberg. I agreed within seconds of being asked. It was a great opportunity to see the Falls and visit Canada for free.

We set off on a Thursday morning after breakfast for the first part of the journey. The "Road Trip Team" featured the oldest group of boys, most of which were in my soccer team and Barry. We followed the bus along Route 191 north before joining Interstate 86 west towards Buffalo. With Jackson Brown and Tom Petty blasting out on the speakers the boredom of continuous motorway driving behind a coach with a top speed of fifty-five miles per hour was somewhat relieved. That was until we reached Elvira.

Just before the exit for Route 14, Barry who had settled in a reclined position in the front seat, suddenly jumped up and announced that we were near his old college Hobart, and that his Frat House was just "up the road" on Route 14. With the enduring popularity of the film Animal House, the Frat House was a colourful symbol of life at an American University.

The boys began to chant "Frat House, Frat House...."

I turned to Barry and asked a simple question "Is it far and do you know the way back onto the interstate?"

His reply of "No it's not far, and yes I know the way," was all I needed to satisfy the demands of the baying crowd. My thirst for adventure had kicked in. It may have seemed irresponsible, but it was a calculated decision. Firstly, it is always better, when possible and practical, to display flexibility where adolescents are concerned. There will be payback at some time in the future and secondly it will provide Barry with an opportunity to entertain us with stories from his college days, giving poor old Jackson a rest.

He did not disappoint with certain landmarks along the route being the trigger for another tale from the past. The drive along Seneca Lake and across country to re-join the Interstate was also a pleasant break. We eventually arrived at the motel in Niagara Falls fifty minutes behind the coach dispelling any concern by stating that someone had diarrhoea, though it was more verbal than physical.

The owners of the camp, Lynne and Sam were happy with the overall feedback from the campers on their return and they asked if I had any suggestion for the future. This was the golden opportunity.

"What is needed to ensure effective use of time and money (always a key issue) is continuity. By limiting the destinations to two areas the trip leader will be able to establish a good knowledge of the area and plan accordingly."

They could see the logic. Just another little push was needed.

"With the two oldest age groups involved in the trip no camper would go to the same destination. A place such as Boston, which I know well, offers not only the Universities but several places of interest both scientifically and historically."

The seed was sown. Within days it was confirmed that the following year the trip would be to Boston and that I would lead the group. Result.

The key to having sixty-plus boys and girls roaming in a large city or across a university campus safely, is to have a broad but simple set of rules and expectations that they all buy into. During all visits everyone must wear the gold camp tee shirt or polo. Midday means midday not 12.15. When visiting an enclosed site, such as a campus, groups must comprise of at least three people, even for "comfort breaks".

From this there can be significant flexibility within the group with campers having an input into the daily schedule. At this point it should be pointed out that "the Schedule" is a programme of activity produced by the camp owners to impress the parents. Some visits are fantastic, such as the amazing hands-on experience at the Museum of Science on the Charles River in Boston, but others are not engaging. Holding the bank, I was able to change the programme to suit the campers. The planned visit to the Salt-water taffy making factory was ditched for a Red Sox game at Boston's legendary Fenway Park. The visit to a craft centre in Toronto was changed to an ascent of the CN Tower and a Maid of the Mist tour at Niagara Falls.

Not every trip was without a hitch. In 1983, I again had to drive a top of the range Air-Bus to Toronto. On this occasion however, it was occupied by my girls' soccer team, a couple of boys and a young female assistant counsellor. They were a lively, boisterous but personality-rich team. The bus was new and luxurious with less than a thousand miles on the clock.

On the return journey home on Interstate 90, black smoke began to billow from the exhaust and the bus started to lose power. I pulled over to the side of the highway where there was a suitable grass verge for the girls to rest. I called camp on the cell phone who suggested I initially seek help from a nearby garage which the map indicated was near the next exit about four miles away. Leaving the girls in the charge of the female counsellor I hitched a lift to the garage. I explained the situation to the mechanic who leisurely threw some tools in the back of his recovery vehicle beckoning me to climb into the front seat before setting off in the direction of the break-down at a steady pace. This was soon to change.

In the distance across the other side of the highway I could see the bus. I could also see (and hear) the speakers placed on the roof blasting out dance tunes, with several of the girls strutting their stuff on the verge. A cross between the Spice Girls and the Dallas Cowboy cheerleaders.

"Jeeezus! Are those your gals?" the mechanic hollered.

"Afraid so," I replied. This was the point when he seemed to speed up until he was able to fishtail across onto the appropriate side before pulling up behind the vehicle.

"Does the noise distract you?" I asked him as he examined the engine to the sounds of Martha and the Vandellas and a group of girls definitely Dancing in the Street.

"Hell no. Your gals got more goin' for 'em than this here bus."

He seemed to take a while before deciding that the problem was a total lack of oil in the engine. Whoever had serviced the vehicle immediately before our departure from camp had failed to replace a draining cap hence the oil had left the engine long before Toronto.

"The only place this is going is to my garage," at which he hooked up the vehicle and then phoned a local contact to take the group to Syracuse, which was about twenty miles away. Lynne at camp instructed me to find suitable accommodation for the Saturday night and a new bus would be dispatched the next day. There was, however, a major problem with accommodation. Most of the hotels in the city were fully booked as the Empire State Games with over four-thousand participants was being staged in Syracuse over that weekend. Some hotels had odd rooms but not enough. The only option was the five-star Hilton.

That Saturday night the girls enjoyed all the luxuries of a top hotel. From bubble baths to a jacuzzi followed by a dinner delight. "Every cloud...."

It was not only the older campers who had an opportunity to enjoy the "outside world". In early August 1984, I was the leader of a coach trip with forty-four twelve-year old boys to a theme park in New York. On the return journey to camp, we stopped at a MacDonald's as a treat. This was to be their only visit to a fast-food emporium for the eight-week duration of camp. It was of course the year of the Olympic Games, held in Los Angeles of which MacDonald's was a major sponsor. Every purchase at the restaurant qualified for a scratch-off ticket. Once the silver covering had been removed an event at the Olympics was revealed and if a medal had been secured by the United States, the ticket could be exchanged for either French fries (bronze medal); Coca Cola (silver medal) or a Big Mac (Gold).

Three weeks prior to the start of the games USSR withdrew, closely followed by East Germany and other communist backed nations. The first two nations alone had sandwiched the USA at each of the previous games, winning on average 112 and 86 medals respectively. In 1984, the USA won 174 medals. It was jackpot time for the boys with many returning with a winning ticket for further food or drink and another ticket. I eventually called time by asking the manager to only give tickets when a purchase had been made, thus stopping the conveyor belt of food and drink which I knew would be regurgitated in the not- too-distant future. Several stops later, including a team vomit, we arrived at camp with a significant number of boys pledging to "never visit a MacDonald's again."

Camp was education without pressure, with minimal red-tape and with a freedom that enabled every child to express themselves at some stage in the eight-week period. It facilitated not only the development of relationships between children but also between children and adults from various parts of the world. Some counsellors seemed unable or unwilling to accept a "child first" ethos. They never seemed to have time for their campers, to play ball with them or listen to them. They were the ones who would return home following a night out to find cornflakes in their sheets or even worse their bed, perfectly made but outside in a nearby tree. A not very subtle seal of disapproval from the boys in their care.

For me personally the kids were like oxygen. I cared for everyone in my bunk. It was my role to make sure they had the best of times and felt valued. On occasions with the older lads, it was a balancing act between mischief and mistakes. At Camp Towanda these included post- midnight raids to the kitchens for food or Girl's camp at the bottom of the hill. One time they "borrowed" from a number of girls' bunks a large number of boots and sneakers, tying them together before attaching them to the Head Counsellor's shack in such a way as to prevent him leaving. Before making a hasty retreat, they turned on the Girl's camp Tannoy system waking the whole camp at 1.00 a.m. with the sounds of Pink Floyd asking, "Is there anybody out there?"

On another occasion, following three days of heavy rain, where the programme was interrupted with spells of confinement to the bunks, there was a certain amount of cabin-fever. Whilst having a little afternoon nap one of the campers persisted in throwing bits of paper and other things in my direction, pretending to be asleep when I looked up. Eventually I caught him approaching me to do further menace. I jumped up and chased him out of the bunk into the persistent shower, wearing only my shorts and him his white Y fronts. He attempted to run down the hill knowing I would not follow him, but he slipped on the wet grass and slid about thirty yards on his rear. Some of the other lads had followed me to the top of the hill to witness the outcome and that's when it started. They looked at me with that glint in their eye. Seeking approval.

I smiled and put my hands over my eyes, see no evil style and walked back towards the bunk. That was enough.

Within less than a minute all my boys donned their underwear to create a large single mudslide in the Pennsylvania rain. I retreated to my bed knowing that it would not end well, but the guys were happy, and it released some energy.

Sure enough, within thirty minutes or so George the caretaker stormed into my cabin.

"Hey Limey, yer goddamn kids are wrecking the hill out there," he shouted.

"Really. I thought they had gone to the gym, so I was just having a nap." I calmly responded. I walked out with George and put an end to the activity and with an Oscar winning performance gave the protagonists a "severe" b*ll*cking. In a contrite manner they all passed George heads bowed, before hitting the bunk in jubilation to shower and soak their underwear to remove the mud. Some just threw theirs in the trash.

It was not just the older groups who provided the amusement. Just before a senior trip I drove the Air-Bus onto the boys camp and allowed a few younger campers to have a ride whilst I gave them a tour of Boy's camp, which basically involved a slow journey of about two minutes covering an area the size of a junior football pitch. Before I had returned to the starting position at Bunk One a queue had formed.

Pop's Tours was founded at that moment in time. For fifty cents they had a tour of the campus with a commentary added along the way. There was the bear that once went into Bunk three…the mystery women that can only be seen from the rear of bunk six across the baseball diamond and the strange noises at bunk eight when there is a full moon. The stories changed at every trip, though the noises at bunk eight remained constant (I would follow it up a few nights later just to give the tour some credibility). The money collected was used to purchase the boys in my bunk pizza.

The amazing thing with the whole venture was that those in line waiting to take the tour, and some did it twice, were from wealthy families used to travelling in style with the best of everything an expectation and not an exception.

My boy's often received pizza throughout the summer on my return from a night out in town. Not only financed by the Tour but other things that happened during the camp. One of the evening activities was a Basketball Free throw competition. This featured not only a separate competition for every age group but also one for counsellors.

The counsellor competition featured Ronnie Morales a regular at camp and a strong basketball player who could often be seen taking shots from around the key that seemed to swish into the net with alarming frequency. He was always the hot favourite to win. American counsellors thought I was crazy to offer even money for him to win the competition with several willing to stake five dollars (maximum bet). Ronnie was magnificent in the early rounds, everyone a winner. However, he could not handle pressure and when he reached the Final he would "choke". He did not let me down. For those final three years he did not win a single competition and my boys got to enjoy nocturnal dining as a result.

The food at camp was excellent and plentiful. The only exception was on the final morning. Every camper was expected to make a sandwich for the journey home. The choice was limited with baloney or peanut butter and jelly on plain white bread plus a piece of fruit. Anyone trying to smuggle cereal from the canteen was spotted by Sam, the owner and sent back. For most of the campers the journey home was between three and four hours. They needed more.

My boys had been amazing throughout the summer making my job easy and very enjoyable, so I promised to buy them all a Sub(marine) sandwich for the journey home from the nearby deli. Word quickly got out and very soon several campers asked if I could also buy some on their behalf. It could all easily become messy. Some organisation was needed, and my boys were just the ones to do it.

On the penultimate afternoon of camp, I sent them to each bunk during the rest period to take orders for a Sub (a choice of four different sandwiches) and a drink from anyone wishing an alternative source of food for the journey home for a five-dollar charge.

By 7.00 p.m. the order was sent to town and because of the volume I was able to negotiate a discount. I arranged to meet the delivery driver just off the road by the back baseball field at 6.30 a.m., which was forty-five minutes before Reveille. With most of my boys awake I transformed into a modern-day Fagin dispatching my helpers to every bunk on Boy's camp to distribute the food. Within twenty minutes part one was complete. Part two was a smaller delivery to Girl's camp, which took a little longer. I helped by carrying a large number in a bag usually full of soccer balls. By 9.30, the operation was complete. Everybody was happy, including my departing boys who received theirs free of charge.

The numbers increased year on year. The sandwiches were not only cheaper than standard, but I was able to throw a drink in for free. That was until the fourth year.

On the final evening Sam called me into his office just before dinner. He had a real Brooklyn accent.

"Some schmuck is getting sandwiches for the kids on the buses. When I get hold of the sonofabitch I'm gonna cut his throat. I want you to come with me tomorrow morning so we can catch him."

"Have you any idea who it could be Sam?" I asked inquisitively.

"No, but he picks up the food at the baseball field early in the morning. We gotta be there early."

Sadly, that year there were no sandwiches with my boys returning all monies collected. They did, however, enjoy a final pizza on the last night as a thank you.

The following morning, I sat in the car with Sam from 6.00 a.m., hidden from general view for over an hour. Nothing happened. He just looked at me, shrugged his shoulders, uttered "Goddamn it," before driving me back to Boys' Camp just before the rest of camp awoke for the final time.

Sam was always threatening extremes, but he would never hurt a fly. One time I started to play music across the campus to wake the boys up after the traditional bugle at 7.15. With the whistling introduction to "The Stranger" being played, Sam rang the Head Counsellor shack.

"Who is that on the Goddamn mic?" he asked.

"It's Billy Joel" I replied.

"I don't care what kid it is. If he don't quit - I'm gonna cut his tongue out, do ya hear!"

Visiting Day at camp was always a cultural shock for many of the overseas counsellors. Some parents arrived in Cadillacs, some in a Rolls Royce or a Bentley and some by Helicopter. For some it was a reality show where affluence was a sign of success. This was manifested in their dress or often in gifts brought for their children, including more candy than a person could eat in a year. Over ninety percent was collected at the end of the day and given to the local community in Honesdale.

The parents of campers who had attended regularly were always the most relaxed and I enjoyed catching up with them. They always seemed to take an interest in my life throughout the year and how things were "across the pond". Many would offer me a place to stay after camp and some offered me employment. There was a highly respected gynaecologist who felt he could use my friendly manner and accent to put patients at ease, provided I didn't "bite my nails!" Another offered me a position with his son in Marine Salvage. My mediocre swimming skills impacted on my decision.

There was, however, one offer which appeared too good to discard. Irwin was a parent whose son played in the soccer team. He was heavily involved in the family business Quartet Fashions, based in New York. The company supplied ladies dress wear to some of the leading stores across the USA, including JC Penney. Irwin was looking to extend the operation into Europe but wanted someone who he knew and trusted on the ground in the United Kingdom to organise distribution. There would be a retainer and commission on sales. He invited me to visit their showrooms and offices in the Fashion District on Broadway once camp finished.

On my return to England I formed a company Henry Zabel, named after one of my favourite campers, to be the sole representatives of Quartet Fashions in the UK. An advert in the Times newspaper invited buyers from leading stores to make an appointment to view the Winter Collection being displayed over five days at the Ritz in London during February. Within three weeks buyers from Wallis, Miss Selfridges, C & A, Richard Shops, Top Shop and several Independent stores had confirmed dates and times. Irwin was delighted.

A Volvo estate car was provided for me to drive to London from Cannock and meet Irwin at Heathrow to load both stock and hanging rails, before moving onto the Ritz hotel for the next six nights. He had a magnificent suite with plush furniture, I was a couple of floors below in a single room with a large bath.

Following a quick tutorial on how to unpack the clothes and display them on the rails in a prescribed order we were ready to rock and roll. Irwin could talk the talk. He rolled out the numbers of pre-orders from some of the stores in the USA at the first meeting, drawing attention to the leading styles. The first buyer was impressed and asked for a second meeting in New York at their offices.

The meeting with C & A appeared to be going very well. They discussed likely orders which appeared to exceed ten thousand pieces. I was beginning to dream. Then there was the first red flag. The buyer asked for a discount to cover the cost of steaming the clothes to remove creases following shipment.

"We send thousands of garments across the USA without any complaint. They are all packed in such a way that there are no creases." The comment was not well-received, with the buyer deferring an order until further conversation with her colleagues. Meetings over the next few days seemed to arouse significant interest from the buyers. The range of trousers was particularly well received.

On the penultimate day we met with the buyer from Top Shop. She was very impressed with the range and going forward could see the group purchasing large numbers of the trouser range, providing adjustments could be made to the crotch/seat to suit the European female. The look on Irwin's face told me that there was unlikely to be a positive response. He took hold of a trouser from the rail and with his voice ringing with contempt addressed the issue.

"Lady, seventy thousand women will go to JC Penney and buy this item. An ass is an ass, whether it's an American ass or a British ass." A stillness descended on the room. With his response the dream of making any money from this enterprise quickly evaporated. Irwin left and I packed the display away. I am unsure if any business resulted from the meetings. I doubt it. The following year his son did not return to camp.

Sometimes a golden moment presents itself at the most unlikely of times in the most unlikely of places. In September 1981, a couple of the handball team joined me for a few weeks in California following the end of Camp. We did all the things that tourists do in Los Angeles from Hollywood Boulevard to Venice Beach and down to La Jolla in San Diego.

One afternoon we took a tour of Universal Studios. Unlike the current tours this was a walking tour where you could engage in conversation with the guide. Midway through the tour we arrived at a studio where the group was scheduled to see some special effects. I had previously answered a question from the guide about the film Chariots of Fire and he invited me to be one of the volunteers for the next part of the tour. I was sent into the studio followed by several others which included children. I was sat in a chair waiting for instructions when a women appeared from the back of the studio and stared at me intensely before disappearing quickly. Within seconds she had returned with another female and a thirty – something male.

"Oh my gawd. It's unbelievable," he cried out in dramatic fashion. I was suddenly aware that I was the subject of the outburst. The two women asked me to stand and quietly circled me before going into a huddle with the male. All I could hear was singular exclamations "Absolutely! Fantastic! Perfect, just perfect and Oh I agree!"

Some of the other volunteers looked bemused about the commotion which was now subsiding to a state of calm. The male approached me and introduced himself as the chief make-up artist for the studio. Following the answers to a few simple questions from him, which seemed to raise a smile, I became aware of the reason for the display of euphoria. For the past three years I had a moustache, and often during my visits to the Fireside Bar in Honesdale the regulars referred to me as "Burt" due to my resemblance to the esteemed Mr. Reynolds. Now with a California tan it was even more believable.

"We are due to start on a film with Burt Reynolds and Dolly Parton, The Best Little Whorehouse in Texas in sixteen days at this studio," he said. "We need a body-double and you would be perfect."

"I am due to return to England soon," I replied.

"I have been with Mr. Reynolds on his past two movies, and we already have two more scheduled in following this. I can guarantee you the work, and it is *very* lucrative," he said

He gave me his card and asked me to report to the studio a week before the start of filming on 21st September.

What was there to think about? I was not in a relationship. My mother could move from Manchester and have some sun on her back. It could be very lucrative he said.

Sat on a patio later that evening with a tequila sunrise in my hand and the sun slowly setting over Huntington Beach there seemed only one answer. Then I had a second drink and more time to think as the curtain closed on the day. Random beach fires appeared almost with the flick of a switch as small groups continued their conversation into the night. Decision time.

Released in July 1982, the film grossed over $69 million at the box office and was the fourth highest earning film of the decade. About that time, I was doing what I do best, working with nine-year old children chasing a ball around a soccer field in Pennsylvania.

Having dipped my toe in the waters of the fashion world I was not sure about jumping into the Ocean that is the film industry. My decision to return to England was not influenced by a second or third tequila sunrise but the realisation that for Peter Bateson, the headteacher who had encouraged and supported me throughout my professional career, the failure to return would have serious implications for him and the school. His belief and faith were not a tradeable commodity.

# Chapter Fourteen

Sport has a unique place in British culture. Once in its seductive embrace you become part of a different world. A world full of hopes, dreams and expectations. A world where the word *"No"* is excluded from your vocabulary.

The tribalism of professional sport, particularly in football and rugby, with fans following their teams through good times and bad is the basis of the special atmosphere which exists at venues large and small. To decline the offer of a spare ticket is paramount to treason and guarantees that you are unlikely to be ever offered one again.

Then there are the thousands involved in the provision of sport for children as young as seven, right through to adults in the latter years of life. The adults all have a common characteristic, the inability to say *"no"*. Only in extreme weather conditions do they refuse a round of golf or a game of football. When asked to run a junior team for a short time they agree, suddenly realising three years later that they're unable to stop. The reward for all their endeavour is that day, that moment when everything goes right. With it comes a rebirth a feeling and belief that it is the start of something better.

In the late '70s and early '80s, there were more than one-hundred football teams playing on a Saturday afternoon in various leagues around the West Midlands and Staffordshire. The quality was often high with many players paid appearance fees. These teams trained during the week. Saturday was for real football.

Once I'd settled in the area, I played on a Saturday for a team called Sherbrook. The manager was an insurance salesman who had one time been a teacher. Great with the banter but his technical knowledge was limited, with his half time talk often ending with the well-worn phrase *"we need to push up and spread out"*. On one occasion we were short of a player, and he volunteered his services. The referee suggested that he wear shin-guards and he disappeared for a few minutes to return with his socks pulled up and padding evident. Handing the referee his glasses, which I think were bulletproof, should have been a warning of what was to come.

His overall involvement on the left wing was very limited during the first half though on one occasion we did have to point out that he was standing on an adjoining pitch (he took the width aspect very seriously). Minutes before half time the ball squirmed through the penalty area where five yards from goal and unmarked, he swung his right foot. He missed the ball completely which rolled harmlessly towards the touchline but The Sunday Times magazine he was wearing as a shin-guard was launched goalwards, while his other shin-guard (a notebook) remained in his sock.

On another occasion, having kicked over a bucket of water which contained the "magic sponge," in frustration at a referee's indecision he was called in to treat an injured player. He ran onto the pitch carrying a white Adidas holdall and immediately began to reassure the player. Kind words alone had to be used rather than actual medical treatment as the bag contained only a single bottle of liniment and a radio (for an update of the afternoon's football scores). He had forgotten to bring the first aid kit. As the player slowly regained his feet the manager assessed him.

"You'll be alright," he said. "Run it off, and by the way, the Baggies have just scored to go one up."

The team had some useful young players who were fit and competitive. In the latter stages of a Cup competition, we played at Bloxwich on a wet and miserable afternoon. It was a game I have never forgotten. A few minutes into the second half, I scored the best goal of my life. Winning possession close to my own penalty area I played the ball wide to the right winger and I went to support him. He returned the pass, and I played it to the centre forward a dozen yards inside the opposing half who played it around the corner for the advancing winger. He carried the ball to the touchline before crossing to the edge of the area where I had continued my run to hit the ball on the volley from eighteen yards into the back of the net giving us the lead.

On my way back to our goal for the restart an opposing player came over to shake my hand. The words *"well done pal"* was followed by his head dropping several inches to make forceful contact with my nose.

"Fucking hell ref! Did you see that?" I exclaimed as the man in black returned to the centre circle.

"I did indeed, son. Fantastic goal."

Unperturbed, I carried on playing. Waiting. Waiting for that time near the end of the game when tired legs would result in under hit passes. With his back to goal my newfound "pal" waited for the ball to arrive, which it did and at the same time I made a tackle that Tommy Smith would have been proud of. In one deft move, I played the ball and 'took out' the player, leaving him buckled in a heap. Shortly afterwards, my "pal" was helped by a couple of teammates from the field of play, a wet and solitary figure slowly limping towards the distant changing rooms. Payback.

A couple of seasons later I had the opportunity to coach and play at a much better standard. It seemed a perfect opportunity. The player-manager had played at a good level but was probably two stone heavier than he should be and a day slower. The team was a mix of experienced older players and some promising youngsters. There was no shortage of characters. Dave Marshall was a huge personality in both stature and character. If you had performed badly, he would gleefully wrap his recently removed jockstrap around your face with the rest of the team glad that they were not the "chosen one". The manager was persuaded to end his thoughts of playing and instead be confined to the dug-out. He had some strange ideas, none more so than the dozen cans of lager he placed in the dug-out on a hot day for a game.

"May as well enjoy the game," he remarked.

I instructed some of the substitutes to warm up even though the game had only just started. I told them to keep active as someone will have an injury before the lager becomes too warm to drink. Indeed, within fifteen minutes Masha was the first (hamstring) followed by another senior player (groin) just before half time. Always an injury that could not be seen. An injury that would force immediate withdrawal.

Crabby was a young player with good technical ability. He was also a character with a great sense of humour. I had taught him and had no doubts about his ability to play at this level. He was, however, often unjustly blamed for the team's poor performance by the manager who would regularly drop him from the team following a loss. On one occasion he was on the bench near to the manager, providing him with the odd chewing gum. Crabby was ignoring me with the gifts and I thought he had got the hump at being dropped. At the end of the game, I approached him to reassure him that the selection for that match was not my doing which he seemed to accept with a smile.

On the following Tuesday, our regular training night, Cliff the manager asked me to take all the training as he had suffered with diarrhoea for the past two days. It was only during the session that Crabby informed me that the chewing gum provided during the game on Saturday was a strong laxative. A personal response to the manager's decision.

Less than twenty-four hours later the landscape changed. More than ninety teams played in the Cannock Chase Sunday league alone. With kick off at 11.00 a.m., the capabilities of the participants ranged from exceptional to comical. Some would arrive at games with their boots as polished as their dreams whilst others would mercilessly hammer their footwear on the changing room floor to remove the mud from the previous week.

Most weeks teams playing in the lower leagues would have a guest player. The one who could not refuse when asked the night before if he fancied a game as the team was short. However, not being officially registered he would play under an assumed name. Surprisingly at the time there were several "Dave Smith's" playing all with the same date of birth with some looking better for their age than others.

What was remarkable was not only the range of skill but the physical capacity. Some players worked on their fitness through running the streets or going to the gym, whilst others preferred short walks from the oche to the dartboard. For some, the pre-game ritual included a cigarette or a pint of beer and in some cases both. Despite this there were many spectators prepared to put on a hat and coat to endure ninety minutes on the touchline hoping that at some stage football would be played. They too could not decline an invitation.

Sunday mornings were pure theatre with characters at every turn. The show would begin in the changing rooms with banter thrown between players with the speed of a tennis ball. No one and no subject were off limits (except for the manager if there were more than twelve players available for selection). This would continue out on the pitch with a wider target audience which included the opposition, the referee and the crowd.

Sunday mornings were my guilty pleasure. They were totally unpredictable. The team kit was often carried in an old and battered suitcase, with a mixed bag of shorts and socks. Only the shirts remained constant. However, arriving early provided an opportunity to select a shirt that fitted, socks without holes and shorts which didn't drop below your knee or fit like hot pants.

Those who played on a Sunday were unaffected by conditions. Games would be played in howling gales and driving rain or on frozen surfaces. On numerous occasions there would be a small lake in the middle of the pitch with teams having to pass around it rather than through it. Only the brave or stupid would try and run through it. Teams playing in the top division often had grounds that received more attention than public fields and were the grounds where cup finals were staged.

Our team, West Cannock, reached a major cup final with the game scheduled for an afternoon kick-off. Throughout the season I combined football with handball on a Sunday. On that particular day, I had play-off finals at Hinckley for handball in the morning and the football final in the afternoon.

The games at Hinckley (which we won!) ran over time into the early afternoon. I had driven the whole team and some spectators in the fifty-seater green school bus to the handball event, but now faced a race against time. Having packed my bag with both handball and football kit there was only one option, to drive directly to the final where the handball team and spectators could watch the game or arrange to be picked up. Some spectators were amazed when the bus arrived on the carpark close to the pitch, fifteen minutes after the start of the game. Within five minutes I was playing in my second final of the day. It did not end in success, with a former student from my days at Norton Canes High School, Adie, man-marking me throughout the game. A token gesture of respect occurred with five minutes to play and with his team four goals to the good when he allowed me to have a kick of the ball and complete a pass which resulted in our only goal.

****

Handball had become a significant part of Sunday sport, with games often played during the afternoon or early evening at a wide range of venues from Liverpool in the north to Ashford in the South. Home games were played at Cheslyn Hay Sports Centre in the late afternoon. Whe playing away, for the furthest destinations, a couple of cars would be used for travel. On many occasions my Sunday dinner was either a burger or a quick visit to "Greasy Lil's" on the A5 for roast beef, mash, carrots and peas and if time allowed apple pie and custard. It was a nutritionist's nightmare; but some fuel is better than no fuel.

On one occasion we had to travel two hundred miles to Ashford in Kent with a man short due to illness. Despite a couple of players suggesting that we call and cancel the game the *"no"* factor took over. A fixture is a fixture. Six players squeezed into my Volkswagen estate for the four-hour journey towards the English Channel.

We adapted our game plan and played some of the best handball of the season to win by five goals. The journey home seemed much shorter. By this time Olympia Handball Club was recognised as a fast-emerging force in the sport, and more importantly they had a coach who appeared unable to say *"no"*.

John Timmins called to inform me that a group of males nearby to Cannock were eager to engage in the sport on a Wednesday evening which incidentally was my only free night. He stated that the British Handball Association would be extremely grateful if I could deliver the sport over a twelve-week period.

Stafford prison located near the town centre was built in 1793. It had towering walls and was occupied by about six hundred inmates. Apparently, a request had been made by the governor following an extensive article in the regional press about our Club's success. The expectation was for me to work with twelve to fifteen players of very mixed ability and mentality whilst upskilling the staff responsible for physical recreation.

Why I was unable to decline the request I will never know. There was no indoor facility; there was no equipment and there was no payment.

The courtyard was surrounded on three sides by high stone walls each with four or five rows of small windows with a fifteen-inch square cast iron grill firmly fixed in the structure. Search lights in each corner illuminated the whole of the thirty by twenty metre concrete pad which was the playing area. Steel goals were firmly anchored at each end. Immovable.

The prison staff were helpful and enthusiastic and when they described the group as "mixed" they were not exaggerating. When the participants appeared, they seemed to represent every type of physical and psychological category possible. From the athletic to the obese; the coordinated to the clumsy; the loud to the withdrawn and the passive to the aggressive.

The one unifying factor was the prison kit of dark green athletic vests and long, washed-out Navy-blue cotton twill shorts and black canvas pumps. It was October and the temperature was about 6°C and dropping. The ninety-minute sessions would be a challenge.

The level of concentration by the inmates was limited with short breaks needed on numerous occasions to diffuse a potential incident caused by a poor pass, a shot striking the defender or an accidental collision. I was on fire-watch in a tinder dry forest, in the middle of summer.

Some could work independently whilst others needed considerable support. When it came to playing a game, they were clueless and had difficulty understanding or following basic rules, which on reflection was unsurprising given their current circumstances. They needed role models and mentors.

Within two weeks and with Home Office approval eight players aged 16 accompanied me to the prison to help with the coaching. It was a culture shock to them. The huge wooden external gates led to a further enclosed area where two prison guards awaited. They escorted us through several closed gates, one at the front opening the gate, and one at the rear closing the gate once we had passed through. Each player had been made aware of a barrage of abuse which would spasmodically be hurtled at the prison staff at the courtside throughout the night from faceless individuals housed behind the grilled windows.

The inmates responded well to the additional help and individual attention they were able to receive, in complete contrast to their normal day. They admired the skill and tactical understanding of the young players. The more able participants were able to model their actions and improve the quality of their play. Progress was being made.

The young players from the club demonstrated a remarkable maturity being able to encourage without being patronising. During gameplay they adjusted the tempo to be challenging but realistic, with the less able receiving passes which they could control readily and make an ongoing contribution. They were able to adapt the level of physicality to the overall skill set of the individual player. There were times when an inmate apologised for a foul committed. There was a mutual respect.

Unfortunately, the group was often subject to change in personnel due to an incident during the week which resulted in privileges being withdrawn. Some incidents were amusing. One of the more capable players also participated in kayaking under supervision each Sunday on a canal in nearby Stone. When re-called to the docking area by whistle, he failed to respond with his canoe bobbing peacefully one hundred yards away, whilst he was bobbing along energetically with thousands of runners in the Town's half marathon. Several days later he was apprehended with his newfound freedom ending abruptly along with his handball career.

Another inmate had his privileges withdrawn for a month for a different reason. With his cell window overlooking the side street he had arranged for a local youth to provide him with fish and chips on a weekly basis at a given time. A fishing line was passed through the window with the money (plus small tip) in the plastic bag into which was placed the parcel for the salivating inmate. The ritual was only discovered by chance when a prison officer was late leaving his shift and noticed the lad delivering the food. It was the earliest form of Uber Eats!

Despite the fluid nature of the squad, the inmates enjoyed the activity and by the end of the twelve-week period the quality of play had significantly improved. With the provision of some basic equipment and ongoing understanding the staff were able to continue with the development of the game. It was testimony to the popularity of the sport and their endeavour that some years later HMP Stafford would face Olympia in the final of the Midlands cup. The Home Office would only allow the game to be played at the Riverside sports centre less than two hundred yards from the prison. The small court was further reduced by spectators from both teams crammed down the sides.

It was the only cup final I have played in where each opposing player entered the arena shackled to a guard before being temporarily released for an hour to play the game. The sad part was that the kit for this special occasion was still the green athletic vests, washed out shorts and black pumps.

In a bruising encounter the game ended in a tie with Olympia eventually prevailing in extra time. For some of the young children spectating it provided an opportunity to see their absent father taking part in something active and purposeful, sharing something achieved, something that for one day at least they could be proud of.

It was the second year in succession that we had played in the Midlands cup final which had ended tied. The previous year we played Warwick University at Granby halls in Leicester. The Warwick team had the three top goal scorers in the competition, all German and all backcourt players. They were all over six feet tall, strong and athletic. We needed a plan to stop the flow of goals. We needed to find a weakness.

Their strength was also actually their weakness. Three players had scored 90 per-cent of all goals for the team. I had noted on many occasions the single mindedness of many continental players. They were gifted and experienced but would often exclude others of lesser ability during games, conditioning them to only provide passes and discouraging them from any attempt to shoot at goal. This mentality would extend into training sessions where instead of utilising their knowledge to help develop the skill level of the emerging players they would instead use the opportunity to sharpen their own set of skills.

With no timeouts in the game, we decided to play the first half without a structured defensive plan making few adjustments despite being four goals down at half time. All the opposition goals with one exception had been scored by the big three.

In the second half we put our plan into place. Each time the ball was played to one of their weaker players out on the wing and close to goal we allowed him time and space. The two nearest German players, however, were pressed by a team of three. There was no outlet the only thing to do was shoot or try to make a long pass which they had never executed in training so the chances of success in a cup final were not good. They were caught between a rock and a hard place.

We encouraged them to shoot relying on their lack of practise and Steve's ability in goal. If they tried to pass it was often intercepted and steadily, we crawled back into the game much to the frustration of the German players. The game eventually ended in a tie with extra time played.

Having played all game without a break the German players began to make the odd mistake. They were a little slower in defence but still a threat in attack. They were becoming frustrated with our tactics and the changes of tempo in attack. With less than a minute remaining of the extra-time period and the game still tied I tried to beat the tallest player (slowest on his feet) and was fouled. From the restart I immediately attacked him again and this time he was clumsy and was sent off for two minutes. His teammates were not happy at the decision.

The game entered sudden death and with Warwick a man short it was vital that we end the game sooner rather than later. Each time I received the ball I attacked the space nearest the angry Aryan who eventually could not resist clothes lining me (an attempt to remove my head from my neck), joining his colleague on the side. With a two-man advantage it was time to strike but nobody wanted to make the decisive move. It was pass-the-parcel time until the captain Joe eventually took it upon himself to dispatch the ball into the top corner for the Golden Goal.

The game ended thirty minutes after the official closing time of the centre. There was no official presentation with the cup containing medals thrust hastily into Joe's hands by the organiser who urged the team to change quickly as a disgruntled member of staff with keys in hand escorted the gathered crowd out through a fire door onto a carpark. No time for applause. No time for speeches and no man of the match award. Freezing cold showers only ensured that the team joined their spectators in record time for the journey home.

# Chapter Fifteen

For some, work is a necessity to meet the financial demands of their life and to provide for family commitments. The nature of the work can often be dictated by income and not choice. For some convenience is key, with salary a secondary consideration

Then there are those for whom it is something more. People who, on a daily basis, offer care, protection and guidance to all in the community through health, welfare and education. For a significant number it is a vocation, a calling. They work for the greater good.

Despite this there are times when the raw enthusiasm wains. The beacon begins to fade. Often caused by under-staffing or under-funding or the onset of further bureaucracy. A time of uncertainty where the question "Is it worth it?" appears with alarming irregularity.

Often at these times of doubt something occurs that re-ignites the fire and draws you back in with energy, passion and optimism. A life saved or a disaster averted. In education it often manifests itself as a year group. A mixture of individuals who provide challenge but have potential. A group of diverse personalities with the desire to engage in the academic, physical and social process within the school. It is a connection that rekindles the enthusiasm and re-generates the mind.

In education that "something" usually occurs in September when a new intake of students arrive to start their life in senior school. In the initial weeks, the talents and the personality of each student begins to emerge. Nowhere is it more evident than in Physical Education.

On the playing fields the challenge is not only the acquisition of a new skill or the mastery of an opponent but the elements. Nature quickly identifies those who will persevere, who will battle even in the harsh conditions that sometime prevail. Our playing fields were located at a high point and open to biting winds from Central Europe. The distance from the changing rooms ensured that running for cover was not really an option in the driving rain. No one was spared, including the staff!

The class register identifies those who attend every lesson fully equipped, ready for action and those who attend many of the extra-curricular opportunities. The rest is down to the teacher to recognise the individual and collective qualities and to provide an opportunity for them to grow into a "special year group" developing not only their sporting prowess and fitness but their character and personality.

Some years have an abundance of characters. Students who are lively, cooperative, good-humoured and reliable but only a few with obvious sporting prowess. Other years have students that are a challenge, a long-term project but who have significant ability. These can be the more demanding of the groups with many factors impacting on their engagement and ultimately their achievement. They can often be seen standing outside the classroom having somehow "for no reason," been excluded from the lesson by the teacher.

Then, with almost cosmic regularity, a year group appears which has the best of both worlds. Usually, as one group departs in year eleven another arrives in year seven to ensure your permanency for a further five years. Excitement and anticipation replace monotony and the seeds of apathy. A plan evolves which integrates your time with their enthusiasm and talents.

There will be some students who shine from day one. They are confident and assured. The transition from a small school to the secondary school holds no fear. Many, however, find the process demanding and at times intimidating. They need time and support to flourish.

The advantage of having a group of talented individuals with enthusiasm and drive is that it impacts positively on many others in the year who are drawn into the various streams of success, slowly developing their latent talents. In some years, these students go unnoticed not because of a lack of opportunity but more the lack of momentum within their peer group. This is not only confined to Physical Education but is evident in all performing arts.

During my first two years at Central Grammar School for Boys it was not the lack of talent in the year group or the support of my peers, but more the lack of opportunity provided for me personally, by those with a responsibility for delivering Physical Education and managing sports teams, which impacted on my development. The transition from junior to senior education was not without its challenges and disappointments which was sometimes reflected in my behaviour.

I was, however, the student with latent ability and determination. Ability that was eventually recognised and given an opportunity. I was the student who, in those first two years found a sense of purpose with a talented group of young footballers who made me feel more valued than any adult at the school.

The students who emerge over time are the prime energisers. They are the ones who provide the greatest satisfaction because their journey is not without difficulty or an investment of time.

There will be many for whom Physical Education was not a pleasurable experience during their days at school. In many cases it will be impacted not so much by resources but by teachers, their enthusiasm and imagination.

All children are different. They have different personalities, different social backgrounds and different interests. No two children are the same. The Physical Education teacher is in the best place possible to establish a conversation with individual students, not just within the lesson but during break-times, at lesson changeover and at lunch-time practices. They have a great opportunity to discover what really matters to those in their care.

Without engaging in conversation with the students how can the teacher expect children to engage in the subject?

Patrick was a fifteen-year-old student who suffered with the condition Spina Bifida. For him involvement in the core programme was limited. He did, however, have a lasting impact on my teaching philosophy.

Each September the final year group were presented with a Leisure activity programme. A diverse range of activities which included swimming, ice-skating, roller skating, fitness training, canoeing and squash as well as photography and craft projects, a dozen activities in all. Students would opt for five areas of personal choice, one for each half-term.

"Is there any activity that you would like to follow that is not on the list?" I asked the whole year group at the first meeting.

"Fishing!" was Patrick's answer.

There was a pause followed by a smile and an almost dismissive exhalation before I responded.

"How many of you would like to see Fishing as an option?"

To my amazement a significant number of hands were raised, and Fishing was included. Sixteen students enrolled for the first block of six weeks. It was agreed that the group would be placed on the Staffordshire and Worcestershire canal at nearby Penkridge, which was also close to the squash courts for another group.

When analysing the list of characters who had chosen fishing there was an element of doubt and concern. This was partly removed when on the first morning of the activity students arrived at my office at 8.30 a.m. with an array of tackle and equipment for the afternoon session.

The group, which Patrick had agreed to supervise, was dropped off first by the school bus, close to steps leading down to the canal. I then drove the bus a mile to the courts where a squash coach would work with the group. Still with an element of doubt, I decided to return to the canal half-way through the session.

Hidden from their view I expected to see several having a fag, maybe even a couple on the nearby pub patio. Instead, I saw sixteen lines set up at regular intervals along the bank with Patrick supervising all catches and offering advice on bait or floats. There was one keep net. It was well-organised, and everyone was engaged. I was so impressed over the next few weeks I sourced other areas within a ten-mile radius for the group to fish knowing that they could be left to their own devices without fear of offence or danger.

Patrick's willingness to speak out had made me realise there is a responsibility to cater for every individual. Where possible, programmes should have flexibility and have the potential for change to meet the needs and interests of the participants. It is not one size fits all, and teachers need to be imaginative and provide for the innate curiosity of children. It is not a product to be delivered but an experience to excite and engage.

Throughout the following years with a mix of departmental staff and external coaches, students were offered rock-climbing, dance and aerobics, boxing, table tennis, badminton, softball with real mitts, street-hockey, American football (touch), lacrosse, orienteering and capture the flag all as part of an expansive core programme which included traditional sports such as tennis, netball, hockey, rugby and football.

With carte blanche, I was able to change the programme at short notice to accommodate guest coaches or adapt to staffing demands and changes of weather conditions.

In Britain we seem unable to deal effectively with any snowfall above four or five inches. Our world stops, as is the case of schools where a significant number of students rely on the provision of transport. The attendance on "snow days" was often less than twenty per cent. Small classes were accommodated but little learning took place. In the PE programme various activities were offered to keep the reduced numbers of boys and girls occupied. Some target games were introduced and various racket games, but there was no excitement. Those who attended were just supervised.

It was boring for me, and it was boring for them. What would the students really like to do? What did my boys do at camp when it rained? Mud sliding. What would the students want to do when it snowed?

I asked the school kitchen to give me six metal dinner trays and dressed for the freezing conditions and the deep snow, tobogganing became part of the programme at the school. Using the natural resources of a steep incline and a series of smaller hills, the students readily immersed themselves in the new activity. It did attract members of the sixth-form, who joined the lesson before it concluded with an almighty snow-ball war. All lessons followed the same format, with students running to the lesson to participate in the snow games.

I joined in with all the activities, particularly the snowball fight at the end of the session. However, seniority has no place in this activity and if you join the battle, expect the worse. It only takes one participant to turn rogue and the others will willingly follow to pound the staff with snowballs from every direction. There were some who remained loyal to the end offering some limited resistance.

Word travelled fast and attendance at PE lessons during "snow days" quadrupled. Some who normally travelled on buses insisted that their parents drive them to school. How could they refuse?

Things did not always go to plan for some. Colin who often faced extreme conditions when rock-climbing, lived several miles from school on the other side of Cannock Chase. With roads impassable he decided to run to school to take part in the activities for the day. With snow peppering down and the lesson in full flow he appeared running across the field, just in time for the morning break.

He changed into some dry socks and his snow gear and joined our group in the staff room for a welcomed cup of tea. Minutes later the "Duke" appeared to announce that he was closing the school for the rest of the day due to the increasing snowfall and that all parents with children at the school had been informed. With no other staff attempting the journey across the Chase there was no option for Colin. Thirty minutes later he was back on the road beating the blizzard. Disappointed would be an under-statement

When new staff joined the Department, they were always amazed at the "Snow Day Activity". There was no lesson plan. It was not included in a scheme of work. There was no "risk assessment". It was pure play. An activity which the participant willingly engaged in with unbridled joy and freedom.

It also demonstrated that some teachers still retain the child within.

# Chapter Sixteen

I had a troubled childhood. There was challenge and conflict.

I was an only child, with parents who could not speak English. Exiled after the Second World War from Yugoslavia they settled in Manchester, the first foreign family in the neighbourhood.

My parents worked long hours at the cotton mills in Reddish and each weekday morning at 7.00 a.m. I was left in the care of a child minder who lived several doors away and became known as Auntie Lil. She had two daughters, Anne and Kathleen and a son Godfrey. They were my only source of conversation, with my parents insisting that I speak only English, effectively disengaging me from any Balkan influence. Every Thursday evening Auntie Lil's husband, a bus driver, would arrive home with a handful of comics. They were my language learning tool.

My early years at school were bliss. The children in my class at Abbey Hey would engage with anyone in anything. It was pure play. No one was excluded. I looked forward to my days at school and I was making significant progress, so much so they decided to move me into the year above, and that's when it all changed.

Within weeks I heard comments about the colour of my skin. I was excluded from certain groups and in games of football I was only allowed to play in goal. Some boys seemed to target me with abuse, verbal or physical and sometimes both. Unfortunately, I responded by hitting out. On many occasions they would hit back, and we would both end up in headmistress Miss Pilkington's office for the strap across our hands and an entry in the "Black book." There were those that initiated incidents but cleverly escaped whilst I still ended up in the office.

Outside school the climate seemed to be changing also. During the summer holidays following my 8th birthday, one of my friends William was going to Southport for the day, and he invited me along. My mother gave me half a crown to give to his parents to cover the cost of food.

We had an active and enjoyable day playing on the sands of Ainsdale and returned home in the early evening. I thanked his parents and left his house, returning seconds later to retrieve my cap which I had left on a chair. At the open kitchen door, I heard his father comment that he was unhappy with his son playing with "that foreign lad." I saw less and less of him in the weeks that followed. I was never invited out again.

In the local park some of the older boys would occasionally push me off some of the playground rides. Kathleen once intervened for which she received a punch in the mouth and a broken set of spectacles. On another occasion I was launched into the air from a ride eventually biting the dust, or in this case the red shale, which seemed to be the common playground surface of the day, several feet away. A quick visit to the hospital at Ancoats, and several stitches in my chin guaranteed that I had a physical reminder of the incident for many years.

I did have a good friend from my class at school who lived about fifteen minutes away. I would often go over to his house and play board games such as Risk and Monopoly with his parents always making me feel welcome. Being a year older he left Junior School a year prior to me but I would still go over to his house. However, his group of friends from the new school we're not so welcoming, referring to me as "the Little Wog". Peer pressure dissolved that friendship.

I was the only child from the year group at my Junior School to pass the 11 plus exam and qualify for a place at a grammar school. Following another incident, I also became the only child in the history of Abbey Hey juniors to be entered in the Black book on fifty occasions, at which point Miss Pilkington indicated that she did not want me in school for the final three weeks of the year. Auntie Lil felt it was best to keep it quiet and not to cause any upset to my parents, so for those final weeks I helped her in the house and read books. They did not have a television.

My reputation appeared to follow me to Central Grammar school. The teachers were very formal and abrupt always addressing students by a surname. I trialled for both the football team and the rugby team. The teacher in charge of the rugby team made his feelings perfectly clear from the start. With only sixteen players attending trials he not only didn't select me but included a couple of players in the team who had not bothered to turn up on the night. I was desperate to be in the football team with all the lads accepting me for what I was rather than what I looked like. The manager seemed to tolerate me but selected Callaghan

(I have forgotten his first name) as the goalkeeper and his father as the linesman. Despite being a reserve player, I turned up for every Saturday morning match throughout the season, changed into my boots, socks, shorts and the blue wool jumper my mother had knitted for me. We turned travelling on public buses to games into a social event. I eventually got my chance in the penultimate game of the season which was a mid-week game against Manchester Grammar School due to Callaghan having a dental appointment. I apparently played well in a 1-1 draw, but obviously not well enough to retain a place the following season.

Despite all my prayers each Friday night for Callaghan's car to break down or have a puncture on the Saturday morning I still failed to make an appearance during the second year.

There were 130 boys in my year group of which only four were from non-British heritage. Kewku, a six-foot Afro -Caribbean, David from Pakistan, Ivor a meek and mild Jew and myself. We were all subject to various degrees of racial abuse and bullying at some stage, other than Kweku who seemed exempt for obvious reasons.

After sixteen months the bullying stopped following an incident on the school yard during a lunchbreak. The school yard was over sixty yards wide and forty yards long and several games of football would take place during the hour. Part of the decision-making skill was knowing who was playing in your game. I had in the past been subjected to verbal abuse and some strong challenges by certain players, (not from the school team) who were part of a small gang. Their leader was slightly taller than me and they were always together, safety in numbers.

On the day in question the leader charged into my back during the game and I fell hard onto the ground. I was not aware of the blood running down my leg from the split knee, but I was aware of the gaping hole in my new trousers which my mother had worked several Saturday mornings to pay for.

Enough was enough.

I started to get to my feet slowly and deliberately as he stood over me sneering. Without warning I exploded upwards hitting him under his chin with my skull. His teeth cracked together knocking his head backwards. The red mist descended, and I grabbed his collar and head-butted the bridge of his nose before my knee collided with his groin. His little gang moved into help, but some of the football team and the rugby captain moved forward preventing an intervention. A swinging right knocked him to the floor and finally to remove any thoughts of instant retaliation I stamped on his right hand. Life at school was a little different from that day on.

I was now old enough to join Gorton Lads club. The situation was not dissimilar, with a group of boys from the secondary school making life uncomfortable. One evening a group of six boys, one three years older, surrounded me as I left the club and started pushing me from one to the other making various comments until one of the group was struck over the head with an implement, which turned out to be an umbrella and another was pushed forcibly out of the way, falling over a pavement. My mother, a five-foot two-inch muscular woman from Montenegro, who was on her way home from Bingo became a legend that night.

It was in the September of my third year at the school that my life changed forever. One man and sport turned my life around completely. The two original PE teachers, both ex RAF instructors left, much to my relief as they both hated me with a passion. If anything was amiss in their lessons the blame would be directed to me. They were replaced by two younger teachers.

Peter Scholefield was my saviour. He was totally different from the dinosaurs he replaced. He was five-feet nine inches tall, weighed about nine stone with a straggly ginger beard. His strength was athletics and the ability to connect. He could talk for England and seemed to have a response, often humorous, to every question.

In the early days he convinced me that he had been a boxing champion in the Navy often bobbing and weaving as he approached me. He would initiate conversation with students and then step back to listen to the banter or comments. He called me Pop.

He was able to engage with all students without the need to bellow instructions, a bi-product of the respect he displayed for every individual, giving them a voice and ownership. He was consistent and fair and never seemed to be rattled.

There was also a managerial change for the football team. A school bursar became the new manager and following a couple of training sessions he selected me to play in goal. Callaghan protested but to no avail. He never appeared again. A couple of clean sheets convinced the manager Mr. Coleman to send me for area trials where I was selected not just for the Central area but for Manchester Junior Boys.

With my new-found success in football, playing for the school each Saturday, for the area in midweek and Manchester junior boys my standing amongst my peers began to improve dramatically. Sadly, some teachers fell short. One at an Area match referred to me as "Darkie", whilst another made reference to the donkey jacket I was wearing, commenting that I "looked more like a coalman than a footballer".

The worst example, however, occurred in the following season when I was playing for Manchester boys at Springfield Park Wigan in a mid-week fixture at the beginning of September. It was the second match of the season and following a hot summer my skin was quite tanned. The crowd behind the goal subjected me to barrage of racial abuse from "black bastard" to "wog". There were the usual calls of *"go back where you came from"* and much more. At half time we were a goal down and I complained to the manager, a primary school head teacher, about the abuse.

"Just deal with it!" was his empathetic and compassionate response. I was fourteen years old and in bits. We lost the game by three goals to one and I was dropped for the next game.

Mr. Scholefield was disappointed but not surprised when I told him the following day. He changed the focus of the conversation completely by asking why the team had only managed to score a single goal?

"What would you have changed?" he asked. It was the prelude to many conversations we had at Monday morning break by the gym notice board about the week-end sport either for the school or Manchester boys.

I realised years later that the whole process was an education in coaching. He had a limited knowledge of football, but was introducing me to the basics of analysis and response. Things that could be improved both individually and collectively. He was discreetly providing me with a platform to develop my understanding, awareness and observational skills.

When I was fifteen years of age, he paid for me to take the Football Association preliminary coaching badge which was being delivered at a local school during the Easter break. This was against all protocol as the course was for adults. The course lasted six days. I did not pass.

The course tutor, Steve Fleet, a former Manchester City goalkeeper informed me that I had failed not due to a lack of knowledge but because I had allowed the fact that the players being coached were of my age or older, to impact on my confidence and authority when delivering the session.

"When you come back for re-assessment act like a twenty-one-year-old. Put six years between you and the players."

Seven weeks later, just after my 16th birthday, I passed to become the youngest ever holder of the award. This was to have a major impact on my pathway in later life.

Within a few weeks of his appointment, "Schoey" suggested I joined the basketball team, which would help my ball handling. He would sit in the gym at break time whilst several boys practised shooting. He organised practises after school and entered the team in the Manchester Schools League. We won the league with Kweku eventually playing for England and I playing for the Manchester Schools team under Bill Beswick who in later life was not only a coach for England at basketball but a sports psychologist for the England football team.

I completely trusted "Schoey" and he gave me no reason not to. On one occasion the school had a final basketball match of the year in Stockport. The league had already been won but he wanted to remain unbeaten, and the opponents were strong challengers. The problem was that Gorton lads club had reached the finals of the Manchester and district 5-a-side tournament which was being held at a later time on the same evening some fourteen miles away. This was a time before school minibuses. Teams travelled to school games using public transport. Getting to Stockport was not an issue, the bus stop was only five minutes from the Grammar school. It was the return journey which would be difficult, as I would need to catch two buses during peak time. He agreed to give me a lift after the basketball match straight to Openshaw where the finals were being held. We won the basketball game scoring 100 points.

I changed quickly and waited at the school entrance for my lift. He appeared a few minutes later driving a large motorbike with box compartments on either side. I was astounded. I expected a car.

"Put your bags in the box and put this on," he said giving me a helmet which was apparently his wife's. We then set off weaving through the rush hour traffic on a freezing and damp February evening whilst he appeared to be singing spiritual songs from the deep south. We arrived at the finals with time to spare and three matches later Gorton lads received the winner's trophy with me saving a penalty in the final game. A pleasing day's work.

The finest card he played however, was when just before he left the Grammar school for a position at a college for further education, he sat down with me one lunchtime to discuss my future post-school. He listened to my thoughts and the advice I had been given by Albert the careers teacher, and then shook his head.

"Forget all that. Your future is in teaching and sport. You have enthusiasm and an ability to relate to performers with a good sense of humour. I think you would enjoy it. Now it's up to you to go out and work to achieve the grades you need."

He later advised me to apply to Madeley College, a specialist physical education college which he himself had attended, agreeing to provide a reference which I am sure helped secure my place. He eventually became a renowned and valued coach of international athletes at Sale Harriers Athletics Club.

All that now remained was for me to live up to his expectations and follow his example.

# Chapter Seventeen

I was nine years old when I first attended greyhound racing at Belle Vue stadium in Gorton courtesy of a local shop owner. A regular at the track which hosted racing on Saturday and Wednesday, he agreed to take me to the Wednesday night meeting whilst my mother enjoyed her weekly visit to the Bingo Hall opposite his shop. It was certainly a better option than staying at home without a television or access to our radio, which my father would take over from 7.30 p.m. each night to listen to the BBC world service news, before retiring to bed at 9.30 p.m.

It very soon became a regular fixture in my life. I developed an affinity with the canine athletes and even had my heroes. Nessie's Mercy, a flyer from trap one or the ambling 86lb Prince of Camus who rarely won a race but always finished with a flourish. I would always attend the meetings when major races such as the Northern Flat Championships were a feature to see the top dogs of the day. I got a kick from inspecting the greyhounds in the paddock to watching them parade around the track before running to Mr. Whitehead and telling him the selection as the hare moved and the traps opened, joining the masses to urge their choice to *"keep going…keep going"* or *"go on my son"* all believing that the additional encouragement would make them go faster. If I selected four winners on a night, I was elated.

All the greyhounds at the track were kenneled at the rear of the stadium situated on Kirkmanshulme Lane, next to my Grammar school. There were six different trainers looking after more than two-hundred greyhounds. One night on the way home from school at the age of thirteen, I stopped at the security office by the entrance gate to ask if there was any work with the dogs over the half-term break. Fortunately a trainer, Stan Mitchell, was in the office at the time and he offered me work for three days in his kennels.

My role included not only mucking out kennels but walking the greyhounds around the perimeter of the stadium. Very soon, with my competence proved I was trusted with four at a time. They became nonjudgmental friends. I would talk to them as we walked. I was completely at ease. I was hooked. Whenever I could I helped with the loading before racing and sometimes on race nights themselves.

The four-storey Grammar school overlooked the long grass paddocks situated next to our playing fields where greyhounds could run loose. I was the only student whose desk contents included binoculars and a notebook to record which greyhounds were receiving the most attention. If my cohort was not in the group, I would sometimes go into the kennels after school and let them out for ten or fifteen minutes to enjoy the freedom of the paddock, particularly on warm summer days.

Thirteen years later and settled in Cannock, I was asked by a friend Alan Satchwell to share in the purchase of a greyhound puppy. It was a no-brainer. Seattle Girl was bred at the Sugarloaf Kennels in Stourbridge by legendary trainer Tommy Chamberlain. She was a fawn bitch, the smallest of the litter but had her mother's head and was not intimidated by larger members of the litter. She was not the quickest greyhound in the world but featured regularly at Willenhall initially before moving to Monmore Green, Wolverhampton, racing at a distance of 480 meters where she would always be finishing her races well but rarely troubling the judge.

When tackling distances of 750 metres and over, she became a star, breaking a track record at Norton Canes and winning a heat of the Cesarewitch Trophy at Belle Vue over 800 metres, before finishing third in the consolation final of the event. To return to my home track, meet with some of the old-time punters and have a winner gave me a terrific feeling. She had stamina in abundance and the heart of a lioness. She won several races over marathon trips before sadly dying following a freak accident before her fourth birthday.

Alan's father Frank owned several greyhounds and was a keen golfer. On one occasion playing at the Beaudesert Golf course on Cannock Chase, he won a greyhound which had been bred by the daughter of Reg Hollinshead, a famous local racehorse trainer. Hobourne's Lad was fifteen months old and as black as the ace of spades.

In a preliminary trial at Monmore Green he was very awkward, turning his head to interfere with one of the other runners. A second trial had the same outcome. Each greyhound has a passport, with a unique registration number (this number is tattooed inside their ear once the litter is registered). If a greyhound turns a head (fights) during a race, the passport is stamped. Two stamps result in permanent exclusion from racing at licensed tracks in England, Scotland or Ireland.

The management at Monmore Green took into consideration the age of Hobourne's Lad and did not stamp his passport but did ask Frank to take him away. Following a further trial at nearby Norton Canes where again he was awkward, I was approached by Alan who asked if I wanted the dog with a view to running at the unlicensed tracks around the Midlands. These were unregulated tracks where passports were not needed, where the names of the greyhound could change from track to track, and urine samples were never tested. They were family-oriented places where people with one or two greyhounds in their care would run them in scheduled races. They were often situated near mining or industrial communities. To be registered at the track the dog would need to compete in a trial race against a couple of others to establish its ability. The faster the time achieved, the higher grade they would be allocated and placed in the appropriate race. Should a greyhound exceed the grading time by a significant amount when in a race, they would be disqualified. The higher the grade the greater the prize money available. Those owners with a fast dog, would run it in an "Open Race" which had significant prize-money, but where trainers from beyond the locality would appear sometimes with greyhounds that had been purchased for two or three thousand pounds.

My first impression of Laddie was that of a quiet and relaxed dog. His litter brother and sister were not only competing in top puppy races throughout the country but winning a fair few. He, however, was immature, a sound frame but lacking the build to go with it. Believing that you get nothing for free in life, I offered Alan 50p which he accepted, and I had a new resident at 99 Station Street.

A year earlier during my visits to Monmore Green to watch racing I had established a friendship with Pat Ryan, a contracted trainer, and his partner Patricia. They had kennels on a farm at Landywood, a couple of miles from my house. I offered to help with the rehabilitation of greyhounds in their care, the ones recovering from injury. For several months of the year, I would visit the kennels early in the morning and take designated dogs on a jog, for about thirty minutes.

The regime fitted perfectly for Laddie. I wanted him to be with other greyhounds and have the necessary exercise. Each morning, we would travel in my Ford Escort on the short journey to Landywood and then, following a quick breakfast to school, where his home for the day was in a little used storeroom with high-level windows inside the sports hall. He soon endeared himself to certain pupils. On clear warm days, a student who was not taking part in a lesson outdoors due to injury or illness was asked to walk him around the fields.

"The best way to recover from injury is with regular and gentle mobilization," I would assure the student. Nobody objected to the request. Some even volunteered to take him on a lunchtime walk around the cross-country course.

Tim, a third-year pupil at the time, was key to this. He was comfortable with animals and worked during weekends for the Hollinshead's at their stables. He would take Laddie three lunchtimes per week through the forest at a gentle trot. On other days Liam volunteered, but for different reasons. He enjoyed a gentle stroll and at half-way a fag break without fear of a teacher interrupting.

I retained my commitment to after-school activities, returning home with my canine buddy after 6.00 p.m. on three or four nights. That was until Jamie, who lived in our village, proposed a solution. He would walk Laddie home each time I had a fixture. Though not an outstanding athlete he did have a great work ethic and was both sensible and reliable. With his mates queuing for the school bus home, he would breeze past them at the start of a two and a half mile walk to my house. It provided a significant addition to the exercise programme designed to improve his strength and overall stature.

During my six-week working break in the USA, he stayed at the local boarding kennels of Humphrey Friel a greyhound enthusiast, before starting his racing career five months after I acquired him. At this time, the option was to race at an unlicensed track, the closest being Chasewater. In a solo trial he performed well, with a fast time. I registered him as St. Joe (named after Joe, the international athlete) and asked for him to be entered in a sprint race (290 metres) around two bends which provided less opportunity to fight. He finished like a train, just losing out by neck, but more importantly running straight. He was now a much stronger and more mature greyhound.

I decided to enter him in an open race against unknown opposition over the standard distance of 450 metres. He again finished second but was beaten by a greyhound purchased for two thousand pounds. I began to get excited. Laddie was now showing his true potential. In a race ten days later, he won readily. I asked Pat if he would take him on board to run at Wolverhampton based on the performances and he agreed, with some reservation (having seen him trial previously at the track). Laddie vacated the wooden garage which had been his home, for the kennels at Landywood in October. He won all three trials without any concerns and qualified to run at the track. Hobourne's Lad made his debut in a grade 5 race over 480 metres on a wet November evening in 1983.

The return to school in September had not been without alarm and concern. The local authority had issued a notice of intention to close the school and relocate the Catholic children to other schools within the Diocese. It was felt that Cannock was not large enough to sustain three secondary schools. The school and its Governors intended to fight the decision, and I decided any prizemoney won by Hobourne's Lad would be given to the Fighting Fund.

He won his first three races with ease and because of such he was moved into a grade two race on a Saturday night. He won that race also which meant he had a seven-race unbeaten record. In an attempt to elevate the mood within the school, I contacted a reporter at the Daily Express (the newspaper purchased for the Staff) on the Monday morning with the back story and details of Hobourne's improved performances. Within an hour, the reporter called to inform me that a photographer was on his way from Birmingham.

I called Pat at the kennels and arranged to "borrow" Hobourne's Lad for the afternoon. Surrounded by a hundred or more students, he behaved impeccably as the Express man secured the necessary photographs, before Laddie was transferred back to his new home.

The first indication that it was more than a small interest item was when I received a phone call just after midnight from the deputy editor of the Daily Mail asking why I had approached the Express. He inferred that his paper would have paid a substantial amount for the story. Paper talk I thought.

The following morning, I was met by a frantic headteacher in reception with newspaper in hand. Two thirds of page three were dedicated to the story, accompanied by an image of the greyhound surrounded by adoring students.

"I have already had Radio WM arrive. They are interviewing students as we speak," he said. "There's also a number from the BBC to ring. You had better take some time to sort it out." He turned, shaking his head and laughing before heading for the sanctuary of his office.

Following a quick interview with the local radio station, I rang the BBC. They asked if I could attend a satellite studio at the rear of an Indian restaurant in Wolverhampton to provide an interview for Radio One and their Newsbeat feature. Everyone seemed to be interested in the story. With the interview for Newsbeat completed I was about to leave the studio when the engineer received a phone call.

"You can't go," he said. "We need you to do another interview for The World at One."

I drove back to school and headed straight for the woodwork room where they had a large radio (usually for Test Match commentary).

"Have I got a surprise for you," I said to Bill, the Head of Faculty. He turned the radio on as instructed and then twenty minutes into the half-hour news programme, the legendary voice of Sir Robin Day declared:

"*...and now we go from the crisis in the Middle East to a greyhound in Staffordshire.*" Three minutes of fame.

By the end of the day the regional evening newspaper had been in touch to carry a feature, and also the local weekly paper. Things would now settle down. At least that's what I thought.

The following morning BBC television called and following a long discussion asked permission to cover the story for Breakfast Television. A director (or producer I don't know which is which) arranged a call to run through the planning, which of course had to be agreed by the head teacher. They wanted to start production in twelve days and include a race featuring Hobourne's Lad. The school was fully supportive. Feelgood publicity is a winner for all. However, I had to ask Pat to liaise with the track to ensure that Laddie did not have a race in the meantime, in order to retain his record, but also to request that he runs on the Thursday evening for filming purposes.

There was another hurdle. Laddie was a runner at a licensed track with strict protocols. He would only be allowed out of the kennel area for a period of four hours with a return within 48 hours of a race. He also had to be constantly supervised by a recognized member of Pat's staff.

Filming began in earnest with Laddie on the front row of morning assembly, attended by Maria, one of my handball players, as the rest of the year sang All things Bright and Beautiful. Very apt. Peter Bateson was interviewed and described him as "their little Champion". All was well.

On the night of the race, I took several lads who helped in those early days and some staff over to the track in the school bus to watch him run. The whole BBC crew asked if he was likely to win. My only response was so far so good. The general public were not so confident, backing trap one, Oakfield, an expensive purchase. Those in the know, including the presenter, lighting and sound crew, invested their cash on Hobourne's Lad at five to two. Oakfield led round the final bend, but the black greyhound in trap six flashed by near the winning line, to make a very happy ending to the beginning of a long and colourful journey.

# Chapter Eighteen

The interest in the story continued well into the new year. Interviews on local and national radio maintained the momentum, with every further win generating more exposure both locally and nationally of the fight for survival by the school. Syndicated Features, a media agency from the United States arranged for a reporter to visit the school, where for over an hour she recorded our conversation. The transcript was eventually circulated to news agencies throughout the world. One Saturday evening a fellow owner at Monmore Green, who had just returned from a business trip, provided a copy of an extensive article from the Kuwait Times with the headline: *The Greyhound Saviour.* The story had global appeal.

The continued success was down to one-man, Pat Ryan. A sociable and affable Irishman who was also a genius with greyhounds. He had that rare ability to identify not only what routine makes a dog tick but when it is likely to be at its best. He could plot, and often did so with precision, a peak performance which would ensure a happy set of owners, particularly if they had backed his judgement with their cash to land a "nice touch".

Following a performance where he seemed stale and awkward, Pat suggested we take Hobourne's Lad off the track for a couple of weeks. During that time, to maintain his fitness I took him to an unlicensed track at Warwick where his trial time was impressively fast (even though I had put him in trap one to inconvenience him slightly) and registered him for future races as McGill. Following a further success at the unlicensed Chasewater, he returned to Wolverhampton, where he powered home in his first race back at the track from trap six cheered on by a bus load of pupils from the school who then collected the winner's trophy.

He then ran (and won) a race at Henlow, following which Pat made a significant observation.

"This yoke enjoys change. He gets bored easily with the mundane and that's when he will mess about."

I had used the analogy of a young, gangly student growing in time into a powerful athlete when speaking to the media, but now there was another analogy from education. The bored student who has much to offer but when not challenged will flick his ruler or paper at another student or pull a chair away. Not malicious or aggressive just annoying. That was Laddie and recognising such was the key to his ongoing success. We needed to move him around, he needed stimulation.

He competed in races at Swindon, Perry Barr, Sheffield and Belle Vue in between his races at Monmore Green. He won at all the tracks he ran at first time except for one. On a freezing cold midwinter night, I drove Cordy, the kennel maid, with Laddie on a two-hour journey to Peterborough where he was running from trap six. A perfect race for him. The locals backed their champion in trap one, believing that a lack of experience at the track would be a major negative and Laddie drifted in price. I then had my £100 bet on him. Just before they loaded the greyhounds into the traps for the start of the race Cordy informed me that the undersoil heating (to melt the frozen ground) was only working for the strip on the inside of the track. The outside was frozen on the bends. He would be skating around them. It was too late to do anything but hope.

The traps flew open, and Laddie was second at the bend, when he hit the frozen ground he cornered like Bambi on ice, coming out of the second bend in joint last place. He flew down the straight to be alongside the leader before the bend appeared and again his back end skidded around the turn almost losing his feet. In the final fifty yards he flew home only to be beaten in a photo finish. The journey home seemed to take forever. We never went back to Peterborough.

Following each success there was an envelope pushed through my home letter box with a five-pound note in it. I had no idea where it came from or from whom, until one morning when I heard the flap rattle and noticed a familiar car leaving up the High Street. My GP at the time had children at the school and I had once told him that Hobourne's Lad always ran well from trap six. He apparently regularly had a bet on the dog and his donation was gratefully added to the fund.

Following the Peterborough experience, we decided to make use of the more local unauthorised (Flapping) tracks. They would serve the same purpose without the time and travel investment. There were several within an hour's drive of the kennels.

Throughout the next few months, I took my canine star to the tracks at Warwick, Hinckley, Coalville and Chesterton. Hinckley was the only track where the hare was fixed to the inside on an extended arm. He was registered as McClean at Warwick, McGill at Hinckley, McCleod at Coalville and Percy at Chesterton. He won his first race at Warwick comfortably. I returned seven days later for an Open race (entries by anyone from anywhere) worth £100 to the winner over a longer distance.

In some cases, the management of the track frame races to cater for a local trainer with conditions to favour their greyhound often in return for regular support. We unfortunately were not in that category. They tried everything to get him beaten. He was leading at half-way when the hare driver slowed the hare causing Laddie to ease down thinking the race was over, which allowed the others to catch him and for a couple to race past him as the hare accelerated again. Laddie regained his momentum and led at the sixth and final bend only for the hare to stop, with the race declared void due to a "mechanical failure." As this was the first race on the programme, the management decided to run the race again as the final race, over two hours later. Laddie seemed fine so we both relaxed in the back of my Passat estate car until fifteen minutes before the race.

The greyhound which had been backed to beat Laddie in the original race (with all bets returned) was withdrawn and another substituted in its place. It appeared that a hasty plot had been initiated to ensure the prizemoney stayed at home. The locals backed the fresh newcomer to win the race. Our lad had second thoughts as he powered up the straight to win by several lengths. Job done. More money in the pot.

There was also a valuable race held at St. Helens in Lancashire with prizemoney of £1,500. Hobourne's Lad had a trial at the track and his solo time was just outside the track record. An amazing achievement for his first run around what was a difficult track. Later that night I received a phone call from someone in Lancashire who had seen him run with an offer of £2,500 for Laddie. He was not for sale.

An injury to a toe side-lined him for several weeks, during which time he returned to my house, enjoying the occasional evening watching

TV but more often in the wooden garage on the bed of hay. There was, however, a problem in that he seemed able to at times escape through the doors and jog down to the local chip shop where he would happily wait to be fed by the customers. On more than one occasion I opened the back door to find an old farmer holding his trousers up with one hand and his belt in the other with Laddie on the end of the makeshift lead. My next-door neighbour Colin, who regularly volunteered to walk the dog was not exempt. One Sunday afternoon he knocked on my door, holding the dog with a tea-towel for a collar in one hand and a deconstructed lump of beef in the other. He appeared to be laughing. Laddie had escaped but had taken the five metre walk next door into the utility room and then snatched the beef joint which had been left on the side to defrost. Colin and Joan had to settle for lamb chops instead.

Johnny Mac and Manny two former students sorted out the issue by building two breeze block kennels with secure doors at the bottom of my garden the following Saturday for the price of a drink.

During this time, the Monmore Green track was in the process of being acquired by Ladbrokes the betting shop group. The management approached me to join an Owners and Trainers group to be part of ongoing discussions and decisions which would impact on the racing. The meetings took place each month and I was elected chairman, with World Cup Final referee Jack Taylor as vice-chair. The Ladbroke team was led by Ron Pollard an icon in the industry. He was a complete gentleman and was open to any ideas to improve racing and the experience for punters at the stadium.

I stepped forward with several ideas regarding races which could be staged to improve the variety and elevate interest, and these were taken on board. A multi-distance championship, with a greyhound competing over sprint, middle and long distances gaining points for their finishing position created an ante-post market as did a thirty-two runner Handicap championships. There were Selling races and first-race/last race sprints. The place was vibrant.

Sadly, the current product caters for volume rather than novelty.

I was now a regular visitor to the stadium on a Saturday night where I would always have a brief chat with Alan Satchwell before joining Pat Ryan and his crew for the craic. After an incident packed race one evening Alan appeared looking excited. I thought he had won the jackpot.

"Did you see the last race?" he asked

The race he was referring to was over a distance of 480 metres in which a greyhound, Burgess Strand, had been knocked sideways at the first bend and was several lengths behind the leaders, but had then accelerated down the back straight to such an effect that he joined the leading two greyhounds at the third bend, before head-butting them both and completely wiping them out, allowing the trailing runners to waltz home at their leisure. Burgess Strand was immediately disqualified from racing at the track.

"Maurice the owner is fuming. He paid £1000 for the dog and just wants to get rid of it. You can have it for nothing," he said.

I took a deep breath. Could lightning strike twice?

"Tell him I will collect it from his kennels tomorrow."

"He wants you to take it tonight, now." With that Alan and I left, he back to the races and me to the stadium kennels to pick up my new resident.

That evening, I travelled home with a hyperactive brindle greyhound (a mixture of brown and black), in the back of my car, who was continually trying to jump into the front. A complete nutter. He seemed to calm down when I opened my side window, standing on the seat directly behind me with his front legs over my shoulders and his head at the side of mine. I was wearing a live jacket. I called him Bozo, which seemed appropriate.

Once he settled into his new surroundings, he was fine, just very enthusiastic. He was not aggressive just playful, and he soon accompanied me to school where he was subject to the same regime as Hobourne's Lad. The pupils loved him. There were times when he would take off with the walker when over Cannock Chase. Great conditioning when you are trying to tow a hundred-pound weight.

Following an extended break from racing we entered him in races at Chasewater (Brando), Hinkley (Bogart) and Warwick (Bond). The idea was just to let him find his feet (or paws) and enjoy the experience. He won a couple of races at Chasewater and one at Warwick.

Almost six months after the breaking of the Hobourne's Lad story, ITV contacted me about the possibility of a story for a children's programme and to follow up on the fight for survival by the school. The only issue was Laddie being injured. I informed the producer and mentioned Bozo, and that he would only be able to run at an unlicensed track. I explained the difference, but this only ignited his interest. The idea of a family running "their pet" at these tracks would be ideal for the story. I needed some time to hatch a plan and get Bozo into peak condition. Twenty days later a large crew converged on the school.

Unlike the BBC, the crew was well populated not only with camera men but experts in lighting, sound and continuity. They were scheduled for four days filming. They interviewed some of the walkers and filmed Bozo sprinting across the field (pursuing a bib being carried by one of my better athletes) and taking Tim for a jog across the Chase. My job was to deliver Bozo (Bogart) in prime condition for his race at Hinckley, a track where he had run three times previously without success.

On the night concerned he was in trap one, giving all the greyhounds a start of up to twelve metres. It was not an easy task, but it was an ideal scenario, it gave him something to pursue. He had thankfully passed them all by the third bend to win by a couple of lengths, cheered on by a handful of students and with a delighted crew nearly three-hundred pound richer from bets placed. Job done.

The six-minute story appeared on national television three weeks later. The following month it was announced that the school would not be closed and that the other two schools in Cannock would be amalgamated. Job done.

# Chapter Nineteen

The year ended well, and the school was now guaranteed a future. With Laddie at the top of his game Pat suggested he be aimed at an event called the Springbok. The race would require the greyhounds to jump five brush hurdles and was restricted to greyhounds who had never previously run over hurdles. It was worth £1,500 to the winner.

For nearly three weeks I would run and jump hurdles with my canine hero. He cleared them all with precision at a jog. A couple of half-lap trials with three hurdles at the track went well and Pat decided he was ready for a full trial against two other dogs. The race took place on a Tuesday morning.

When I visited the kennel after school to see how the trial went, I nearly cried. My eyes filled when a solemn Pat took me to Laddie's kennel, and he struggled to get to his feet to greet me. It appeared that during the trial, he was so far ahead of the other two runners that the hare driver slowed the hare slightly to allow them to catch up, at which point Laddie tried to dive through the gap at the side of the hurdle which allowed the hare to pass through to get the slowing hare, badly injuring his shoulder.

Pat had taken him to the vet, who examined him and though nothing was broken he felt that the injury was serious. It could be anything from six to eight months to recover, if at all. I sat in the kennel just stroking his head. I was devastated. I felt sick.

The following few days I went to the kennels in the morning and evening just to be with him and walk him gently on the grass. He always seemed happy to see me, but he was in some pain and discomfort. I needed to do something to help him.

When I was in the United States the previous summer, I had purchased a small book about alternative approaches to the treatment of sports injuries. I remembered reading in a half-page section on the use of DMSO in the treatment of shoulder injuries in quarterbacks in American Football. Mr. McKinnon the vet had heard of its use in horses in America, but he had no knowledge of it being used in the United Kingdom. He ordered a small bottle of the substance, dimethyl sulfoxide which technically was an industrial solvent and a bi-product from the manufacture of paper.

I was instructed to shave the area around the shoulder and apply the liquid gently with a soft brush twice a day. With very little information, it really was a desperate attempt to both relieve the discomfort and repair the shoulder. During the first application I noticed a vapour rising from the area and I thought it was heat, but Laddie was unmoved.

I had also read a chapter in the book which focused on passive movement within 48 hours of a sprain or strain. The author used circus acrobats as an example, who if spraining an ankle, would ice the area but within 48 hours begin movement of the joint. Increasing the range daily until they were able to train and perform again, usually within a short time frame. If they did not perform, they would not get paid.

I followed the same process with Laddie. Gently moving his leg following application of the DMSO. Each day the range increased without any discomfort or pain. Within fourteen days he was walking soundly again with a sparkle in his eye. His racing future was on hold and was secondary to his welfare and well-being. During the next four weeks I gradually increased the distance we would walk. I would pick him up from Pat's kennels and drive him to nearby Cannock Chase where fallen leaves and pine needles were soft underfoot making it a safe area to jog. The change of scenery seemed to bring him alive. Ears pricked and bouncing, his black coat shone like a guardsman's shoes.

Eight weeks after a serious injury, Hobourne's Lad returned for a solo run around two-bends to assess the extent of the damage and establish if he would ever be able to race again. The time was moderate but most importantly he was sound and well. He was ready to race again.

Colin, my next-door neighbour, enjoyed the occasional flutter on the horses. He had been both helpful and tolerant living next door to me. Timmy who often exercised Laddie during his lunchbreak and attended greyhound races with me was determined to pursue a career as a jockey. He worked during the weekend and during the holidays at a local racing stable which had launched the career of some outstanding jockeys. They both needed some reward for their endeavours. Something meaningful.

On the third Thursday in March Hobourne's Lad was scheduled to return to the track, running in race five at Monmore Green. It was also Gold Cup Day at Cheltenham. A great opportunity for a double header. I pulled a "sickie" and arranged to take them both to the races followed by an evening meal at Monmore Green to watch our hero's return. With two-hundred pounds in my pocket we set off for one of the World's best racing experiences.

"Don't worry boys," I said. "I have won on the past three Gold Cup Days," as we joined the packed stands. Six races later I had not backed a winner or had any return on my investments.

The journey to Wolverhampton was uneventful but quiet. On the plus side there had been some terrific racing and the whole experience of Cheltenham with its fierce Anglo – Irish competition and the roar of the crowd was on a different level. Michael Dickenson had trained the first five home in the Gold Cup, a feat never repeated.

We arrived at the greyhound stadium in good time to enjoy our meal in the restaurant. Having paid the bill, I was left with just under twenty pounds. I went downstairs to speak with Pat about the chances of Laddie who was running from trap five. He also had another dog, Hilltown Law, running from trap six.

"Yer fella is well, but I raced him in a trial with the 'six dog' on Sunday and was beaten by five lengths. Save your money and see how he goes on. The six dog is a fair animal."

The information must have become common knowledge as everybody was backing Hilltown Law who was a short-priced favourite. Hobourne's Lad was ten to one. I invested a tenner on the Lad for old times' sake.

Just before the hare started, Stan Hughes a popular bookmaker offered odds of twenty to one - a price he felt was a truer reflection of the Lad's chances. I threw him my last fiver.

When the traps opened Hilltown Law flew out and by the second bend was about four lengths clear of the second dog who in turn was three lengths clear of the third. The third dog was Hobourne's Lad. By the final bend, the lead was reduced to three lengths and with a storming finish Laddie stuck his head out were it mattered to win by the narrowest of margins. Job done.

Timmy and Colin collected the trophy and I "went past Go" and collected two-hundred pounds. A great day of sport, paid for by our four-legged friend. His win also saved a bookmaker a large four figure pay out with his gratitude being the purchase of a new playing kit for my handball team.

Hobourne's Lad was without doubt the gift that kept on giving.

Throughout the next twelve months we visited a number of different tracks with mixed success but always returning to Wolverhampton for two or three consecutive races. He seemed to sense the big occasion. When my mother attended for a birthday meal, he put in another great performance to win a trophy.

When Peter Bateson, the headteacher who had been so supportive of me and my endeavours decided to retire I organised for a large party of teachers and Governors from the school to attend Monmore Green. Almost half the restaurant was taken up with the group and I arranged to sponsor a race – the Peter Bateson Retirement Stakes. Hobourne's Lad was engaged in a race later in the evening. For many it was the first time they had been to a greyhound meeting or seen Laddie run in the flesh.

His task was not an easy one from trap five and there were three runners ahead of him in the market, including a hot favourite in trap one. I placed £20 on him, more out of loyalty than expectation. The female PE teacher confided she had never placed a bet in her life and never intended to do so after that night. She jumped in with a £50 investment at odds of five to one. Many of the group had no idea what to do so they each threw five pounds into the hat totalling eighty pounds for me to place on the school saviour. I was hoping for the best but expecting the worst.

Hobourne's Lad did not have a good start and was fifth of the six runners at the second bend. The group looked disappointed. They did not know what he was like. That he needed a target in front to chase. He closed on the leading group down the back straight and from the final bend produced an explosive run to pass the three in front to win by a head. He seemed to know exactly where the finishing line was.

Peter Bateson collected the trophy and everyone had a sense of euphoria, not to mention a small, and in one case not so small windfall to send them home with a smile.

Hobourne's Lad was a once in a lifetime greyhound. Not always the fastest, but when it mattered, he produced the performances that mattered. He retired from racing a few months before his fifth birthday to live at home with Diane, my future wife and I, until he sadly died after being diagnosed with throat cancer at the age of eleven.

It was testimony to his impact at Monmore Green that many years after his retirement regulars at the track would approach me to enquire how he was.

****

During the period with both greyhounds and my involvement with Pat Ryan I was privileged to meet many characters in the sport who contributed in different ways to the unique atmosphere at Monmore Green at that time. There were the punters, Jimmy the Fish, Potato Billy, Mick the Scrap, Elderberry Pete, Paul the Gent and Riceman Chris, battling the bookmakers Harry Nixon, Barry and Lee Hughes, Mick Williams, Paul Beard and Tony Campbell. Each trying to get ahead. Win or lose, every Saturday night they would converge on the bar after racing, two teams united to sample the seafood of the day supplied by Jimmy. There was speculation and rumour, and everyone seemed to have a story which made for a colourful tapestry. The performances of the night were discussed with "touches" (wins) quietly acknowledged with the amounts won never discussed and "setbacks" (losers) where the amount was often known immediately after a race in a form of news flash. It was here that small groups with their "ifs" and "buts" of the night began to plot their "how" and "when" of the future. The battle was lost but not the war.

The unlicensed greyhound tracks were known as "Flapping Tracks" and there were several within easy reach of Cannock. They were unregulated and had extremely basic facilities but always provided eight races for the public to enjoy. They were well supported by greyhound owners and the public and often had several local bookmakers trading.

The track manager's role was to ensure that the races at each meeting be as even as possible and he would always treat trial times with caution, suspecting that the animal would improve once in a race. They would often place a greyhound in two or three grades higher for its first run, making it extremely difficult to win at the first time of asking.

My reputation to get greyhounds fit enabled me to be given care of a bitch who had just completed her seasonal break with a view to landing a touch. She had not raced for nearly ten weeks. It usually takes a couple of races for a greyhound to find their form following enforced rest. I trialled her at Hinckley where she achieved a moderate time and named her Bardot.

Over the next two weeks, we would walk and jog to improve her fitness. At her peak Blackstock was one of the fastest bitches in the Midlands.

The plan was to run just one race at Hinckley and then return her to racing at Monmore Green. The owner had given me two-hundred pounds to place on her. Once I thought she was fit enough. I asked the track to enter her in a race on a Saturday night. They placed her in trap three in two grades above her achieved time.

For many years I was employed by an organisation that placed students in American Summer Camps. My role was to travel to venues and interview students to verify their qualification and assess their qualities and capabilities for work with children. On this Saturday I was scheduled to interview in Liverpool until 2.30 p.m. The race at Hinckley was not until 8.30 p.m.

I boarded the afternoon train at Lime Street, Liverpool - heading for Stafford, changing at Crewe. At Crewe I asked the guard for the train to Stafford and was directed to a waiting train which had a final destination of London Euston. About twenty minutes into the journey the guard announced:

*"Welcome to the London Euston Express stopping at Watford Junction."*

I was mortified. All my plans were up in the air. I walked down the train to find the guard who was walking through the carriages checking tickets. He was a six-foot three Afro-Caribbean who weighed in excess of 220lbs.

"I have been put on the wrong train," I said. "I need to get off at Stafford." He seemed unconcerned.

"The next stop is Watford Junction, you have to get off and get a train back," He casually replied, without even lifting his eyes from the tickets he was clipping.

"You don't understand," I urged. "I have some very important papers in this case which need to be transported tonight for delivery in New York tomorrow." He looked unimpressed.

"I have a car waiting for me at Stafford to take me to Birmingham Airport (a necessary fabrication) and I am going to pull the Communication Chord to stop the train at Stafford." This got his attention.

The fine for pulling the chord was fifty pounds and I took the cash from my wallet to hand to him, at which point with the whole carriage engaged by the conversation he beckoned me to follow him.

With the train hurtling towards Stafford at speed he pulled the chord, and the train braked dramatically and grinded to a halt approximately fifty yards past the end of the platform. The guard opened the door, enabling me to climb down onto the side of the track.

"Next time man, take the bloody bus," were his final words on the matter.

Several bemused people and the station master waited on the platform as I walked with briefcase in hand along the track. Some recognised me and others looked with suspicion as the station master approached. I accompanied him to his office.

"Could you explain what happened?" he calmly said.

I explained that I had been guided to the wrong train by a guard at Crewe.

"So why did you pull the chord?" he asked.

"I didn't. The guard did." At that point, the interview was terminated, and I was free to complete my plans.

I picked Timmy up and drove to Hinckley with Blackstock (Bardot). She won the race by a couple of lengths, and I had placed our bets on to return six hundred pounds in profit. However, before I could collect the money a racegoer colleague of a bookmaker from Hall Green Birmingham recognised her from the distinctive markings on her chest. He conveyed the information about her being a top-class greyhound to the track manager who declared the race void (red light) due to *"the significant improvement made,"* by our greyhound. Our stake money on bets was returned. The plan was thwarted but pride was the only casualty.

The following day I relayed the story to Pat. He smiled as he tapped a pen on the table. I knew he was thinking of a repost, particularly when he looked out of the window and in his soft Limerick brogue said:

"We'll have to see what can be done."

Fifteen miles from Hinckley, a former farm worker, now in his early sixties, lived on a rundown small-holding. He had in the past been involved with greyhound racing at the local flapping tracks. The animals in his care were either slow or getting older and their owners had let them go to a good home. He was a carer rather than a trainer and his success rate was very poor. For him it was a social occasion, providing a reason to go racing.

The two greyhounds we gave him were slow. They both looked good and had been well-kept at the kennels, but they were more like pets than racing greyhounds. We suggested he grade them at Hinckley and enter them on the card whenever he could. He was delighted. For the following six weeks they raced without ever troubling the judge, with the closest finish being a third.

He was then asked to enter a greyhound in an open race at the track, with a £100 purse likely to attract a decent entry. He decided after much deliberation to call the runner Lucky. The greyhound concerned belonged to an owner who had gone AWOL without paying substantial bills and was top class. The greyhound was transported to the small holding on the evening of the race with an instruction to the farmer to arrive at the track only thirty minutes before the race start and that he talks to nobody and walks the dog around the track personally before putting him in the traps. If asked he should only say that the dog is the faster litter brother of one of his other dogs, neither of which had ever won a race.

There were five bookmakers at the track who began to trade on our race with a couple of runners being strongly supported by the large crowd. Having not had a winner for more than eighteen months, there was very little confidence in "our trainer" and the price drifted. Just before the greyhounds were loaded into the traps and with the price at eight to one, the four friends who had travelled with me, placed fifty pounds bets with each of the bookmakers who seemed happy to take the late, easy money. That was until the second bend with Lucky three lengths clear and drawing away.

'The victor belongs to the spoils!' Our man retained the trophy and the prize-money and we returned the greyhound to its usual residence, bills paid.

The battle was won. The war was over.

# Chapter Twenty

By the beginning of the eighties, when the intake from my early years had departed, the level of commitment by students seemed to wane. There was a lack of urgency and fulfilling the fixtures both during the week and on Saturday became increasingly difficult, not helped by the declining numbers of Catholic children in the area. We did have a successful gymnastics club, and we still provided two lunch-time practices per day in a variety of sports for those interested enough to attend.

Then it all changed. Two of the major feeder Catholic Primary schools provided a small group of talented and committed students. The leader of the pack was Nick from Rugeley. A tall, well-made individual who was very confident. Never afraid to question but always respectful. Then there was Steven, a quiet and unassuming student until he tackled you during a football match. Each led by example. Suddenly the numbers attending the practices increased and so did the success.

Though a good football team, they developed a particular interest in handball and basketball. Within two years they were part of the team winning the National Schools Under 15 Championship in handball and the District Championship at basketball. It would be the start of a long run of success for the school in sport.

With strong support from John Timmins, the schools' competition for boys was established in the early eighties. The enthusiastic and ebullient secretary of the British Handball Association explored every avenue for sponsorship, sometimes without looking at the implications. During the late seventies following the success of the young Olympia he secured a sponsorship offer for kit and a leased minibus for a season. He couldn't understand why I would turn down the offer, but being based at a Catholic School, sponsorship by Durex was to echo the words (almost) of Chuck Berry a case of "No, Johnnie No."

He also negotiated a deal with Wilkinson, the razor manufacturer, to sponsor the schools' competition. Most people would have accepted a decent silver cup. Not John.

The trophy for the winners of the handball competition was a metre-long sterling silver ceremonial sword donated by the sponsors with Wilkinson Sword being a household name. It was the type used for conferring a knighthood and in the wrong hands could be lethal. Though mounted on a mahogany board it was never displayed at the school, with the insurers placing a value of more than two thousand pounds on it. For the next six years it would remain in the headteachers office, only leaving the school when accompanied by a team to compete in the finals before being returned to Cannock.

Within two weeks of winning the Championship the team ventured across the Channel to play in a tournament at Merksem in Belgium. Eight clubs from across Europe competed in our age section, where we eventually played Metz (France) in the final, defeating them by 11 goals to 7 and becoming the first English team to win a major tournament on mainland Europe. The entry to the tournament was last-minute with players asked to contribute £5 towards the cost of transport, food and accommodation. I made up the balance from a couple of successful punts at the greyhounds. The French team were disappointed as they expected to win. They asked for a return match in Metz and a date and time was fixed which slotted nicely into the return journey from our next handball adventure.

The Duke had already agreed earlier in the year for a team to participate in the prestigious Interamnia Tournament held annually in Teramo, Italy at the beginning of July. There were the usual conditions that the trip would be self-funded and that parents be appropriately informed. The date of return (as always) remained fluid.

A twenty-four-hour sponsored handball match raised a significant amount of money which contributed towards the purchase of kit and payment for a minibus as I no longer had a contact. It also enabled the cost per individual to be capped at £45 for the planned twelve-day trip.

With a total of eleven players, aged 12 to 14 years, several large boxes of Frosties and Sugar Puffs and a map we departed from Cannock on the 1,300-mile journey. No phones, no emails, just an address in Teramo and a phone number. What could go wrong?

Seven years earlier I had made part of the journey into Italy and had a general idea of the direction I needed to take. If there was a doubt I would follow signs to the Adriatic coast, head south and turn right at Giulianova.

The journey through Belgium was uninteresting with many of the players preferring to sleep, only waking for a quick snack. Prior to the handball trip to Merksem, only one player from the group had travelled outside the United Kingdom or Ireland. Their first culture shock occurred near Friedburg when we stopped at a road-side canteen for bratwurst and frites. The players looked disappointed at the "skinny chips" as they were referred to but were completely taken aback when asked if they wanted mustard or mayonnaise on their frites. Open-mouthed, some just froze as if a cobra was about to strike.

"Welcome to Germany," I said, with a smile. "I'll have mayonnaise please!"

There was no over-night stop planned. We agreed to sleep in the bus. I pulled in a lay-by on a quiet mountain road near Andermatt and climbed on the roof of the van where the luggage had been neatly placed to create a soft sleeping area for me. I slid into my sleeping bag for a restful night's slumber.

Once the warm sun peered over the mountain top, I awoke. All the lads were asleep. I had a quick drink and began the final part of the journey to Teramo. Twenty years later the silence was broken when one of the players informed me that they had all woken an hour or so before me and descended down the mountain side to have a splash about in the stream below, scurrying back just before my return to the land of the living to resume their sleeping mode.

We reached Teramo by late afternoon and settled into our camp chalets near the beach in Giulianova. Over the next few days, playing games on carparks and in sports halls, we won all our games to finish top of our league to reach the quarterfinals.

With a break in games on the Sunday, I decided to take the team on the two-hour drive to Rome, where we could not only visit some of the sights but celebrate mass in St. Peter's Basilica. The mass of course was delivered in Latin, not that it would have impacted on many of the players who slept all the way through despite a real fire and brimstone sermon.

The following day we defeated Valle Handball Club from Columbia in a tense and at times physical game. Nick led the team into battle, a rock in defence and a constant threat in attack where his combination play with Seamus was outstanding. The Columbians seemed to have a significant number of mean-looking supporters who became particularly vocal when Nick clattered into their star player when making an interception from which we scored. We left the court quickly and I drove the players to a restaurant to celebrate. I introduced them all to Pizza. They were underwhelmed.

"Why doe they 'av chips sir?" Sean the captain asked.

"Because Sean, this is Italy where pizza and pasta replace pie and chips," I replied.

The semi-final was due to be played in Teramo at 4.00 p.m. against the hosts. We travelled to the court from our base, a thirty-minute drive and began to warm up, though with temperatures in the low thirties there seemed little need. With ten minutes to throw off a young boy arrived on a bike and gave me a note. The game would now be played at 7.00 p.m. at the indoor court in the town. We had no alternative but to stay in the town and kill time.

By 7.00 p.m., some of the boys were drained not only by the wait but by the heat. We eventually lost to the hosts by five goals, with three occurring in the final minutes as we visibly wilted. We did, however, qualify for the play-off for third place against Ajax of Copenhagen.

Leading by four goals at half-time I decided to climb on the minibus to video the rest of the game. It was at this time that the phrase "It's not over till it's over" resonated. The Danes slowly clawed their way back into the game. Once I had decided to end my Spielberg adventure they were leading by a goal, and we had lost our momentum. Despite our gallant efforts they managed to retain their single goal advantage until the final whistle.

The team must have created a favourable impression as the mayor of a small town in the north of the Abruzzo region asked if we would travel to play their team on our homeward journey, with food and accommodation provided. It was another cultural adventure for the boys. The town was situated in the mountains with several old streets converging like streams into a square whose main feature was a church. Just off the square was a small school with a playground area. On the Saturday night this was transformed into an entertainment centre with food, music, dancing and games. However, the population was entirely made up of women and children. All the men of the town gathered in a bar at the top of the hill, some playing cards, others just talking. They only appeared to descend the hill when the music was no more, and the activities below ceased.

The following day was Sunday, the town was quiet, and we played a couple of games outdoor before beginning the long journey home via Metz. Following another night in the minibus parked by the lake at Lucerne we travelled through the winding roads of the Ardennes, reaching the hall in Metz sixty minutes before the agreed time. We were greeted by the caretaker and a young boy who was the interpreter. Having travelled over 890 kilometres I was informed that some of the Metz players were on holiday so they would be unable to play. It was hard not to shoot the messenger.

Our overall achievements and the manner of them had impressed many at the tournaments and during the next months I received several requests to attend tournaments throughout Scandinavia, Germany and France for the following year. We eventually settled for an Easter visit to Neuss, a suburb of Dusseldorf, where the players would stay with a host family for five days, playing a game against the local team and participating in their tournament at the weekend.

Following their first night in their new homes the team met at a local sports centre. Three of the team, all housed in the same place, were excited and confused.

"The house is massive, sir and even has a lift. There is a swimming pool in the basement and a small games room. But there is no telly," Michael said.

He continued, "I asked the dad what they did at night without a television, and he said they train for handball and football and in the home, they swim, play board games or talk." The idea that a family could spend the evening talking seemed strange, almost alien to them.

The people of Neuss were very hospitable and the tournament very well organised. We would visit the town on many occasions during the proceeding years where Manfred Buschgens was pivotal in the organisation.

On one occasion Seamus and Sean had to sit an examination at school a day after our departure. This was not any examination. It was a Religious Education examination, which for a Catholic School, was of paramount importance. They were mortified. I jokingly suggested that they could get a train from Birmingham to Dusseldorf once they had taken their exam. Without a minute's hesitation their parents approved the idea and the fifteen-year-old boys who had previously travelled to Italy, Belgium and Germany booked their one-way tickets.

I drove the minibus at midday to meet them at the station in Dusseldorf with the remainder of the squad. The train arrived but they did not. Panic. I asked the guard where the train next stopped fearing that they may have fallen asleep, and he informed me it was Hamburg which was four hundred kilometres away. Maybe they had missed the train?

I allowed the rest of the team to wander around the nearby square where the sportswear shops seemed to fascinate them whilst I sat nervously in the Minibus and waited for the next train into the station. With relief they arrived, having got off the original train at Dusseldorf south rather than Central. They were oblivious to the state of panic that was tearing at me some thirty minutes earlier.

The trips to Neuss also provided some other insights to sport in Germany. Firstly, that the restaurant and bar we frequently visited was owned by the sports teams of the town, with profits going to support not only the handball but basketball and volleyball teams. All participants at the tournaments were directed there to eat and drink and provide ongoing income.

One afternoon, during the tournament a few of the team went outside the sports hall to cool down. It was a warm day. Outside on a handball court with a tartan surface, four boys were practicing their football skills. They were nine years old and for twenty minutes they went through a routine which included ball manipulation and turning, passing and shooting without any supervision and guidance and more significantly with a high degree of execution.

I was impressed and questioned the group why they were so focused.

"It is the work set by the coach for each day," replied the tallest and presumably the oldest of the group. The handball players could not believe the level of application. They were six years older and still, for most of the time, needed to be monitored at training sessions.

The trips to Neuss became an annual event, with teams from across the continent requesting to be placed in our group, not because we were an easy touch, but because it would be their first ever game against an English side. We played games against teams from the Soviet Union, Czechoslovakia, East Germany, Hungary and Poland in addition to the usual suspects from Germany, Holland, Switzerland and Belgium.

Despite this there was still an element of wanderlust. With a new mini-bus and the Neuss tournament taking place at the beginning of the Easter Break I asked the team if they would like to play another game after the tournament before our return. They agreed unanimously. I told them that the game would be in France and that the trip would be extended by four days with a small additional charge.

Parents were informed some weeks before travel about departure and return (provisional) and that we would be playing games in Neuss (Germany) and at Villefranche-sur- Soane (France). In Germany we would be accommodated in classrooms whilst in France we would be camping. A good friend, Tom Smith, who was the secretary of Brentwood Handball Club heard of the proposed trip to Neuss a few weeks before our departure, following a senior game against Olympia. He called me and asked if we would allow his son James to play. His son was a sociable and well-mannered player I had seen at England trials. I provided Tom with a brief outline, with the caveat that the return date was flexible. Without hesitation and complete trust, he arranged for Jim to be picked up on the North Circular Road in Essex on the way to Dover.

I borrowed a huge scout tent for our trip which along with my three-man tent was adequate. The players had no idea where the final destination would be. The plan was to drive to a site near to the French border and set up camp for a night or two before moving closer to the game venue. However, the rain was torrential, and we spent the night in the bus before moving on to the mystery destination early the following morning.

Annecy, one of France's most picturesque towns is set on the western bank of its largest lake. We settled nicely in our new environment by the lake where the open spaces and lake were ideal to keep the group busy during the downtime.

On one evening visit into the town an accident had just occurred on the lakeside road involving a motorcyclist who looked severely injured. The gendarmerie had just arrived at the scene and immediately stopped the traffic. There was a significant amount of blood.

From the back of the bus, I heard a voice call out.

"Sir I think his foot is back there." The bus was stationary at this time, and I turned to clarify what had just been said.

"I saw a boot with blood on it in the road just as we slowed," he said.

I left the bus to inform one of the officers of the grim observation, before eventually being allowed to move past the scene into town. The whole episode did little for the appetite of the team most of whom settled for frites and ice cream.

The game against Villefranche the following day involved a two-hour drive. We lost narrowly, but following the game they provided an amazing chicken chasseur which everybody devoured, and I was given a dozen bottles of Beaujolais. Results sometimes come in different forms and with the weather being sunny and warm I decided to extend our stay by a couple of nights.

The whole adventure was a success with the boys seeing differing areas of Germany and France and returning home in time for the start of the summer term. There were no reports to make, no forms to complete the only task was to fill up the minibus with fuel for the next driver. (I did give a bottle of Beaujolais to Peter Bateson, Dave Roberts, the deputy head and Tom Smith). The rest found an appreciative home in my new wine rack.

# Chapter Twenty-One

Following treatment for skin cancer the small, well-spoken, polite and approachable Peter Bateson decided to retire (he eventually lived into his early nineties). He had without doubt "hooked" me into the life of the school to such an extent that leaving was not an option. I felt free, valued and supported. Soon that was all to change.

His replacement was short and stocky with a lazy eye and wiry hair that never seemed to grow. For the first few weeks he seemed to vacate his office moving swiftly around the school, making mental notes of the modus operandi and the fabric of the building. He would sometimes enter classrooms to scan not only the pupils but the member of staff delivering the lesson. Nowhere was out of bounds including the staffroom, where the Duke always knocked before entering. "Freddie" as he became affectionately known in the Department, would burst through the door, look at the notice board, and then turn to review the few staff who were either working or taking a well-earned free period, leaving without saying a word. When questioned about his frequent visits into the staffroom he declared that he was as entitled as any other member of staff to use the room.

He had within days, informed me that under no circumstances would any dogs be allowed on site, which I accepted without concern as that story had been played out successfully. He also expected staff to arrive at school at least ten minutes before the start of the day. Reasonable I thought.

I had been elected as the staff representative on the Governing body of the school four years earlier, serving throughout the threat of closure. I would, when necessary, canvas the views of staff and if appropriate when asked by the Chairman for guidance I would express the consensus of opinion on a specific matter. I was only excluded from Reserved Business where confidential items were discussed.

The first Governors meeting attended by Freddie was held at the end of September. During the meeting, the Chairman asked me directly for an opinion and I expressed it on behalf of the staff. From across the table I was aware of a one-eyed glare and the grating of teeth. Someone was displeased.

The following day I was called into Freddie's office and informed that I should not speak again at a Governor's meeting.

"I have always been part of the process," I said. "I am there on behalf of the staff, to represent their views."

"*I* will express their views," he said sternly. "You are there to support *me!*"

The next few weeks were a little fractious. I avoided him and it was a busy time for fixtures. Then one day during lunch (I was often one of the last in the dining room due to lunch-time clubs) he sat down next to me as I was in the process of devouring my pudding. There was only a scattering of pupils around the room when, looking out of the window, he declared:

"You are not my type of PE man. I want someone who teaches rugby and volleyball. I think your time here is limited."

Not the kind of comment you want to hear when enjoying your last mouthful of spotted dick, but quite appropriate timing I thought.

I took my time to respond, I stood up slowly, gathered my plate and dish and said quietly,

"Really," shaking my head as I left the room.

Things did not get better in the new year. A visit by the Archbishop of Birmingham to the school was seen as a major event. Having celebrated Mass and met with some of the children His Grace was guided by Freddie into the staff room to meet the teachers during an extended break-time. He moved around the room slowly, making polite conversation before he was introduced to me.

"You are the one with the greyhounds," he said excitedly. "Tell me how they are doing?" and at that we both ambled towards Moira our tea lady, where fig rolls and chocolate digestives lay waiting, leaving Freddie fuming whilst we discussed the finer points of greyhound racing.

Following the Governor's meeting in the Spring term, where again he was Mr Angry, Freddie called me into his office. I was instructed to resign from my position on the Governing body as being an "unmarried parent" at that time was, in his opinion, damaging to the ethos of the school. Unbelievable. I wasn't prepared to be a puppet, so I resigned. There was no election. He replaced me with a female member whose silent support was far more acceptable. The staff were only informed once the transition had been completed. Elections became a thing of the past.

I realised from that moment that I would need to make changes. The things I once took for granted would be no more. That every move or suggestion would be scrutinised and the strong support I had enjoyed for the past eleven years was rapidly deteriorating.

One Friday evening I received a phone call from Colin with a warning that Freddie was after me and to be prepared on Monday morning. I did not have a lesson to teach during the final hour of Friday afternoon and did not have any form responsibilities. Fifteen minutes before the end of school I had packed my car with several footballs to take to the local sports shop for repair. I left early to avoid post school traffic. On seeing me leave through the gates, he immediately contacted the caretaker and instructed him to activate an impromptu fire-practice. The fire alarm was set off and the whole school and its staff gathered on the top playground – except me.

On Monday morning at 9.00 a.m. I was issued with a first written warning. There was no opportunity to explain. I walked up towards the Sports Hall only stopping to dispatch the letter into the bin with the rest of the trash. The following year I was given form-teacher responsibilities and never again allocated non-teaching time on a Friday afternoon.

The on-going battle was a side-show. My responsibility was to the students and in every year group there was a significant number with talent and enthusiasm. They had personality and were far more genuine and transparent than the Fat Controller. My department was committed and incredibly supportive. The Staff provided the day-to-day banter so necessary in a healthy working environment. Avoiding him and his unwanted attention was key to my enjoyment of life.

Handball was still a major sport for the boys but in one particular year, a group of girls aged fourteen had started to play. I managed to include training sessions for them with games initially against the boys. I was at the time receiving mail from across Europe inviting the school to play in tournaments. One invitation arrived from a team in Orleans,

France. Unfortunately, the timing of the tournament did not fit in with our school year, but they did have a girls' team and I suggested a short visit of four days to play a couple of games. My future wife, Diane, agreed to act as a chaperone and a five-day trip to France was organised for the first week in May.

The mini-bus journey was smooth, and the club were fantastic. Each girl was partnered with a family (some families took two) and the local Catholic school was used as a central meeting point. We played two games, one on Friday evening and one on Saturday afternoon. Though we lost both matches there was significant improvement from game to game. On Sunday morning all the girls went ice-skating.

During the lunchtime on Sunday, I received a call from a worried host. One of our girls, Joanne had developed a huge swelling on her ankle and lower leg. She was not in pain and had no idea how it had happened. A neighbour who was a doctor had suggested she should visit the hospital immediately.

Diane and I drove the minibus to the hospital to meet Joanne and the family. She sat on the bed smiling with the "elephant leg" slightly raised. The hospital took x-rays and some blood samples but were mystified as to the condition or cause. Several hours later a specialist consultant arrived to examine her, again with no logical or medical explanation regarding the swelling.

At 8.30 p.m., seven and a half hours after being admitted, she was discharged and ordered to sleep with the leg raised. With the group leaving the following day, the hospital provided me with all the X-rays and notes to enable the case to be transferred to a hospital in England on our return.

By the time we arrived back in Cannock the ankle was back to normal. I instructed her to visit the hospital just as a precaution. She was discharged without any further investigation. Five weeks later she was playing handball for the girls, winning the National Championship against a very strong team from Salford Handball Club. The school became the first (and only) team to win the boys and girls championships in the same year.

The weekend before the Finals, Diane and I got married. Kerry and Lisa, two girls from the school arranged for several volunteers to form a choir. Geoff (metal work teacher) was the organist and Peter K was the photographer. Joe, my handball captain and a former student was an usher, along with a great friend Alec Graham. It was a great day which ended with several male guests, including my best man Joe, sat on the four-poster bed in the honeymoon suite watching Northern Ireland versus Spain in the World Cup finals.

Freddie had already denied my request for three days leave for a brief honeymoon stating that getting married during term-time was not acceptable. Out of the blue, on the Thursday before the wedding, I received a phone call from my GP asking me to attend the evening surgery. Following a quick examination of my eyes and chest he declared that there was a problem with my back, and he issued me with a sick note for seven days. I am unsure of how he knew about the situation, but it was his wedding gift and a "thank you" for the success of Hobourne's Lad.

In spite of my "problematic back" the wedding was enjoyed by all, and I returned to school on Thursday, following three days of rest, in time for a handball training session with the girls.

Two weeks after our success in handball, I was summoned into the Headteachers office. Present was Dave Roberts, the deputy-head. It looked serious. Freddie handed me a letter and informed me that it was a final written warning for a severe breach of the terms and conditions of my contract. That on a recent visit to France on a school sanctioned trip I had failed to take the girls to Mass.

I tried to explain the situation which occurred on that Sunday, but Freddie remained tight-lipped and unmoved. I sensed that this action was not supported by Dave who later in the day advised I consult my Union.

The Union were very supportive and following a meeting with the area representative they arranged for a formal meeting with the headteacher and the Parish priest from whom the complaint had derived at the beginning of July. My representative was the full-time secretary for the Midlands division of the Union.

My statement was based on the notion of "loco parentis", a duty of care to the students with their health and welfare paramount. My focus on that Sunday afternoon was Joanne. To leave the hospital where her condition was unclear for two or three hours, to collect all the other players and take them to Mass, would have been a dereliction of my responsibility. In the event of any surgery, emergency or otherwise, I would need to provide the authority to proceed.

The Priest did try to impress the representative on the importance of Mass to the Catholic community, but he was unmoved. A short recess followed before Freddie called for our return. His offer was to drop the word "final" and just issue a written warning.

"In that case we wish to appeal your decision and would ask that you convene an emergency meeting of the Governors to take place in twenty-eight days as stipulated in the regulations for appeals," was the response of my learned friend.

Freddie looked agitated.

"That's not possible," he said. "I've a villa booked in Tuscany."

The response was swift and sweet.

"Well, my advice is to unbook it then!"

Ten minutes later, a red-faced headteacher emerged to confirm through gritted teeth that no action would be taken and that the warning would be withdrawn without prejudice. With his one good eye glaring at me with laser precision, I gently moved my head from side to side, raised my eyebrows, and said nothing.

I may have succeeded here but I knew there would be other times when life would become uncomfortable. He would not give up easily on his one-man war, and from his reaction even a glass of chianti on a Tuscan terrace would not appease the situation.

# Chapter Twenty-Two

During the summer break of 1986 I toured the United States and Canada with my wife, Diane and young daughter Verity. We initially stayed with my good friend Murray and his wife Roz on Long Island which was a great base for our visits into New York City. My daughter, not yet a year old was the centre of attention wherever we went due to her amazing likeness to the Cabbage Patch Doll which was a global phenomenon at the time.

We travelled to Toronto in Canada with an overnight stay at Niagara Falls. No visit to the Falls is complete without a trip on the Maid of the Mist, a small boat which takes you as close to the Falls as possible, but parking nearby was an issue. Following an unsuccessful twenty-minutes snaking through streets searching for a space, I decided to park in a disabled area (of which there seemed to be many unoccupied). On leaving the car with the pushchair, I walked with an exaggerated limp - as if I'd been a recent patient in a badly conducted hip replacement operation.

The trip was a great experience with the thunderous waters of the Falls cascading across the vessel with its passengers protected by thick black ponchos. However, on my return to the vehicle I forgot to limp, a fact that was noticed by a traffic cop who then started to issue a parking ticket. Without any hesitation I turned to my wife and exclaimed:

"I've been cured. My lameness has disappeared. Blessed be the Falls. It's a miracle!" which had absolutely no impact on the outcome. I did, however, retain the ticket which to this day remains in a box of souvenirs from my travels – unpaid.

Having visited Toronto, we travelled eastwards towards Boston where I received another ticket this time for speeding (65 miles per hour on an Interstate where the permissible maximum speed is 55 mph). The issuing officer instructed me to slow down and then advised me with a smile to: "Mail the fine once you return to England." Another souvenir for the box.

Boston is one of my favourite cities in the world and nearby Cape

Cod is one of America's jewels. With its splattering of small towns and villages with very English names such as Barnstable, Truro and Plymouth where the Pilgrim fathers first landed on the Mayflower. We stayed in Falmouth for five nights at the Elm Arch Inn, a beautiful old Inn with beamed ceilings and warped floors and a framed hole in the dining room wall made by a cannon ball from a British vessel during the War of Independence.

On our final day we walked down Main Street and cashed the travellers' cheques (over $700) to pay the hotel bill and for the final leg of our trip to New York. On the way back to the hotel we stopped for breakfast. The waitress brought the check, and I asked Diane for the purse with the cash. At this point she looked down at Verity in the pushchair who had been handed the purse to "play with" but who was now munching a blueberry pancake. The purse was missing, causing a rapid change of my facial skin colour from healthy tan to insipid grey.

I retraced our steps entering a couple of stores without success. The third store was a pharmacy, and they produced the purse which had been found on the sidewalk outside and handed to the staff. Nothing had been removed and my pulse rate began to return to its normal rate. I never discovered who carried out the act of kindness, but on further visits to Massachusetts later in life I always travelled to Falmouth and the Elm Arch Inn. A place of calm and serenity. A reminder in a world becoming more self-centred and frantic of the importance of life in the "slow lane" for not only the values of care and community but for any individual's mental health and well-being. It was also the place where we discovered, following the regurgitation of a sea-food feast of scallops and clams that Diane was again pregnant.

The return to school was a mixture of excitement, optimism and apprehension. The events of the final weeks had resulted in Diane withdrawing any future support for school trips abroad, reminding me on, a daily basis to be on my guard. Through the many years of our marriage, she would prove to be a great sounding board, not always giving me the advice expected, but always expressing her view.

I treated Freddie as a distraction. I had a great set of students in every year who were not only enthusiastic but had personality and talent. My responsibility was to provide them with the optimum opportunity to develop their ability. To give them credit they made my job easy and enjoyable.

When strike action was called in 1987, I refused to leave the premises during lunchtime and would not work to rule. I understood the reasons behind strike action and did not criticise any colleague for their action. However, in Physical Education I had seen the devastating impact the strikes of 1984 had on extra-curricular sport. How the staff who had once enjoyed having responsibility for a team had overnight withdrawn their support. They were the oxygen of inter-school fixtures.

I had often said to the talented players that this was their time. Their time to develop the physical abilities and characteristics through sport which will serve them well in later life. How could I now, regardless of the length of time, consider abandoning them at such a crucial time?

School fixtures were suspended for a time, though the department did provide a couple of after-school clubs, and the youth club did continue. Once the action was over it was back to normal with the football, handball and hockey teams enjoying great success both locally and nationally.

I had managed to avoid any confrontation with Freddie. However, in the final week he called me into his office to inform me that Sports Week, the following year would be replaced by a traditional Sports Day. He was not prepared for some staff to "have a jolly" with the extended lunchtimes and he wanted "middle-class parents" to enjoy watching their children perform on the track, which some of the parents of talented performers already did through inter-schools' competition and the local Athletics Club. Parents only attended sports days at Junior School. The introduction of a house system with six small groups in each form further eroded the community ethos which had been created not only by the students but often by their form-tutor.

There was no consideration of the young girl who had won the brick recovery competition at the swimming baths to give her form victory or the boy whose school-life was changed when he saved a penalty in the final of the handball competition. The week had provided many average ability performers with an opportunity to excel and feel valued by their form. It was their platform, their moment. The final days sports assembly, with the cumulative scores as safely guarded as the winner of an Oscar and the final presentation to the outstanding boy and girl, a culmination of effort, fair-play and performance had been the fabric of the final week at school for ten years.

I was also told to remove the plaques from the wall by my office. The plaques which celebrated the success of forms and were a reminder for parents and visitors to the school of the individuals who were part of it. It eradicated a record of events before his time. He eventually relocated my office to the storeroom in the sports hall; with Mel my colleague being transferred to the small drying room and store cupboard.

The following year the Sports Day took place on a warm afternoon with seventy percent of the school sat on the grass bank watching, along with two parents. Staff who did not volunteer to officiate were instructed to keep order. The result of almost every race or event was predictable. It was sterile.

Inter-house competitions in football, netball and handball were organised during the year, but they lacked the intensity and focus of the Sports week.

The whole saga seemed to illuminate not only his disconnect with me and my ideas but also the values of our department which were very much geared to inclusivity and participation. He did not appear to appreciate the holistic value of the many activities which we endeavoured to introduce and develop. Physical Education was not just for the gifted and talented.

His underlying contempt was demonstrated clearly at a meeting in his office which to this day remains one of the most self-centred and baffling comments I have ever encountered from a parent of a child in my care.

"Why are you playing my son in the school football team?" he demanded. "He is no good and you are doing it deliberately to embarrass him and me."

For a moment I was speechless. Over the years, I had received calls from parents asking why their son was NOT in the school team but never the reverse.

"I have a football practice every week. Players who turn up at the practice are selected in the squad for the next game," I said. "That is the way we work. Your son has attended every practice and if he continues to do so he will remain in the squad, whether you like it or not!"

I turned and left. His son appeared in every game that season.

The school was slowly gaining a strong reputation in football and hockey, where the diminutive Mel, who had responsibility for the girls' programme demonstrated exceptional commitment. Though only five feet three inches she exuded drive, energy and determination. Not only was she an outstanding hockey player but had the ability to throw a cricket ball further than any male in the staff cricket team. She provided a pathway to club hockey for many girls in her care who would otherwise have been lost to sport and activity. She continued to play club hockey way beyond her fiftieth birthday.

With the school opening its doors to non-Catholic families in the area the numbers attending the school began to rise. The smaller class sizes and the caring manner of many of the staff provided a significant pull for many new parents.

The school had several exceptional teachers, of which Colin was one of them. Having been part of my department for over ten years he was now teaching maths (and still rock-climbing every weekend). His A level groups achieved high grades, and his O level passes were way above the national average. Despite the success, when the post of Head of Mathematics became vacant his application was dismissed because he "was not a Maths graduate."

It was a kick in the teeth for one of the most talented teachers I worked with. His departure a few years later was a great loss to the school. He had been a valued and trusted colleague who would always give an honest appraisal.

Another member of staff, Dave Roberts, was also a trusted and valued colleague, who for more than fourteen years watched over me and helped during some turbulent times. He was the Deputy Head teacher who witnessed some of the actions against me personally and the department.

He was a good sportsman who appreciated the efforts of the whole department and the importance of physical education. He would direct me to available sources of funding and always asked about the progress of individuals and teams. He was also my annual betting partner for Cheltenham and Ascot where our daily multiple bets and placepot attempted to acquire untold riches. The fact that we both worked till retirement age is indicative of our success.

Dave would discreetly inform me of tasks that needed urgent attention or aspects within the department which were being scrutinised. This would range from pupil reports to curriculum planners and minutes of departmental meetings. It kept me ahead of the game and frustrated the hell out of Freddie.

Without his help and support I am sure that the consistent efforts to undermine me would have caused significant emotional stress and damage. He would always take time to listen and advise. He understood the deep upset when Diane mis-carried and was the first to congratulate me a year later when she gave birth to Stefan, my youngest son.

David would not always tell me what I wanted to hear but his response would always be in my best interests. He made it an even playing field. The rest was up to me.

When he eventually retired in 1999, I had to do something special to mark the occasion. He was a staunch Welshman who had previously worked at a school in North Wales where one of his students was Ian Rush. One of my colleagues Tony had a contact at the Football Association of Wales and he was dispatched to Wrexham where the team were training to receive a signed football shirt.

A couple of days before his retirement presentation, I decided to contact another famous sports personality who had just retired, Jenny Pitman. After all we had backed several of her horses, including Burrough Hill Lad, at the Cheltenham Festival. Her partner answered the phone as she was currently on the gallops but passed on the message and he suggested I ring another Dave Roberts (AP McCoy's agent). Within two hours of making the call I received a fax (way before e-mails) from Jenny addressed to Dave wishing him a long and happy retirement with lots of winners.

Amazed by the positive and timely response I went into overdrive. Dave was an avid rugby supporter and regularly attended international matches. Through a contact at the Sports Council of Wales I was given a direct telephone number for Gerald Davies, the legendary winger for Wales and the British Lions. He answered my call and agreed to send a fax, he also suggested I call Gareth Edwards and JPR Williams and provided their contact numbers. JPR was a consultant at Bridgend Hospital at the time and his PA agreed to pass on the message. Gareth

Edwards was out of the country at the time on business, but his secretary suggested I contact Derek Quinnell. On a Monday afternoon at 5.10 p.m., I rang the number provided and asked for Derek Quinell, with the responder shouting out "Da it's for you" (one of his famous rugby playing sons).

Derek Quinnell not only answered the call but took time to ask about Dave Roberts, his career in teaching and his passion for Welsh Rugby. Five minutes later he provided me with Phil Bennett's phone number, though he said he would call him also.

Less than twenty-four hours after the start of my quest I had received messages from AP McCoy and all the rugby players contacted. Phil Bennett had taken the time to draft a personal, hand-written letter to David on his personal headed notepaper which featured rugby posts.

What it did demonstrate was the complete integration of rugby players in Wales with their community and fans. An appreciation of the importance of the sport in the lives of villages and small towns throughout the country and a willingness to take the time to give something back.

# Chapter Twenty-Three

One of the advantages of teaching Physical Education is the flow of traffic that passes by the office or changing rooms each day allowing banter to take place. Monday mornings were always vibrant with football results and the performance of local teams was always a topic of conversation, with the Wolves boys having a go at the Albion supporters and the Villa boys laughing at Birmingham with Walsall supporters out on their own.

There were those who delighted in telling me the Manchester United result whilst asking me the Manchester City result, knowing full well that they had lost. It was also an opportunity to ask students in different sports about their performances. The athlete's for Cannock and Stafford Athletic Club. The hockey players at Cannock or the boxers from Rugeley.

It was not always about sport. Music was also in the mix along with local events. These were the times that laid the foundations for the tone of our department.

The staff often gave up a substantial amount of their time and at their own expense to ferry players to District or County trials and matches. Mel would often be accompanied with two or three girls every evening to play hockey for the school or club, not to mention at the weekend where she would arrange to travel from West Bromwich to pick up some talented hockey players to play league hockey for her club. Other staff at the school were always willing to help by dropping players off at fixtures. It was a community that cared and shared.

I lived in the heart of our catchment area by choice. Not only was it convenient but it enabled me to establish a rapport and a connection with those who I taught. During the hot summer of 1976, when I was washing my car in Bracken Way, Rugeley I would turn the hose on the young kids playing in the street who would run squealing with delight before entering the "firing zone" again minutes later to tempt another dowsing. Several years later one of the young girls turned up at my school in year seven reminding me of those days. She in later life reminded her son

Elliot who became a key member of my football team of those events.

It was the advantage of staying in a school beyond a single generation. Older brothers could be approached if there was a problem or a concern about a younger sibling. Parents who I had taught were always accessible and understanding. There was no drama.

It worked both ways. If they had a concern they could contact me at any time. When I was a very young child I remembered our local GP, Doctor Chadwick, who would ride through Gorton on his push-bike. A pillar of the community. He made himself available, regardless of the time of day or night, to care for his patients. A humble man respected by all. He set the bar.

One Friday evening I received a phone call from the mother of a student. Her son, Brian, was a keen Liverpool supporter and from a conversation I'd had with him during the week he'd mentioned that he was going to Wembley to see the League Cup final (Liverpool v Nottingham Forest) on the Saturday.

"I hope you don't mind me calling but Brian is distraught," explained his mother. "His Dad has been called into work tomorrow so he can't go to the game, and I was wondering if you are free tomorrow. Would you be able to take him?" she asked.

When you have no responsibilities or commitments on a certain day the decision becomes a lot less complicated. I agreed, picked him up from Burntwood and drove to London, and for the only time in my life spent a warm afternoon in March with Liverpool supporters at Wembley singing 'You'll Never Walk Alone'.

There were times when I would take some of my developing goalkeepers to play squash during weekends or school holidays to improve their reactions and speed of foot. Talented footballers in the upper school were recruited to my adult teams. Sully played for years in both Saturday and Sunday teams with me as did Crabby, Laff, Gord and Stevie T, with the latter having a long and successful career in non-league football. They all eventually made several appearances in my Veterans team many years down the line.

During my visits into the town centre, I would often see students and always try to acknowledge or engage with them. Many years ago, I was walking past a group of teenage boys, when one of the youth men called out "Alright Sir."

"Hello John, how are you? Are you still playing any football? What are you up to today?" I replied

"Yes sir, still playing. We are going to Hednesford Park to an event..." at which, another member of the group interrupted the conversation.

"You don't have to call him Sir. You're not at school...."

"It's because he *is* calling me sir that we are having this conversation," I said. "It's called mutual respect. You should try it sometime." After which, John and I continued our brief chat.

It was a feature of the early football games playing alongside ex-students that they would call "Sir! Sir!" or "Man on! Sir" - much to the amusement of referees, some of whom, no doubt, thought I was a titled person. I wasn't a titled person, but I was blessed. I was surrounded by a group of kids who would do all they could to help. They were like an extended family.

Whenever possible I tried to help them. I used my contacts at Camp Towanda to provide jobs for Johnny B and his sisters Anne and Mary. I arranged for many more to apply successfully through the BUNAC programme I was involved with along with my great friend Graham Hesketh. The programme provided them with opportunities to travel and work in North America during the summer holiday. Heskey would go the extra mile by funding one of his disadvantaged students to travel and work at his two-week soccer camp in Manchester, New Hampshire each year.

It was not always the outstanding students with whom you built a rapport. There were some individuals who were always the first to change and enter the gym or sports hall. For them it was an opportunity to engage in conversation, one-to-one with an adult. It was perhaps, at times, something lacking at home. They were often the ones who stayed till the end, clearing equipment without being asked. They needed to feel important, to feel valued and they were.

One student searching for acceptance was Matthew. He was a powerfully built individual who appeared to be quietly simmering, often pressing his lips together as a sign that he had your measure. He had the potential to fall on the wrong side of the line. At a Parents Evening when he was thirteen his father asked me to help him as he feared he was losing control and Matthew was becoming less cooperative. He was beginning to associate with groups that had a negative reputation within the local community.

The issue with him was that he looked "hard". Some people would try to challenge him for no reason other than his look and stature. Many discovered that the looks were not deceiving. I managed to persuade him to join the boxing club at Rugeley, which he really enjoyed and attended on a consistent basis. Tony Bates, who did so much for the Rugeley area provided a focus for his energy. He later joined the local Rugby club.

When I was made aware of a vacancy at the Football Pools Office on a Friday evening it was an opportunity to further divert him from "the streets". The role was to help secure and deliver the bundles of bags that contained the dreams of thousands. I recommended Matt. I was tasked with driving the bags to Liverpool each Friday night and if there was one person I would want to be by my side it was the fifteen-year-old rock from Hednesford. He received a significant payment and for nearly three years he was my partner before entering the Marines where he became an outstanding soldier.

The other benefit of those long journeys to Liverpool was the intelligence gained about people and events happening which directly impacted on the school and some of the students. It provided me with an opportunity to intervene at a very early stage and stop potential incidents from escalating. The inside information frustrated Freddie. He felt undermined and at one stage suggested that I was involved with the "Cannock Underworld". He remained unaware of the reason the late-night disturbances outside his family home suddenly disappeared. No one deserves to have the sanctuary of their home life invaded or impacted by anti-social behaviour.

It is not only the social aspect which distinguishes physical education from other subjects. It provides an opportunity for some to achieve something memorable. In maths or science when a student solves a problem, nobody remembers. In sport there is visual recognition, an event or achievement that remains in the memory long after the day, particularly for those who have witnessed or achieved the "impossible dream."

Andrew was a small, lean and very quiet student. His interaction with the rest of the group was very limited and his general co-ordination was poor with a lack of refined motor skills. Despite this he regularly participated in lessons which were a major challenge, except for cross-country. In his silent world he was one of the best in the year group.

Ray Collins was an economics teacher who was assigned to the department for a few periods a week. He was keen orienteer and a member of Walton Chasers, renowned nationally for their achievements in the sport. Ray encouraged Andrew to join the club helping him adapt socially, providing continual support and guidance. It was a door opened which he stepped through eventually being part of the junior team that finished third in the National Club Championships.

I cannot recall him speaking other than to answer his name during the five years in my care, but he did smile the time I clumsily high-fived him and congratulated him on his bronze medal.

Odhran was another student with significant difficulties. He was a quiet and nervous student who was overweight. His ability to run was very limited and this restricted his contribution within some of the game activities. One day he volunteered to play as a goalkeeper during a handball match. I am unsure whether it was his bulk or just his inability to move out of the line of a shot, but he was very effective. It changed the whole dynamic. When students selected a team, he was now one of the first to be chosen, knowing that he would play in goal and would be an asset.

His confidence improved and he was encouraged to attend handball practise with a group of players who at the time were the best school team in the United Kingdom. He was valued and protected by his peers despite the limited verbal interaction. He did eventually play in the final of the National Schools Under-15 Competition, conceding only four goals as the team cruised to an eleven-goal victory. To some it was a gold medal. To Odhran it was symbolic of so much more. The bravery to step into the line of fire; the courage to attend the practise with so many talented individuals on the shared determination to overcome his fears and improve. His involvement in the sport may have been short lived, but for one day in June he was a King.

Graham was another student with an immense hurdle to overcome. He was 13 years of age and weighed over 190 pounds. During his first year at school, he had declined to take part in any gymnastic lesson. However, in his second year I insisted that he take part and that we would aim to improve his overall motor skills over the term. At first any rotational movement along the ground proved difficult, with forward rotation seemingly impossible.

After several weeks of work on progressive exercises he had the confidence to try a forward roll with the help of a thick mat and makeshift chutes to help keep him straight. He developed the confidence to take the weight on his hands and without any support and discomfort roll in a straight line. Now was the real challenge. I had to convince him to attempt the movement along a vaulting box. I assured him that I would always be there to physically support him when necessary.

At first Graham was apprehensive, but initial manual guidance either side helped him enormously and soon he was rolling, not only along the box but dismounting (with a little help) onto his feet. By creating a platform for a take-off, the same height as the vaulting box, he was able to comfortably complete the neck spring on the cross box. There was just one final stage and only one week left in the module. Each day in form time I reminded him of how far he had progressed. In the final lesson I challenged him, in a now or never moment, to achieve what he thought was impossible.

The first attempt was a non-starter where he hit the springboard but remained firmly fixed on the take-off side. He was nervous. The second attempt looked very promising as the take-off was perfect but then he froze and instead of bending his arms he locked them causing his body to perform a handstand. At that moment he was a human version of the Leaning Tower of Pisa, but he was leaning the wrong way. Disaster threatened, and I dived quickly to put one arme under his neck whilst the other grabbed the back of his shorts and pulled him over the box. 190 lbs of flesh, bone and sinew landed on top of me. Some of the group were amused, whilst others looked concerned, waiting for some movement from below. Graham walked away as if nothing had happened, and I slowly crawled of the mat and on to my feet.

"Almost Graham" I said, thinking of trust and death in the same breath. "Just relax, bend your arms and go for it. Please, give it your best shot." There was almost a sense of pleading in my voice.

With the whole class watching his final attempt he bounded towards the springboard and planted his hands. His hips came through and with an almighty push he extended them to land on his feet, with a minimal of support. Job done. Gold.

He left the gym for the changing rooms to rapturous applause with a sense of pride and euphoria. I left the gym for the First-Aid room with a black eye, sprained wrist and throbbing thumb.

Peter was another student to overcome a great physical hurdle. A road traffic accident at the age of thirteen had resulted in life-changing injuries with the amputation of his left leg. Following eighteen months of rehabilitation he returned to school. Always a lively student before his accident he insisted on joining in with some sports, including handball and football where he volunteered to play in goal.

On one occasion he made a tremendous diving save in a football match with the ball being deflected for a corner. Just before the kick was due to be taken Peter shouted.

"Hold up Sir, m' leg's come off!"

He was smiling whilst players looked on as he re-attached his leg for the game to re-start. I had to smile with him, and it remains one of the most humorous moments I ever had. He was a great example to others in his year who tried to avoid activity with his maturity and determination to be the best he could be. He went on to live an active life and become a very competent rock-climber.

The start of the school year in September is always hectic in any Physical Education department. Fixtures in several sports must be completed in a short window before the clocks go back, with the new intake providing hope and possibility. Following a six-week break the staff were primed for action.

For my family the summer break of 1990 had been a joyous occasion with the birth of a son, Stefan in late August. We were all on a high.

On Friday 21st September 1990 it all came crashing down.

At 10.45 a.m., the shell which for many years, through emotional challenges and physical battles had remained intact finally broke. Walking towards the staff room at morning break through a canteen populated by hungry students, I was approached by Anthony, a member of my basketball team. In a quiet, solemn voice he said:

"Mr. Popovic, I have some sad news. Nick Bates died in a car accident last night."

I looked at him momentarily in disbelief before tears rolled down my cheeks and I began to cry. I went to the toilets and remained there for the whole of break unable to regain composure. Unable to think of anyone else but his family. Unable to think of anything else but "Baz."

For the rest of the day I was in a strange place, seemingly oblivious to what was going on. The students sensed something was wrong and, as they often did, managed themselves without any drama. The regional evening news reported on the two-car collision which had claimed the lives of four people on the outskirts of Rugeley as I sat in silence. My wife Diane understood my pain and was there to support me in addition to having three young children to care for.

I had known Nick for half his life. We had travelled throughout Europe to handball tournaments over several years, with significant success. He was a popular member of the Great Britain team.

Once during a National League handball match an opposing player committed several excessive physical challenges on me without any retribution from the referee. Nick, then seventeen, who always played alongside me, picked me up after one challenge.

"You look after your game, and I'll look after his!" he said. During the next attack there was a clash of bodies, with the said player having to receive significant treatment before continuing in a far more subdued manner.

He would often volunteer to accompany me to meetings of the England Handball Association in Milton Keynes. On one occasion we were travelling south on the M6 motorway when a vehicle in the process of overtaking us suddenly veered behind us hitting the raised bank before overturning.

We pulled onto the hard shoulder and went to help. The two-seater sports car was upside down with the driver trapped but conscious. The passenger crawled from the wreckage where he informed me at a snapping sound had occurred and the steering became non-existent. With other drivers stopping to help I asked the passenger for the driver's name.

"I don't know. I was just hitching a lift," he replied before adding "I don't suppose you are going anywhere near London, are you?"

Nick and I looked at each other and shook our heads. Eventually when we returned to our vehicle, we could not stop laughing about the mercenary hitchhiker who had spent the whole time at the scene searching for a lift, whilst the driver kind enough to give him one was being secured in a neck brace on a stretcher before being taken to hospital in Coventry.

"The ambulance into Coventry might have been his last resort," said Nick with a smile.

He was without doubt one of the great personalities of his time. Unafraid to speak his mind but immensely loyal and respectful. More than five-hundred people attended his funeral, recognition of the light he brought to so many lives.

Thirty-five years later, his flame continues to burn.

# Chapter Twenty-Four

The final few years of the Eighties had settled down a little. Strikes by the teacher unions had decimated school sport and I was uncomfortable with industrial action. I, like many in the profession, was struggling to pay bills, but at the same time I could not help but feel for the students. This was their time. They would never get it back. The damage could not be repaired.

I left the Union and joined a non-political association which provided public liability cover only. On reflection it was the worst decision I ever made. I thought I was now on a wide path, but in essence was still walking a tightrope, but now with no safety net.

Freddie had made some significant improvements to life at the school. A school uniform was introduced which included a black blazer and some of the buildings were modified, including the provision of a secure office extension in the sports hall and a staff workroom. The discipline within the school improved, though this was primarily due to the energy and enthusiasm of several staff who through their diverse interests would engage very effectively with challenging students. It was a very caring environment.

Despite this, measures were introduced to put pressure on some colleagues. Directed meetings for the first three Mondays of a half-term and staff briefings twenty minutes before the start of the school week extended the day considerably for some staff. Additional monitoring of schemes of work and demands for formal and comprehensive lesson plans further increased the workload of staff and some incurred significant health problems as a result. The pressure forced some to leave the school or even the profession.

For a few years, the focus of Freddie's attention was on others, even though sometimes I would cause him considerable discomfort. During staff briefings I would sometimes look for an opportunity to lighten things with a witty remark, which some of the staff found amusing. These would often be followed by a glare, a sudden hush, after which he would slam his book closed and stomp off leaving the meeting in stunned silence. The colleagues in my corner of the room would laugh and try to estimate the length of time from the event occurring to me being called to his office.

Even with the disconnect he would amble over to "our corner" of the staff room to make conversation, though often I suspect with the intention of information gathering and observation rather than engagement.

On one occasion I walked into the staffroom and there were three male students sitting in our corner waiting to be interviewed for a post. The first was called into Freddie's office, the second for a meeting with the head of department and the third was left alone in the staff room where I was doing some work. He was quite self-assured and confident. Within minutes I knew his life story. He could talk for England.

Once he had realised I had been at the school for several years, he whispered - though I am not sure why as we were the only people in the room:

"Have you got any tips for me in the interview? Is there anything about the headteacher which will help me?"

I smiled.

"He has a dodgy eye and he becomes very conscious of it, so try not to look straight at him," I said. "He is also deaf on his right side so try and speak into his good ear as he can sometimes become frustrated and annoyed. Best of luck."

I never saw him again.

The following morning, I heard Freddie discussing the candidates with some colleagues. They had failed to appoint anyone, and the school would re-advertise the post later in the year.

"One of the candidates was very strange," he said. "He had difficulty making eye contact and seemed to have a neck problem. He was leaning permanently to one side and was very loud."

I made a quick exit.

On the final day of term before the Christmas break the children would finish school at midday. The staff would then gather in the staffroom for any formal presentations to leaving staff and enjoy some food and drink provided by the school. For over ten years it was also the time when dressed in the appropriate headgear I would present certain staff with awards. Dave Roberts was always "Santa's little helper."

The awards and presents often reflected something humorous that the recipient had either said or done throughout the year. Stupid as the presents often were, the accompanying narrative was always greeted with laughter and was something that they seemed to enjoy. No one was offended with some even waiting in anticipation to be included, and some disappointed not to be.

Without warning, late in November I was asked by the secretary to drop-in and see the head-teacher. He informed me that I would no longer be providing the awards at Christmas which he did not find amusing. A Secret Santa would be introduced in its place which all staff would be invited to take part in.

Christmas was not the same again.

The numbers entering the school each year increased, with non-Catholic children being accepted. The quality of athlete also improved, and the PE Department responded by entering as many competitions as logistically possible, from orienteering to hockey and badminton to basketball. The school was gaining significant recognition for its achievements in sport within the local area. Not, however, with our leader.

When the first Ofsted inspection of the school was announced he approached me and with a glint in his eye, the good one, and informed me that this would be the time when I would be "found out."

The officer designated with the task for our subject was in her mid to late-fifties and was a former vice-chair of BALPE (British Association of Lecturers in Physical Education) who had substantial experience not only in school Physical Education but was recognised as a leading lecturer in the subject at university, preparing students for the profession.

Following four days of intense scrutiny the department was judged "Outstanding." With the school being assessed as "Good" overall.

Sadly, the Fat-Controller failed to acknowledge the recognition the Department had received. His only comment was made with bitterness and sarcasm.

"Another women you've managed to sweet-talk. What did she know about PE?"

He seemed disappointed. I was delighted but not surprised at both her judgement and his reaction.

The department pressed on. We had achieved our goal. We did not expect or need any adulation. There were more games to play and more kids to engage.

In 2000, another Ofsted inspection took place. On this occasion the person responsible for Physical Education was a former Olympic athlete who had been a head teacher at a school in Hackney until he was 68 years of age. With due respect, nobody can survive the pressures of inner-city education for that long and until that age unless they are the very best of their profession. It was probably a reason why he had been awarded an MBE for his services to education.

The inspection lasted for three and a half days. He attended the early morning clubs and the after-school fixtures. He talked to the students with enthusiasm, and he engaged with the staff without intimidation. He was a genuinely affable character, the type you could only dream of working for.

Once again, the department was judged to be "Outstanding with a genuine concern for all students."

Sadly, Freddie made only one derisory comment, "What does a man of his age know about Physical Education." Perhaps I should have mentioned that until two years previous he was responsible for a school twice the size of ours and with significantly greater challenges, but it would have been wasted.

Between the two inspections much happened within the department. For many years during the eighties, GCE PE was not included in the option choices for Year 11 students. Instead, I delivered it after school for an hour on a Friday evening to a group of boys and girls. It was a select group with each having the physical capabilities to achieve a good pass. For the less physically able there was no time in the curriculum to work on the skills, hence the elite nature of the group.

The results, as expected were high and eventually the subject was included in the option process. With further success the subject was introduced as an Advanced Level for students in Year 12 and Year 13. I taught the social study aspects and Mel taught the scientific aspects.

Though we both taught Year 13 students we were never allowed to attend the Prom, the occasion celebrated by students and staff at the end of the school journey. The head of senior school did not appear to fight for our cause. Freddie ruled.

Then late in the nineties a group of students from the A level group, many of whom had travelled across Europe to play handball with me in previous years demanded that Mel and I be invited. David, Tom, Matty, Ant and Smithy put significant pressure on the management and they, through gritted teeth, issued an invite.

The evening was going quite well with a pause for some formal speeches. However, at the very end of the Little Man's address, David (never short of confidence) stepped forward, making an impromptu speech and presenting me with an award for outstanding achievement over the past seven years. I had no opportunity to respond as Freddie rushed over, blood pressure through the roof, foaming at the mouth and blurted out:

"Get you and your boys out of here NOW!"

There was a notable silence with some staff looking bemused and students staring at each other.

We quietly exited to a back room with a shrug of the shoulders, a smile and disbelief. Thirty years later we still talk about that night and the trophy is still on my window ledge at home.

The headteacher at any school is in a powerful position. Some, on occasions, use their position to manipulate and intimidate colleagues. Bullying in this workplace was not uncommon.

During the mid-nineties we interviewed several male candidates for a position in the Department. One of the candidates was Mike. He was six-foot four inches tall, black hair, tanned complexion with not a blemish in sight and he spoke with an accent straight from the Sean Connery Finishing school. The girls would freak out I thought. However, it was not the girls I had to worry about. It was the staff.

Within fifteen minutes of his arrival the female RE department had called me over to their corner in the staff room with a simple order – appoint him or forget about any future cooperation or dialogue. They were serious.

Thankfully, he turned out to be the best candidate by a mile. Good for our school. A good communicator and popular with the staff and the students. He was a good teacher.

Sadly, his time at the school was short. Mike had been at the school for several months when Freddie called him to his office. The conversation was short.

He was asked to record my day-to-day activities and report back to him.

Mike refused.

"If you want to know what he is doing I suggest you ask him," he said, at which point he left the office. He would not be bullied. He would not do anything he felt was unethical.

A few weeks later, Mike discovered the Times Educational Supplement in his pigeon-hole with a job at a local school circled in red ink. Later in the day he was "strongly advised" to apply for the job (which was not a promotion). The school lost a committed, competent teacher because he refused to be manipulated.

With Dave watching my back I was always a step ahead. Freddie asked others, such as the caretaker and IT technician to monitor my activities. Sometimes his actions were bizarre and desperate.

One Friday afternoon he called me into his office to question me about absences through sickness. He had accessed the records from the past sixteen years and informed me that during that time I had been absent for a total of fourteen days. He had detected a pattern in that seven of those days had been on a Monday and three on a Friday. I had no absences on a Wednesday. He informed me he would be monitoring my absences going forward.

I couldn't believe it. I did not even attempt to offer an explanation. I just asked for clarification.

"So, what you are saying is that I cannot be sick on Mondays or Fridays, but Wednesday is fine?"

I didn't wait for the answer.

Three days later he called me into his office and apologised. Someone, somewhere, had strongly disagreed with his actions. Sometimes a couple of days of domesticity can reset your thoughts.

It would be unfair to not acknowledge that there were times when he did grant or respond to requests. He did approve of leave (without pay) for certain sporting and personal events such as in my case the Mystique era which took me into a totally different world.

# Chapter Twenty-Five

Many people at various stages of their life have a "light bulb" moment. A thought or an idea which has the potential to be both useful and commercially successful. The hugely popular TV programme Dragon's Den is based entirely upon such people who present their products to a panel of investors in search of financial and marketing support.

My moment occurred one Christmas in the early nineties. I was tasked with devising a simple party game for adults. With Trivial Pursuit firmly established and Pictionary on the rise, I settled for a facial recognition game. Searching old Sunday Times magazines, I removed photographs of famous people and cut them into six segments. Initially one segment was revealed with others added as teams answered questions. Teams could submit their identification at any time, with a reveal when all teams had completed the process. The team quickest to identify the personality received maximum points.

It was both entertaining and engaging. A seed was planted.

During one of the rounds a cousin of my wife, identified a personality correctly from just a segment of his ear. She confessed later that it was not the ear but the background of the photograph which had provided the clue. It was then that my light came on.

Over the following months I developed the concept with the help of several others. A former handball goalkeeper, Steve Derry, provided me with a contact at the Express and Star newspaper from the illustration department. His speciality was drawing people, and he would often attend major court cases to provide sketch drawings of the proceedings. His speciality was a style of line drawing perfect for the game. He agreed to initially provide twenty-five faces for a fixed fee.

Mark, a colleague at school who worked in the Design and Technology department, produced a bespoke wooden hexagonal casket with six triangular lids. The casket would hold the face cards which were 7'x 5' postcard size.

I began to test the game with staff in "our corner". Players in turn rolled a couple of dice and if landing on a double the corresponding numbered segment would be removed to reveal part of the drawing. Each player could submit one guess only. Some rounds were longer than others.

Someone suggested that once seen an image would be remembered. I dispelled the thought by repeating the same image within a couple of rounds, with recognition on the second occasion only being made with the removal of the fourth segment. If the game was commercially successful, further face cards would become available.

I developed the game further to include information cards related to the specific personality. The four categories included male/female, dead/alive, nationality and area of fame. All the personalities came from one of six areas – cinema; sport; television; music; public life or the arts.

There were two dice, one black and one white. If when you rolled the white it was higher than the black you were able to take one profile card and retain it. The aim was to have the full set of four cards for the personality before the final lid was removed at which point the round ended. A double would result in that number lid being removed.

During the round, a player or team could make an identification at any time, writing the name on the slip provided and inserting it into the plastic sleeve. This could not be amended at a later stage. These were then revealed at the end of the round. The first team to have identified correctly achieved maximum points, with others awarded in descending order. Teams also secured points with the correct profile cards, making their way around the simple board to the end line.

I decided to call the game Constellation and contacted another former student, Anthony, who was a graphic designer. He agreed to design a play board for the game. I was now getting excited. Perhaps too excited.

This is the time when there is a need for a cool business head. Someone who has been there before and got the tee shirt. I jumped in with two feet to protect the intellectual property rights an expensive and arduous process. My best man and close friend Joe agreed to invest in the project, and we set about producing a sample version of the game.

A plastic casket was produced locally and was stunning, but so was the price at three-hundred pounds. With the printing of the cards and a box there was little change out of a seven-hundred pounds. The "one off" tooling costs and setting for the print accounting for most of the expense.

Once the sample was produced, I applied for a stand at the British Toy and Hobby Exhibition at Earls Court in January 1993. The stand was the minimum available and was basically a kiosk, about 1.5 metres square with two chairs, a coffee table and a front desk with partitions on three sides able to accept Velcro attachments. It was placed near the back of the hall in a place affectionally known as Death Row.

Within minutes of my arrival my stand was complete – a couple of posters and the game placed on the front table for the world to see over the three days of the exhibition. I then took a little stroll along "Death Row" which was populated with like-minded people all hoping that their one game would be the next Trivial Pursuit. Many looked apprehensive realising the magnitude of the task. They were competing against some of the largest players in the world with bottomless budgets. Some had re-mortgaged their property or invested their pension, failure really was a life sentence.

Being inquisitive I asked some of the exhibitors to explain (or sell) their game idea. One game had that many different things going on after five minutes of explanation I politely left. Another exhibitor looked more upbeat, after all he had spent nearly £90,000 bringing it to market. It had to be successful.

I returned to my stand a little more confident and ready to put my idea across in under a minute, with all the cards carefully placed to ensure a lively and quick demonstration.

The days were long and repetitive - with my 'salesman mode' at full throttle on the first two days, and slightly less so on day three. Nevertheless, there was a significant number of visitors to the stand, many seemed impressed with the concept and some left business cards for future contact.

One individual, Iain Kidney, was particularly positive. He had once been the head buyer for WH Smith but had now set up a consultancy called Games Talk to help companies bring a product to market. He suggested we choose a different name for the game as it inferred horoscopes and astrology and this would divert many away. He suggested I visit his office north of Swindon at some time to discuss ways to improve the product.

A few weeks later I travelled down to the office and over a coffee we discussed the game. I had taken time to think about his initial advice and suggested two names, Photofit and Mystique. He felt the latter was a strong name, and following a quick search we discovered it was not a registered name. Iain then suggested I change the name of the company. Henry Zabel sounded like a fashion brand.

A week after our visit he called to suggest Pharos Games (based on the Lighthouse at Alexandria, one of the wonders of the Ancient World). I registered the company and acquired a copyright for Mystique.

There was also a company, Brandmakers International, based in the Midlands who were extremely interested in the game. They already had a couple of games in their portfolio, and this would sit well alongside them. A preliminary meeting was arranged at a hotel near Cannock.

The two principal directors were smooth and oozed confidence. They had just signed a deal with ITV for the rights to produce a game based on the series Chancer and already had produced the 64,000 Dollar Question, a game based on a long running TV quiz show. They appeared to be very credible and their claims that the game would be a strong seller made both Joe and me very optimistic.

I managed to secure some funding moving forward from a friend, Peter Brittain through his company Force One. However, at the second meeting, Brandmakers asked for a significant upfront payment to produce the game and also for entry into a catalogue for distribution in late September to both the retail trade and public.

Joe agreed to make the funds available having discussed the proposal with Barclays Bank. They were asked to conduct due diligence and within days they had endorsed the Company, referring to it as a "stable and expanding" concern. £15,000 was paid to Brandmakers International to produce and market the game and the original seventy-five characters made available for printing.

The following few months were quiet. Phone calls assured me that the product was near completion and would be ready for the Christmas market. A meeting was arranged at the end of October to reveal the product at an office in Manchester, just off Albert Square. It appeared to be sparce with limited furniture and very little evidence of day-to-day activity. There were no staff, which was a cause of concern.

The two directors produced the finished game. The quality was appalling, with a flimsy casket using similar materials to those used in the packaging of small electrical items. The profile cards were on different coloured card the type freely available at stationery and craft stores for young children to play with. It was a product that would only sell (if at all) on markets or in discount stores and was a million miles from my perception.

The suggestion was that the games be sold for under ten pounds where the overall quality would not be questioned. I disagreed. To add insult to injury they asked for a further advance to produce the game in large numbers. I never met with them again.

A couple of years later an article appeared in a quality newspaper about a company involved in the boardgames industry taking vast sums of money from inventors under the pre-text of producing and marketing the game. One lady had lost £89,000 in her venture. It was only on reading the article I realised that Barclay's Bank had provided venture capital into six figures at the beginning of the nineties for Brandmakers International. It perhaps suggests that their assessment of the company as being "stable" was not without prejudice.

I don't know how many games they produced. I took six but was embarrassed. I gave a couple away instead of a bottle of wine, they were that cheap.

To my knowledge none were sold over the Christmas period, and I wallowed in self-despair. Not only was I in debt personally but Joe had invested a significant amount into the project.

A phone call in February 1994 re-ignited the Mystique project. Iain Kidney, who had attended Toy Fairs in London, Frankfurt and New York called to ask about Mystique, still in his eyes a game with potential.

A meeting was arranged where the sample of game produced was systematically torn apart from both the quality of materials and the printing. He agreed to completely re-design the game around the concept for a moderate fee. I would, however, need to source the plastic casket.

A year earlier I had met at Earls Court the owner of a company that manufactured games components and toys in Hong Kong. I had his details on file and contacted him. Within weeks he had sent me a sample which was ideal. He confirmed that a minimum order of 3,000 landed at my address in the United Kingdom would be priced at 35p per piece. Far removed from the original casket. The lead time would be twelve weeks.

The ideas produced by Games Talk were well received. The design for the box had a classic look about it, with three colours to consider. Eventually I settled for a royal blue. The game cards carried through the box design pattern and were all contained in a small box. It had a chocolate box feel about it. Something that would not look out of place on a bookshelf. It was a product which could be realistically sold in stores for £19.99.

There was one hurdle. I needed investment to take it further. I was at a dead-end. The only exposure the game was getting was at school, where the staff enjoyed a weekly session, and my form group a couple of rounds every Friday morning.

One evening at a school function an old friend, Noel Sweeney, who was a highly successful and much respected businessman approached me and asked how things were progressing with the game. All but his eldest child had been in my forms during their years at school. Apparently, the girls had played the game during form time (when I should have been establishing their direction in life) and commented on how good it was. I briefly told him the stage we were at, and he invited me to visit his house to discuss the possibility of financial help and support.

Following a three-hour meeting which concluded after midnight Noel agreed to provide the investment needed for a share in the Company. The holding at the time was 75%/25% between myself and Joe, with me being the majority shareholder. Noel suggested that the company be re-structured 51%/49% with Joe paid a fee to relinquish his shares. I couldn't accept that. Joe had been in at the beginning and eventually we settled for 50%/30%/20%, with Joe only relinquishing 5%. Many years later I discovered that the initial suggestion was a test of my morality and ethics. Noel valued loyalty above all things, including money.

With several dummy boxes, a top-class sample and a large promotional aid I attended the Toy Fair in London which had moved to Olympia. Mark had made an ultra large hexagonal casket which could hold an A3 size facial print. The casket lid was solid with only one piece removed. It was a very significant piece for the personality I would use. We had strong supporting material and there was highly significant interest both from buyers and other games companies. Hasbro made a verbal offer to buy the idea which was derisory. David Berglers, the legendary magician and mentalist visited, interested greatly in the name Mystique as it was a term often used to describe him during his days on television. His son Marvin was launching a range of magic products at the exhibition.

The large casket provided all who visited the stand with an immediate idea of the game. The open segment revealed part of a cheek and the eye of an extremely well-known television personality who had starred in two of the most iconic shows in the history of comedy. Visitors to the stand were asked to name the personality on the reverse of their business card and leave it in the collection box for a chance to win up to a million pounds. For some it was easier than others. The winning card, drawn after the final day received five entries in the following weeks National Lottery.

During the afternoon of the first day there was a gathering at the stand next to ours when a famous TV personality arrived to promote their game. When the media interest had subsided, and the footfall had dropped slightly the personality popped his head around the corner. I was pleasantly surprised.

"I know him," he declared excitedly, his eyebrows jumping for joy. He scribbled the answer on the back of a business card. Terry Jones was smiling as "Basil" glared down at him. Together they had starred in Monty Python and the Life of Brian. He asked for a demonstration of the game.

Throughout the afternoon whenever there was a quiet time, he would peer around the partition with only his eyes and significant eyebrows visible, asking on one occasion to guess the personality before playing a round of the game. He called it addictive. It certainly seemed more appealing than the game he was being paid to promote.

The whole exhibition proved remarkably successful with commitment from some of London's top stores. Hamley's, Selfridges and John Lewis. Some large independent stores such as Jenner and Beattie's were also prepared to make significant orders along with a dozen or more smaller toy and game shops. Tesco and Toy's R Us were very interested and asked for further discussion.

The following week Iain rang me to inform me that the game had appeared in several magazines with very positive comments and one London newspaper had voted it the best new game of 1995. Taking into consideration the positivity emanating Noel sanctioned the production of 2000 games. They would be stored in an office near to his main place of business in Chasetown.

I arranged a visit to the head buyer of toys and games at Tesco during the school-half term and a call with Toy's R Us. It was then that the realities of engaging with larger stores with a nationwide reach were made clear. The buyer at Tesco predicted that they would sell between two thousand and four thousand units but would expect a discounted price. Their major issue was opening an account for a company with only one product. We needed a minimum of five products for them to proceed.

Toy's R Us were a little more aggressive. The conversation was very much one way. They would require 5,000 units delivered in August with discounts. Settlement would be on games sold over the festive period, with any unsold to be returned with arrangement by Pharos Games. In essence, we would be extending six months credit without an accurate financial return.

Despite this setback significant numbers were ordered by larger independent stores and toy shops. A large article appeared in a regional newspaper about the game and the hurdles to market, following which was an appearance on a local radio show. The exposure within a few days of each other resulted in the Beattie's store in Wolverhampton selling their complete stock of 180 games in one day. It was the fastest selling game in their history, beating the record previously established by Trivial Pursuit. A repeat order was quickly dispatched to them.

Most stores retailed the game at £19.99, with the elite London stores selling at £24.99. It appeared to be the appropriate price point for the product. Most clients settled within sixty days. Several stores made repeat orders within weeks.

With the credibility of the game in the marketplace I arranged to meet with the one of the commercial team at Manchester United with a view to producing a bespoke game for the club. I was given a tour of the warehouse where items from scarves, clocks, bags and even a settee adorned with the face of Ryan Giggs were stored. Almost every household item incorporated the club badge or a player's image.

When I asked what happens when a player leaves the club, the response was simple, the stock is returned to the producer. Manchester United only pay for items sold.

The discussion over lunch was very revealing in many ways. Firstly, over 3,000 people visit the club shop every matchday. The game would be perfect for their fan base and they would expect to sell in the region of 30,000 units per year. They would require "top up" deliveries when requested within forty-eight hours of order. Payment would be made against monthly sales, with settlement in sixty days.

With the prospect of regular sales this would not be an issue. The concern, however, arose with the pricing. Our selling price was between £9.50 - £12.00 depending on volume for the mainstream game. We were prepared to reduce that to £7.75 for the Club. This discount reduced our profit per item to a little over £3.00. It was not acceptable to Manchester United's commercial team.

Without reducing the quality of the product, they would not pay more than £4.00 per unit. Not only did they want the game at less than half the normal trade price, but they would then sell in store at £29.95 a mark-up of almost seven hundred percent. In essence our return on the terms stated would be less than 25 pence per unit with considerable initial outgoings. With no room for negotiation the deal was left open. We received no further contact from the commercial department at the club.

The game sold steadily throughout the Christmas period, and we even had enquiries about follow-up packs of faces. In our original plan this was the area where maximum profits would be realised. Sadly, without concerted advertising and promotion the game did not sell through in numbers to justify this. A further 1,000 games were produced but trickled into the market the following year where only 800 were sold. We were a small fish in a large pond.

Eventually the rights to the game were sold to Toy Brokers, a group with a long-standing reputation and a catalogue of products, who used the format for their Question of Sport and Top Gear games selling a combined total of over 14,000 in the first year.

Noel was philosophical. If you don't have a go, you will never know. It was a journey into the unknown. Many years earlier in 1981, the team in Montreal who devised Trivial Pursuit faced many of the same hurdles, initially producing eleven hundred units at a cost of $75 per game. They hawked the game around the country selling them to retailers and at promotional sessions for $15 over a two-year period before a leading book company recognised it's potential and formed a commercial partnership to launch the product Internationally.

There are many who have taken the journey with personal investment of time and money. Each with a dream that they too could become a major player in the market. The only thing that we all have in common is the realisation that in the games industry there are more snakes than ladders.

# Chapter Twenty-Six

The early years of a career in education or health are often a struggle financially. Many teachers with young families often search for additional income. Some take on private tutoring, some drive taxis and others proof-read or mark examination scripts.

I supplemented my income with summer trips to Camp Towanda in Honesdale, Pennsylvania. The only negative was the impact on my playing career in football. Being away for July and August denied me opportunities to play pre-season and though physically fit could not replicate the fitness gained through game time. A good friend, John Donnelly, suggested I focus more on coaching than playing and offered me an opportunity to do both at a club, Burntwood Institute at which he was the Chairman.

The Club played in an extremely competitive league but had a limited budget. They could not afford to pay me directly, but John who at the time was a Concessionaire for Littlewoods Football Pools offered me a job as a part-time area manager. I would need to be available every Friday evening from 7.00 p.m. to 1.00 a.m. to monitor the performance of twenty-five main agents each with their own sub- team of coupon collectors in specific areas of Staffordshire and Shropshire.

Each week thousands of people throughout the United Kingdom would try and predict from a list of fifty-two matches, eight football games which would end as a score draw. For a small investment, a client could win up to a million pounds. Their coupon was either collected from their home, their work or deposited at a shop.

For some of these Main agents it was a full-time commitment with significant commission to be made. Each Friday they would be responsible for the recording of coupons received from every individual collector (some had over fifty) before ensuring that the monies received balanced and was ready to be banked using a night safe facility.

Once all collectors had submitted their sealed envelopes, some with a hundred coupons, they were securely tied in bundles and delivered personally to the main office in Hednesford, where they were checked and placed in mail bags which were then locked until arrival later in the night at Littlewoods headquarters on Edge Lane, Liverpool. The security of each coupon was paramount. At a time before the National Lottery, it was the one opportunity for an individual to win amounts that could be "life changing" on a weekly basis.

It not only provided an income that enabled my wife Diane to enjoy our children during their early years without financial restraints, but it also afforded some memorable personal incidents and stories from the Littlewoods security team who were always in attendance on a Friday night.

Part of my role as an area-manager was to temporarily cover a main collection during a transitional phase. This could be anything from a couple of weeks to a month during which time I had to ensure the continuity of the service. Telford was a case in point. A long-time door-to-door collector resigned due to ill health but had informed me that a client was keen to take on the role. I arranged to interview the client at his house in Brookside on a Tuesday evening to go through the roles, responsibilities and renumeration.

Finding the address on the housing-estate proved almost impossible with numbers seemingly nailed or painted on doors at random. Eventually a local youth, in return for a "finder's fee", guided me effortlessly to the house, which without his help I would not have located before the weekend.

The door was answered by the applicant's wife who invited me into the hallway. Not being judgmental from first impressions but the site of a motorcycle in various stages of repair with parts scattered around the floor did not instil me with confidence. The air freshener was made by Castrol.

I was shown through into the lounge where her husband was eating his evening meal from a tray on his lap, whilst watching the evening news. A normal situation, except he was naked. I was unsure of what to do until he invited me to sit down and asked if I fancied a cup of tea. I declined the offer.

He appeared totally unconcerned and unmoved. Bob Warman

continued to read the news unperturbed and unaware of his disrobed viewer. Following a brief introduction and explanation of the role, his only questions related to money. Currently unemployed he would be able to start immediately but would need someone to collect the sealed envelope from his home once he had completed the collection as he had no means of transport. The motorcycle, I guess, was far from completion.

I looked around the "living room" and noticed various items scattered around from old newspapers to a couple of empty food containers, plates, cups and a shopping bag. Every surface seemed to have an item or two sprawled along or across it. It was not a sterile environment, and I was unsure that the collected coupons would be safe.

Then, out of the corner of my eye I noticed a movement on the back of a sofa on the far wall. I glanced across to see a ferret crawling along the ridge. It paused for a while and looked across, no doubt being inquisitive about the guest, before turning and disappearing. That was the final nail.

I envisaged headlines in the Shropshire Star "Ferret Eats Winning Coupon" or "The Million Pound Ferret". I could not sanction a place which was a combination of garage, café and zoo and that was only in two rooms.

I thanked him for his time. Assured him that I would show myself out and would be in touch.

"No need to get up," I said (pleadingly).

Fortunately, I was able to fill the vacancy without any further drama.

During those times most people dreamt of winning the pools, much like the lottery in the present day. Most say winning would not change them. However, the response to winning can bring out different emotions and reactions.

The jackpot winners were identified by Monday midday. Some clients would put a cross in a specific box to indicate no publicity if the coupon was a winner. Littlewoods would then try to persuade the winner to change their mind by organising a champagne reception at a leading hotel in return for a photograph to appear in the National press later in the week.

Early one Tuesday morning, John Donnelly received an instruction to visit a "no publicity" jackpot winner in Telford to persuade him to change his mind and inform him of a large win. A women answered the door of the maisonette and identified herself as the client's wife. She asked what it concerned.

"I am here on behalf of Littlewoods Pools to inform your husband of some great news regarding a substantial win." At this point she disappeared up the stairs shaking with excitement. Moments later a rather solemn, unshaven gentleman in a vest appeared, pulling the door behind him. When told the news and the amount of his winnings his response was unexpected.

"I asked for no publicity," he stated in a rather serious tone.

"I can assure you that no one knows about ..." but before John could finish, through gritted teeth he uttered:

"She fucking does!" before turning back inside and slamming the door closed. There was no champagne reception that week.

During a postal strike it was my responsibility to deliver cheques whose value exceeded a thousand pounds directly to winning clients. One Sunday morning within twenty minutes of two deliveries I saw the two sides of human nature.

The first delivery was to a flat in Bloxwich. The occupant a single male in his early sixties was dressed in an old navy jumper, cotton trousers and slippers. The flat looked tired and the furniture was old and worn. It did not take acute observational skills to establish that this was a home in need of some TLC. If there was any disposable income it was not evident.

Having introduced myself I handed over the sealed envelope with the cheque inside. I instructed him to open it as he had to sign to acknowledge receipt. The amount was nearly £16,000. His re-action was muted as he signed the form.

"The first time I have got eight draws - and this is all I fucking get!"

No elation. No thank you. He had just won an amount that most people would not earn in a year.

Five miles further down the road in Walsall I pulled into a large Victorian detached house on the Broadway. A lady in her sixties answered the door and from the hallway I could see her husband lying on the floor playing with their grand-child and his train set. The house was tastefully decorated with tiled floors and lush carpets. It was warm and inviting with several pictures celebrating life in the family.

The husband welcomed me into their lounge, and I explained why I was there and handed him the cheque.

"There must be an error," he said. "I only have a couple of goes on ten homes (predictions for the home team to win) and four aways. It's only a bit of fun."

The value of the cheque was £1,090. He was delighted. He called out to his wife. She asked if I would like a cup of tea and some cake. He promised his grandson something for the train set and he let out an elated scream. The whole atmosphere was one of joy. He obviously did not need the money. For him, his weekly bit of fun had provided an unexpected but very welcome return. On leaving he handed me a bottle of whiskey for my troubles, but I handed it back. The past ten minutes was reward enough.

All jackpot winners are offered financial guidance by the Pools companies. Their advice was often quite simple. Pay off your mortgage; buy the car you want and go on your dream holiday. Invest the rest.

There were many examples of winners who ignored the advice. The biggest mistakes often involved hospitality. People with no prior knowledge of the trade would invest a massive percentage of their winnings buying a Country Pub or restaurant without any clear plan. Over a period of twelve to eighteen months they would haemorrhage money, before selling at a huge loss.

Then there are those who will attempt to cheat the system for financial gain. The security men would talk of people climbing on the roof of the main pools building on Saturday night and drilling a small hole in the roof before rolling up a coupon with all the correct draws marked and pushing it through, allowing it to float merrily to the floor. The intention was for an operative to pick it up and treat it as a coupon which has fallen off the desk at one of the checking stations.

Unfortunately for the hopeful climber each envelope received into the building has a coded iron needle passed through it before opening. A coupon without this authentication is not accepted.

During the summer Australian Football fixtures were used. One local client appeared to be winning on a regular basis before it was realised that his entry was always delivered at the main gate minutes before the deadline, blaming the fact that he was a shift worker.

Following investigation, it was discovered that the deadline was only fifteen minutes before the end of games in Australia and the "successful" punter had a telephone contact relaying scores at the latest possible time. It didn't always highlight the drawn games, but it did indicate which matches were unlikely to be drawn. The deadline time was revised to coincide with kick-off.

A major fire at the Glasgow headquarters resulted in over a hundred phone calls from individuals claiming that their coupon with eight draws had been destroyed in the inferno. Their dreams dying in the embers, their truths living in the dust.

The introduction of the National Lottery severely impacted on the pools business. People had a convenient choice. The potential earnings for collectors decreased and so did the client base. Having collected coupons personally at different periods of time and in different locations I did see the important contribution the service made to the life of the clients aged sixty plus who lived on their own. They would spend time deciding on their selections. Completing the coupon maintained their dexterity and ability to write. A weekly conversation with the collector provided temporary companionship and a welcome relief from loneliness. An essential and valued part of their weekly life.

BUNAC was a non-profit organisation providing opportunities for people to travel to various parts of the world to work and live. Established in the late 1960s, its main market was America where the summer camp system provided an almost insatiable demand for English counsellors and workers. Part of the attraction was the accent, which most Americans adored. Those from rural Northumberland did seem to struggle mind but after eight weeks even they were appreciated. Those from the United Kingdom who worked as counsellors with children were often far less competitive than their American colleagues. They encouraged children and listened to them and were more willing to get involved.

Following a strong recommendation from the owners of Camp Towanda BUNAC approached me to work on their behalf by travelling to pre-arranged sessions throughout the United Kingdom to interview prospective candidates. There was a large pool of Interviewers, many university or college lecturers and teachers who had experienced life in America and the summer camp programme. There were many characters.

Eddie Robinson, Don Curry, Tim Kedge, Tom Jones, Pam Brawn, Peter Harrison, Rachel Thompson and Graham Hesketh who became a life-long friend and my BUNAC brother.

The role of each interviewer was to establish the suitability of an applicant to work with children and of their ability to integrate into the camp programme providing purposeful guidance in the areas of expertise indicated on the application form. There was also a need to assess their capability to work under strict rules over a period of eight-weeks, sometimes in remote areas.

At the beginning of each interview season (usually October) at the annual meeting the application forms of those who failed to see out the entire programme, either resigning or being fired, were passed around for scrutiny. The reason for the departure was provided and the whole group were asked to identify any red flags. Sometimes questions were asked directly to the Interviewer if they were present, about the candidate. These were never judgemental but often the responses were hilarious. It was a process which did help the organisation become the recognised leader in the provision of quality services.

Interview sessions were normally arranged for a weekend at a city centre hotel. There was always a minimum of twenty and often over forty applicants per day, with two or three staff overseeing the process. Interviewers were paid a set fee for every candidate interviewed, accepted or declined.

Don Curry was renowned for being notoriously quick. Always the first to arrive at a hotel he had often interviewed three people before the rest of the team were in place. He would often answer his own questions to speed up the process with the candidate sat there nodding in agreement. On one occasion he interviewed identical twins together, commenting that their answers would, in all probability be very much the same.

However, the funniest example of not wasting a moment occurred in Manchester when the hotel fire alarm was activated with the candidates and interviewers told to evacuate the building and gather on the hotel carpark. Don with his receipt book in hand, began collecting forms and interviewing candidates as we all waited for the fire service to check the building. He even persuaded one of the hotel staff to complete a form and attend an interview at the end of the day.

For me it was further additional income and afforded a chance to meet and make conversation with a wide range of personalities in different parts of the country whilst developing my skills to observe and assess. There were some interesting moments.

First impressions are vital and over the years there were several applicants who immediately excluded themselves from being accepted onto the programme. They were the ones who arrived at interview unprepared (sometimes hungover) with forms that were either incorrectly completed or untidy. When questioned it was obvious that they had not read any literature supplied and had no idea of the demands of camp life.

There was the mother who asked to sit in the interview with her twenty-year old son because he was nervous, and it would be the first time he had travelled away from home for any length of time. The fifty-four-year-old single male who had no child-related experience but fancied a career change, not to mention the great many who on the application form indicated that they could "teach" any sporting activity as an "expert", even those in which they had no participation experience.

The most daunting, however, was the thirty something male who appeared for interview at the end of the day in Manchester. The other interviewer had departed, and I was alone. He walked into the room and sat down (without invitation) and passed across his completed application form, informing me that he was a black belt in karate. His form indicated that he wished to be an overnight expedition leader.

He had no formal qualifications and did not work in education. His form did indicate that he had organised several expeditions with boys in their early teens. As with all candidates he was asked about the expedition, the planning involved and the considerations of participants with regard to their previous experience and physical capacity. His confident response was astounding.

"There was no formal planning as such. The groups would meet and be taken onto Dartmoor to camp for a week and learn to live off the land. They would be taught to hunt and fish and cook whatever they caught. Each day the group would move camp and hike across Dartmoor. It was the whole rustic experience."

The stops were not planned or pre-determined. Camp for the night would be a random stop following several hours of hiking. He had not established if any of the participants had a pre-existing medical condition and neither did he have a formal First Aid Award. At this point he seemed to read my mind.

"All participants were shown how to deal with minor injuries, including lacerations," he said. Then rolling up his sleeves he revealed a couple of scars on each arm. He informed me they were self-inflicted wounds during the expedition, with the boys expected to administer the appropriate treatment which in one case included stitching. He assured me that nothing beats practical experience when it comes to learning.

Following a few further insignificant questions, during which he reminded me twice he was a black belt in Karate, I concluded the interview at which point he rose and leaned across the desk his face only a foot away from mine and in an assertive voice said "I can you see you're impressed."

In all cases where there was the likelihood of confrontation, I would always inform the candidate that the BUNAC officers in London made the final decision. When he finally shook my hand, he attempted to reduce it to the size of a golf ball. He was a catastrophe in waiting.

For the few that were rejected there were many who were exceptional. Some would undersell themselves. They not only had great personalities but had significant experience working with children. Art students were often quiet but usually brought examples of their work to the interview and once asked to display their work they became confident and enthusiastic extending the discussion into projects they could initiate at camps, often using basic materials.

There were also candidates who were musicians, mainly piano or guitar. They could provide a unique and valuable contribution to camp life, either round a campfire or with support for camp shows. If art students produced examples of their work at interview why not ask a musician to play? The fact that someone has attained an RCM grade does not necessarily indicate that they have the competence or confidence to play to an audience. Those with nothing to hide brought along their guitar. One candidate in Nottingham even informed me that after interview he was busking in the town centre to "earn" the fee he had just paid to BUNAC for membership.

With pianists I would, whenever possible, locate a piano in the hotel and ask them to play a favourite song or piece of work. It gave me the opportunity to make a valid and accurate assessment. It did, however, cause a major headache in Liverpool one Saturday afternoon. The piano at the hotel was located in the tearoom, an elegant and popular venue for city centre shoppers. With the manager's consent the candidate agreed to play. Within seconds it was obvious he was exceptional, playing a Beatles number to engage the audience followed by my request for Summer of 42.

The problem was the very appreciate audience would not let him leave. He seemed willing and able to play their choice of song. The interview which normally lasts twenty minutes was now into thirty-five minutes. Eventually I managed to drag him away to the displeasure of all in the room to complete the process. The whole episode impacted dramatically on my schedule.

I missed my train home. For eighty minutes I sat and waited in Lime Street for the next train with a sandwich and the strains of the Michel Legrand classic running through my mind.

The most amusing incident, however, occurred at the Midland Hotel in Birmingham. A young man in his early twenties entered the room, introduced himself, and sat down. He was carrying a blue A4 folder and a laminate.

"Good afternoon, John, and what have you got for me?" I asked as he lay the folder on my desk. He then stood up from the chair and moved away from the table and took a deep breath.

"Be not afeard: this isle is full of noises sounds and sweet airs that give delight and hurt not. Sometimes a thousand twangling instruments...."

I sat in complete awe and probably motionless, unable to interrupt. Paralysed by the intensity.

".... The clouds methought would open and show riches ready to drop upon me that, when I waked, I cried to dream again." He slowly walked back to the chair and sat down relieved.

I asked for the completed BUNAC forms. He looked at me with the astonishment of someone who had just witnessed a murder or a miracle. There was a short pause before the realisation that he was in the wrong room finally registered. He looked deflated more than embarrassed.

Without the hint of a smile, I thanked him, wished him the best of luck and then directed Caliban to the room along the corridor where auditions for a travelling Shakespeare Company were taking place. It took me several minutes to regain my composure before the next candidate.

BUNAC was an organisation that put the candidates first. Historically they were the highest paying organisation but also offered the best support. Each summer twenty interviewers would travel to the USA and over a period of three-weeks would visit every camp with a BUNAC placement to ensure that all was well and discuss any concerns with the camp directors. This allowed the interviewer to build a unique and personal knowledge of the camp and of its ongoing requirements. On my several visits to different States I was able to establish strong contacts with camps and throughout the interview season was able to direct candidates to certain camps in the knowledge that they would both enjoy the experience and provide the camp with a memorable service. Many would often return for several years. Some even moved to the United States permanently.

The whole BUNAC experience was really an extension of my work in school. Opening doors for young people to travel and meet people of differing cultures. During my time I interviewed over three thousand people, some exceptional personalities and talented individuals. People whose enthusiasm and energy revived me following a week at school and whatever that had thrown at me.

When BUNAC was eventually sold it was a sad day for all, with the new owners preferring to focus on profit and not opportunity.

# Chapter Twenty-Seven

For many years throughout the United Kingdom there were hundreds of teachers of Physical Education who not only delivered activity during the normal school day but gave their time voluntarily after school and at weekends to provide additional opportunities for students of all ages to participate in sport at both local and county level. They provided the foundation of the performance pyramid without any financial reward and quite often without recognition. They instilled a passion for sport in children and very often the will to succeed.

The Cannock Chase area was no exception with regular competitive opportunities in football, basketball, netball, hockey, cricket, athletics and handball. The top players from each of the fourteen schools in the area would then have the opportunity to represent the district in games against other towns and cities, with some representing the County or eventually competing for England.

The provision for football was outstanding with five league and cup competitions, small -sided tournaments and seven-a-side games for the most senior students. There were District teams at Under-13, Under-14 and Under-15 age groups, playing games at weekends and occasionally in mid-week against other teams from Staffordshire, Shropshire and beyond. The Cannock Schools' Football Association as it was known would meet on a Monday evening at the beginning of every half-term to discuss the games ahead and any issues. District managers would deliver a report on the progress of the team or individual players. There would always be a presentation evening at the end of the season to celebrate the successes of individuals, school and district teams.

An annual general meeting would take place each July where officers for the following year would be elected. Unless there was a resignation, the existing officer was elected unopposed. Applications to manage district teams were considered and successful candidates duly appointed for the year.

Bryn Scorey was a former well-regarded non-league player and a teacher at a local Middle school. He was elected as secretary to the Association in the mid-seventies, a position he held for over a quarter of a century, whilst also managing several different District teams. For several years he managed the County team. He was passionate about football and his ability to work with young players was exceptional.

In the late nineties Bryn was appointed manager of the Under-13 District team. For two seasons he nurtured the team, assisted by his young daughter and the parent of a player. The team responded well to Bryn's positive and calm manner which was reflected in the results. They won the Staffordshire County Under-14 league competition.

During the season, Bryn became unwell, and despite the demands of frequent hospital visits, endured the demands of his role and was able to celebrate with the team at the end of year presentation. With the continued support of his wife Sue, his daughter Hannah and some of the parents Bryn was determined to continue into the following season with "his team".

During this time, I was the Chairman of the Association and spoke often with Bryn to assure him that if he needed some rest or recovery when he was unwell, I would manage the team personally until his return.

Sadly, Bryn lost his fight against cancer early in 2000. It was a great loss not only to his family and friends but the whole of the school sporting community in Staffordshire. Through a lifetime of selfless dedication and the years since his passing I have yet to meet anyone that was not touched by his warmth, kindness and enthusiasm. A letter from the Prime Minister prior to his death recognised his outstanding contribution to schools' football.

Most of the committee endorsed my managing the team for the rest of the season. I arranged to meet with the parent who had helped Bryn over the past two years to invite him to continue in the same capacity on match days if he so wished. Unfortunately, he was less than happy. He had been "assistant manager" and was disappointed not to have been given the opportunity to manage the team. He knew all the players and had successfully guided his local junior school Under-11 team to a final.

I managed to navigate the situation by explaining that there was a conflict of interest. He could not be the manager whilst his son was playing. If he wanted to manage his son would have to withdraw from the team and the County team. He chose to remain in a helping capacity.

The team embarked on a run of victories, some narrow and scruffy, others playing teams off the park. We had a couple of strong central defenders, a solid and energetic midfield and a couple of decent strikers

Matty was a diamond. Not the tallest or most physical of players but he had an instinct for goal. He was quick, agile and intelligent. The personal quality that set Matty apart was his humility. He, fully supported by his parents, refused the offers from established clubs in the North and Midlands remaining at Walsall, the club who had nurtured his talents from a young age.

Following a decent run of victories of which the last two were decided by a single goal, the team reached the quarter-finals of the English Schools' Inter Association Cup, the longest running school sports competition in the United Kingdom first held in 1906 with nineteen teams taking part.

With only eight teams from the 128 entries remaining, Cannock were drawn at home against competition favourites Sheffield. The Yorkshire team had already defeated Liverpool, Manchester and Barnsley. The team were undefeated, having never lost a game at any age group. The game was arranged for Monday 5th March 2001 at Keys Park, the home of Hednesford Town.

I decided to call the managers of the teams who had suffered defeat and ask a few questions about Sheffield. Liverpool refused to answer any questions referring to my actions as totally unprofessional. Manchester and Barnsley, however, were far more forthcoming. Both highlighted the same attacking strengths – an outstanding midfield player (International) with a great passing range; a left-winger who destroys teams with pace and trickery and a centre forward who is physically robust but becomes agitated if things do not fall for him. Defensively the full backs were very average.

I began to plan for the game. I needed to ensure that the winger did not get on the ball. I needed him to feel uncomfortable and perhaps go into unfamiliar areas. I needed someone to stick to him like flypaper. I had two right-backs of equal ability, strength and speed. This role would require a special attribute. The ability to concentrate for the duration of the game. One task and one task only.

Nine days before the game, Cannock had an away fixture against Tamworth, one of Staffordshire's weaker teams. On a bleak and cold Saturday morning as the teams were warming up, I noticed the usual following of parents plus two men in thick sports coats standing slightly removed from the main body. The fixture was unlikely to be attractive to scouts from professional teams. I ambled over within earshot of them talking as the players were warming up. I smiled. Upon closing my eyes for a moment, I detected the distinctive tones of Sean Bean's finest performances. They were from Yorkshire.

I quickly called the lads together for a team talk but did not mention the Steel City spies.

"Going to make a bit of a change today lads," I said. "The opposition are down to the bare bones, so it gives us a chance to try something different."

They looked bewildered when I moved Matty to right of midfield, with an instruction not to advance more than fifteen yards into the opposing half. The centre-back was given the opportunity to play centre forward and the midfield dynamo, a small but aggressive player was moved to centre-back.

"Just go out and play but enjoy it," was my final remark.

The two right backs would each play one half. With the opposition unlikely to test them, I decided on another tactic. The player in the first half was given a simple sentence at the start of the game – "Fall in Vermont is the best time of the year to visit," and asked to remember it. I asked the second player to do the same task at the start of the next period.

Towards the end of the game, with Cannock leading by five goals I asked the starting full back to repeat the sentence which he did. At the final whistle, with the men from Yorkshire looking quite smug with a spring in their step as they walked back to their car, I asked the full-back leaving the field to repeat the sentence. He couldn't remember. My selection issue was resolved.

Once the players had changed and the crowd had dispersed, I explained the bizarre positional changes to the players and the reasons for it.

On the Monday of the game, I wanted the players to feel special. Each was released from school early and gathered at the Premier Suite in Cannock. The owner, Scott Murray, a great supporter of local sport had arranged for an appropriate meal of chicken and pasta to be provided to ensure optimum levels of nutrition. The players were told to wear school ties and be smart. The meal was served following a short introduction about standards and expectations. These included ensuring that the facility was left in the manner in which it was found.

The game plan hinged around some key elements. Firstly, the right-back would need to man-mark the Sheffield winger regardless of how deep he dropped. Other players would cover when necessary. Secondly the midfield would need to double-team the star man, forcing him when in possession to continually play right, away from the two danger areas in attack.

The two managers from Yorkshire looked bemused when we lined up. Matty was in his striker role, the centre forward from the Tamworth game was at centre-half and there were two "new players" in midfield, one of which played centre-half in the game they had watched.

The lads were fantastic. By half-time they were leading by two goals. The left winger did not receive the ball for the first twenty-five minutes and when he did his touch let him down. The opposing centre-forward was starting to complain at the lack of service, with the Sheffield star smothered. Changing roles throughout the game the two players in midfield gave him little time on the ball, forcing him to play side-ways or backwards.

The second half resumed in the same manner, with the Sheffield midfield player dropping deeper to try and find space but the markers moved with him and the winger tried unsuccessfully to move inside before retreating again to his role as a spectator on the touchline. Matty celebrated his 15th birthday by scoring a second goal before a late penalty conversion provided some consolation for the journey back to Yorkshire.

For the first time in their history Cannock had reached the semi-final and were now favourites to lift the trophy, having been drawn at home against Swindon.

Sadly, none of the local professional clubs or even Hednesford Town would agree to the staging of the semi-final over concerns about the impact on the playing surface. The only offer was from Bilston Town.

I secured sponsorship for a completely new kit, replacing the existing old kit which seemed to have shirts from different generations, a mix of shorts of various makes and sizes and socks of differing shades of green, including two pair of wool socks. The old forest green and black stripes were replaced by a vibrant green with a black horizontal stripe, green shorts and green and black socks. The team had a professional look.

I again arranged for the boys to meet at the Premier Suite in Cannock. However, on this occasion I was delayed by thirty minutes at school and when I arrived there was chaos. Players were sat all over the place, unlike the tables of four on the previous visit. The "assistant manager" had told the kitchen to send out the food and the behaviour of some players fell short of expectation, with eating areas left in an untidy manner.

The first part of my briefing was spent reminding them of standards. It was not a good start. I had gained some insight into the Swindon team who had a couple of useful strikers, one quite quick but the rest of the team were ordinary. The goalkeeper was small and unable to kick any distance.

The early evening rain finally stopped about thirty minutes before kick-off, and I went to check the pitch. When I returned to the dressing room the players were changed but there was a sombre mood. The atmosphere was totally wrong. I then discovered that Dave, the assistant manager had read out a letter from Bryn's father which was very emotional and had obviously upset some of the players who looked forlorn.

Things went from bad to worse. Against the run of play Swindon broke away to open the scoring. A long pass on the right-hand side seemed to go out of play before the wind carried it in. The full-back allowed the ball to run past him waiting for the linesman to flag, which he never did. During the next twenty minutes we struck the post twice and missed a simple chance when the ball stuck in the sanded six-yard area which resembled a bunker at St. Andrews

At half-time a couple of players complained of feeling unwell, one of which was Matty Fryatt who had stomach cramps. He agreed to continue playing. The second half continued very much like the first. The Swindon goal seemed to be charmed. A couple of half-chances rolled past the post and with five minutes remaining a long clearance was missed by the centre-half and Swindon were on their way to the finals.

Football is one of those funny games where if the team win, it's down to the performance of the players but if they lose, it's down to the manager. In this case it was my fault. Some parents blamed my team selection for the game. The only change from the previous game being the introduction of an attacking midfield player who had the ability to score from outside the penalty area. Against a team who were both technically and physically weaker it seemed the appropriate course of action. They failed to realise that selection was on a game-to-game basis and a major consideration is not only the strengths and weaknesses of our own players but also the opposition.

However, the most ridiculous comment made by some parents was that my introducing a new kit for the game had "jinxed" the team. They had under-performed due to the kit they were wearing. Give me strength.

The end of season presentation evening was a little subdued as it was the first one held without Bryn being present. His team were crowned county champions until this day progressing further in the National competition than any other team from the area. Players in every age group received pin badges with the oldest group receiving ties.

As chairman of the Association, I had to deliver a speech in which I thanked all the players for the work they had done throughout the season and of course for the parents for their support. I also made particular mention of a teacher, Jon Brandwood, a Football League referee who regularly called upon his contacts to officiate games with no charge. Very often, Premier League referee Alan Wiley would officiate at mid-week games, including the Sheffield victory. Mark Warren, linesman at the 1996 World Cup final would often step in at the last minute to help out. They were a vital part of the success of the Association.

I spoke passionately about the role of District teams in the development of players both technically and personally. Providing opportunities for all regardless of race, class or colour in a calm and ordered environment. The size of the Association is inconsequential. During my time with Manchester Boys in 1966 with Internationals Lenny Cantello and Tony Towers, we lost 2-1 to Ashton, a small area to the east of the city with only five schools to select from in the National Inter-Association Cup. A couple of weeks later we beat Liverpool (eventual winners of the National cup)5-1 at Goodison Park in the Lancashire Cup, such is the unpredictable nature of the game. They provide, however, the moments that the players will remember and recall long after their ability to strike a ball has gone.

Sadly, in recent years the number of District Association teams has declined considerably, impacted by the rise of professional football Academies and the introduction of Saturday morning leagues for junior players.

NB. Matty Fryatt embarked on a highly successful professional career playing 364 games for Walsall, Leicester City, Hull City and Nottingham Forest scoring 116 goals. At Leicester he created several records including the fastest goal ever scored (9 seconds) in a match against Preston. He represented England Under-19 on six occasions, scoring a hat-trick against Serbia and Montenegro at the European Championships in 2005.

# Chapter Twenty-Eight

The success of the Cannock Schools' team did not go unnoticed. In June of that year, I received a phone call from Glyn Harding, a coach and welfare officer at Wolverhampton Wanderers Football Club. Glyn had delivered a UEFA B license coaching course which I had successfully completed. He asked if I would consider working as a coach at the Club's Academy.

It was a paid position and involved working with elite players for two evenings a week and coaching games on a Sunday. It provided a great opportunity and challenge which was not available in my normal teaching life. With the support of my wife and the proviso that any Cannock players would not be prevented from representing the district on a Saturday, I agreed to an interview. I eventually met with Mike Smith, a former manager of Wales who was the Assistant Director of the Academy at the time. Following a thirty-minute meeting where we discussed differing coaching styles and player management, I was offered the position coaching the Under-12 team which had just won a prestigious tournament in Japan. No pressure. It would prove to be one of the most eventful and enjoyable periods of my sporting life.

The signs that this was going to be a totally different experience became evident on the first evening of coaching. When I arrived at Aldersley Stadium I was given three carrier bags with different clothing in them. These included a tracksuit, a wet weather top and bottoms, a winter coaching coat, three pairs of shorts and socks, a training sweat-top, two training shirts and a jacket. I felt a million dollars.

The group were exceptional in every way. They were all keen to learn and willing to listen. They worked for each other and engaged fully in all the tasks set for them with enthusiasm and energy. The captain, Elliot Bennett was a leader in every respect. Often the first to training and the last to leave. He was determined to succeed, and he did, enjoying a long professional career at a variety of top clubs, including Brighton, Norwich City and Blackburn Rovers.

Ironically, he provided my first real test. At the time he was playing right-back in the team, and I decided to move him into midfield where he would be more involved in the game, have more touches and develop a greater awareness of both attacking and defensive phases. One of the senior scouts came to watch a game and questioned why he was playing in that position.

"He is a full-back and will always be a full-back," he commented. I explained my rationale that only when you open the cage can you see how high the bird can fly. Many years later Elliott became a highly effective and valued midfield player.

There were some great characters on the coaching staff. Some weeks into the season I was joined by Des Davis, a former professional player who was well known in the area. Not only was he extremely knowledgeable with keen observational skills, but he had a good sense of humour which he often used to great effect when dealing with both adults and players. He was a dream to work with, ready to share his thoughts and experiences but always with discretion. He stretched me in the best possible way by making valid comment and significant contributions at every session and game.

A few weeks after the start of our partnership we played at Liverpool. We won the game 3-1 despite the attempts of the referee to give the home team a helping hand. Mike Smith approached Des and I after the game whilst the players were getting changed. He looked quite stern, with pursed lips and his head shaking. We were obviously in trouble. Being a former headmaster, he had retained an authoritative voice.

"It would appear that you have upset Mr. Heighway," (the Liverpool Academy manager) he said.

"We did get a little excited," I replied. Des was trying to recall if his reference to the referee as a "cheating twat" had been overheard.

"That he accepts, but beating his Golden Boys has upset him and he is not happy. Well done!" At that he turned away smiling.

They were not the only big-name club to be annoyed. Manchester United complained our team was too physical following a win at Carrington. We called it competitive.

All the journeys to away games were in luxury coaches. Parents were not allowed to travel with the players and those who wanted to see the games would need their own form of transport. Though most of the games were in the Midlands, there were still games at Cardiff, Bristol, Blackburn, Manchester and Liverpool to play. In some cases, the journeys would take over two hours. With coaches equipped with video machines it was possible to occupy the young players with DVDs of football matches featuring top teams from around the world. If, however, there was no working video player I would supply football coupons to those who wish to take part in a competition to predict the results of the following weekend's Premier League games. Some of the coaches took part also.

The following week a winner was declared. This was the person who had predicted the most results correctly, either a home win, a draw or an away win. The prize (a Mars Bar) was irrelevant, it was the winning that mattered and very often it was won by one of the younger players. Experienced coaches never seemed to get it right.

Within five years the need to occupy the players disappeared with the emergence of the Game Boy and video games. Players now disappeared into their own world. A world without banter and often without any thought of football until they disembarked from the coach.

Parental support is vital for any athlete to succeed and progress to elite level. Some parents would have two boys in the Academy system, training on different nights of the week. With journeys ranging from ten to fifty miles it was a huge demand both time wise and financially.

Most parents were easy to deal with and were very approachable. A significant number, however, seemed to believe that their attendance at games was a major factor in team selection. That if the family had all travelled the hundred plus miles to Bristol, I would be compelled to play their son for a longer period of time. I continually tried to reassure them that this was not the case and that all players would be treated equally, family or no family in attendance. Their time investment was immense already, why compound it with the need to give up the whole day for one game? What about younger siblings and quality time devoted to them?

Occasionally some parent would call me over on arrival for a game to inform me that "Johnny" had not been too well during the night but was determined to play. In other words, if he has a moderate game, there is an excuse. For my part I would try and make them understand two things about performance and assessment. Firstly, that players are not machines, they will have good days and bad. Only the mediocre player is always at his best. Secondly that any assessment made is over several games or a season, not one game.

For every Elliot Bennett there are a hundred that will never progress to the elite level. Some do not have the technical ability, some lack the drive and dedication whilst some are dealt the cruellest hand of all, serious injury.

James Parsonage was a twelve-year old who had previously trialled at the club without being accepted. His father had written to the club asking for another trial. Bob Bennett, the local scout asked me to look at him over a four-week period and decide. He was a tall player for his age, very approachable and he informed me that he played as a central striker.

He was a strong player, but his first touch was not good enough for the level and he struggled to retain the ball when under pressure with his back to goal. However, he was quick, and he would often recover to regain possession of the ball. During the third of his four sessions I asked him to play as a central defender for the second half of the session. He had an innate ability to win the ball. I informed his father that night that I wanted James to play for the Academy on the Sunday at Compton.

The proud and delighted father was somewhat bemused when James started as a centre-back and not as a striker. He made a very promising debut, winning many of his duels with the opposition forwards. It was the start of a highly successful season where he rapidly adjusted to his new position where his speed and agility were major assets. Many visiting clubs noted his performances.

The following season I called the parents together on the carpark at Compton as the players were changing to express my concerns at the number of players wearing blades, a new trend in football boots. Though they would help with forward movement they are not designed to aid turning or moving in a lateral direction and football is not played in straight lines. I advised the parents to return to conventional footwear at the earliest opportunity.

Seventeen minutes into the game, James was pursuing an opponent and managed to intercept the ball. As he turned to play the ball his foot remained planted. The blades had remained in the turf and his knee ligament was ruptured. Following major surgery and a long-fight back James eventually recovered to begin playing again at the elite level. Unfortunately, the injury reoccurred and despite further surgery and the ongoing support of the club a future playing career at professional level was halted. I have no doubt that with his ability and desire he would have enjoyed a long and successful career in the game. He eventually qualified as a physiotherapist.

I felt valued at the club with the full support of both Chris Evans, the Academy manager and Tony Lacey, a legendary coach and scout who in his days at Stoke City had nurtured future international players Lee Dixon and Steve Bould. When Chris asked me into his office one Sunday, I thought it was to discuss a player. It was, however, to offer the financial support to undertake an Advanced Licence coaching qualification. The year-long course comprised of two residential sessions with several in-house coaching sessions to be delivered and evaluated. The cost of the course was over £4,500 and would not have been a consideration without the support.

The irony was that in 1976 I engaged in a course at Lea Green in Derbyshire as preparation for the award. The course was delivered by Howard Wilkinson, the last English manager to win the Premiership. There were fifty candidates, with over 75% having played professionally. Each had to deliver a couple of coaching sessions, which were evaluated and marked. At the end of the course, I received my marks and feedback. I had the third highest combined marks with a comment from Howard that I "had a good chance" of achieving the Advanced award.

In the years following I had numerous conversations with firstly Allen Wade and then Charles Hughes who were Directors of coaching for the Football Association about my application to undertake the course. Due to my commitment with Summer Camps in the USA, I applied for the course traditionally held at Lilleshall Hall, Shropshire at the end of the football season in late May and early June. They continually denied the application as I had never played at a professional level and that the players would "intimidate and embarrass" me. They diverted my application on a regular basis to the course held at the end of July and beginning of August which was primarily for those involved in education. Now twenty-eight years after Lea Green, with the weight of Wolverhampton Wanderers behind me, I was finally accepted onto the course in May 2004.

Freddy willingly granted a week's leave without pay, particularly as I informed him that Wolverhampton Wanderers had offered me another job should I succeed. He saw this as an opportunity to contribute to an exit strategy.

In the first year at Lilleshall there were approximately twenty-eight candidates, many of them in the final stages of their professional careers and a couple from overseas. For two weeks we would participate in or deliver sessions, attend coaching demonstrations and spend a significant amount of time in lectures studying games and playing styles. The day started at 9.00 a.m. and concluded at 8.45 p.m. with an hour for lunch and an hour for dinner. There was no day off.

One of the first classroom-based tasks was to present a programme for the week at a club at which you have been appointed as head coach/ manager. We were divided into designated groups of four. My group was composed of Dean Smith, Rob Newman and Brett Angel, three personalities with 1,769 games between them across all four divisions. Into the furnace.

They were sociable and welcoming. They of course had either played with or against each other, I was the outsider. We discussed various aspects of training and analysis using their vast experience and I suggested input from sports scientists, the delivery of afternoon sessions with advanced Pilates, nutrition, relaxation and meditation. They thought it was a great idea and as the scribe I was nominated to deliver our programme to the group. We were the first of six to present our ideas.

There was total silence as I ran through the mornings and then enthusiastically explained the afternoon sessions and the reasoning behind the programme. All seemed to go well until I asked for any questions or comment.

*"I play golf on Thursday afternoon for my relaxation,"* was the first reaction, followed by *"You need to talk to my wife about nutrition not me."*

I tried to explain that these were initiatives which could extend their careers.

*"If I don't take my missus shopping on Monday afternoon, I won't have a career."*

Then a final comment from one player which seemed to get more heads nodding than a fleet of cars insured by Churchill Insurance.

*"With all this afternoon stuff, who is going to pick my kids up from school? I wouldn't sign for your club."*

I turned to look for support. The three were smiling. I had been stitched up. The tutor thanked me and asked for a final word.

"It just needs a bit of tweaking," I said, and my buddies began to laugh along with several others in the room. I sat down shaking my head. Robbie shook my hand.

"I thought it went orright Pop," he said in a soft West country accent. I was not embarrassed or intimidated, but I was now certainly part of the group.

Throughout the two-weeks my experience in education proved invaluable to some players particularly in organisation and planning. They were nervous, though they knew the technical and tactical aspects the limited time they had devoted to coaching resulted in them sometimes forgetting to consider smaller details, the type of details which I applied daily in teaching and which if overlooked could result in marks being deducted. It was not a competition. We were in this together.

Each coach had to deliver two sessions each lasting between twenty-five and thirty minutes. The remaining candidates acted as players, where everyone was expected to be available to take part unless injured. For the more talented players this would involve five hours or more of football each day. During the sessions in which I participated I would often exaggerate a fault enabling the coach to identify and correct before moving on to his next point. On some occasions if a coach being assessed was nearby, I would quietly remind him of an aspect or point he should be aware of during the session, usually concerned with their positioning.

Some of the sessions were very good and informative. Dean Smith delivered a defensive phase of play which was exceptional and still only scored 74 from 100 possible marks. It was no easy task.

During the two weeks I became part of "our group's" nightly rest and recouperation in the bar where stories were exchanged with several other players, including Mick Tait, a legend from the North-East with a long-playing career, Mike Jackson (later managed Burnley) and Chris Beech. They were all great company.

It was Dean Smith, however, that I developed a long friendship with. He was a local lad and an avid Aston Villa supporter. He valued what I had to say and at the beginning of his coaching career sought my advice. Eventually he became the manager of Walsall, the club he first captained and where I would help with the provision of the school's artificial football pitch for training when his Broad Lane base was unplayable following heavy periods of rain. With highly successful spells at Brentford and Aston Villa, he remains one of the most astute English coaches in the game with a great eye for raw talent and a level of integrity that is often under-valued.

In my two presentations during that first year, I scored 58 marks and 64 marks, which took me above the 120 mark threshold for participation in year two.

The following year the group size had expanded to forty. This was due to the final (and most crucial) assessment task involving an 11 v 11 game. With each candidate having to coach, there were forty games staged over a four-day period During the final week Mike Jackson participated in thirty-four games, each lasting thirty minutes.

The group now included players with international experience on a world stage. Tony Adams and Steve Bould, part of Arsenal's Invincibles and Steve Hodge, the first player to be beaten by Maradona on that amazing run to goal at the 1986 World Cup.

Gary Ablet was also on the course. He was one of the few players to win the FA Cup with two differing teams, in his case Liverpool and Everton. Not only was he a quality player, but he was sociable and approachable. He selected me to play in his assessed session at fullback.

At the time I was wearing boots supplied by Umbro which had a tongue with an elasticated band which fitted under the boot, securing the tongue over the laces. Unbeknown to me the band on my left boot had worked loose and as I tried to receive a pass to move left my right foot was holding the band in place. The result was a catapult effect, and I collapsed dramatically.

Gary ran across as I lay on the ground, looking for a hole to hide in.

"Fuckin' ell Pop, I thought you'd had a heart-attack," he said in his soft scouse accent. The rest of the players were laughing. I apologised to him, picked myself up ready to go again. It did not impact on his performance and the session continued to be delivered with purpose.

That evening when I returned to my room, I cut the elastic bands from the boot tongue.

My initial session on year two went quite well, with a score of 59. I would need to score 61 or more from my 11 v 11 assessment to pass.

My task was to coach a team to play against opponents that would be set up with a man-to-man defence and a sweeper. Mine would be the thirteenth session to be presented and would take place immediately after lunch on Wednesday. A day earlier Tony had approached me and offered to be involved in my teams. Several others, including Gary volunteered their services. I got a little carried away and billed the game as England versus Italy (a country renowned for playing with a sweeper/libero).

I made a quick visit home on Tuesday evening where my son Paul, had produced a programme for the game with the teams listed in the formation they would play. Every player involved was given a programme at lunch and the team list was pinned on the board in the main hall and in the wooden pavilion by the fields.

The England team featured a back-three of Jackson, Adams and Ablet, a mid-field four and a front three. The opposition included Brett Angel, Scott Sellars, Robbie Van De Larne, Dean Smith and Andy Awford.

During the game, the coach must interact with every player at least once, offering appropriate guidance or direction. Usually, it is easier to start at the back and move through the lines.

All was going well when Gary played a simple pass across to Tony Adams from the left. With an opponent moving to pressure and Tony facing the pass I was ready to intervene and question the former England captain.

"Stop!" I cried, at which point Tony with the outside of his right foot hit a forty-yard pass to the centre forward, Richie Barker, who chested the ball and hit the back of the net with a superb volley. There was silence everywhere. I had to react quickly.

"Well done, Tony. That was excellent, but what else could you have done?" I asked.

With a smile he replied:

"I could have opened my body up and played the ball across to Jacko."

"Exactly." Some of the players were shaking their heads and smiling, thinking how the hell did he get out of that. The rest of the session went very well, with two wingers creating space for a mobile midfield, the "England" team scored four further goals. Some of the players who had taken part in the session were very complimentary, including both Tony and Dean who insisted I had "smashed it".

Unfortunately, a senior assessor did not share their view. I was asked why I had decided to play with three defenders instead of the conventional four. I suggested that with only a lone striker, there was no need for four defending players.

"But that is not the way Dick Bate would have done it," was the reply. "He would have gone 4-4-2 with a man in the hole!" Dick Bate, I was later informed was a respected coach who had held various positions with the Football Association.

"I am not Dick Bate, and I felt my tactics worked and that the session was purposeful, and the objective achieved." It was then that I realised that this was not about innovation but preservation, following the prescribed and conventional path. The assessment team were not prepared to acknowledge a challenge to convention. It was ironic that they finally asked if I had learnt anything from delivering the session.

"To expect the unexpected and not jump in too quickly to make a point," I said with a smile referring to Tony's "worldy".

A couple of days later following a short one-to-one with the course director I was asked what my plans would be going forward if I achieved the "A" Licence.

I commented that Wolverhampton Wanderers had funded the course and that I would continue to work in their Academy. It seemed the right and proper response. I was soon to learn that obvious and ethical have little currency in this game.

On the Saturday morning before departing each candidate had a brief feed-back meeting where they were informed if they have passed and are given back their personal logbook, with the session scores and comments. I had scored 59 marks, two short of the total needed to pass. One of the disturbing features, however, was the mark I received for organisation: 2 out of 5 - with a further comment stating that the bibs were not laid on the ground in the differing formations to inform players of their playing positions immediately before the start of my session. The thirty programmes with the information clearly displayed, distributed to all players and on show were apparently not good enough. Then the final insult suggesting that if I return to be assessed "with the teachers" three months later in August I would pass.

Only fourteen players walked away successfully from the course. I never returned or requested to be re-assessed. For four weeks of my life, I had been immersed in football and had considerably developed my knowledge of the game and its culture. I had been part of the team, the banter, the games, the stories and received a Darlington shirt from Mick Tait. Nothing comes close.

# Chapter Twenty-Nine

One of the great opportunities of education is to broaden horizons. Imaginative teachers can, through their enthusiasm and drive, ignite the flame which exists in us all. There are many teachers who give up their time selflessly to enable students to have experiences that ordinarily they would not enjoy.

Our school was no different. There was a highly active Celtic music department which regularly arranged trips into mainland Europe allowing the school Swing Band to perform. Clanna Gael was a Celtic influenced group that played at many venues throughout Cannock Chase. The driving force was a pocket-sized music teacher called Yvonne. She was demanding, persistent and enthusiastic. All the qualities an outstanding coach needs, but sadly which some teachers lack.

In our department we were always looking at opportunities for the students beyond the confines of the school. Handball trips to Germany, France and Italy were an annual feature. Ski-ing trips were organised and often over-subscribed.

The school introduced an end-of-year activity day with a rich array of experiences to choose from.

One activity which Ray introduced, initially for sixth formers only (due to a legal restriction at the time) was Paintballing or Skirmishing as it is known in the USA. The activity was very much in its infancy at the time and the nearest site was near Stone. I volunteered my services to support on the day. As with the "Snow Days" once you are in the field, respect or rank disappears quicker than a rat down a drain.

During the afternoon in a "Last Man Standing" contest I reached the latter stages. With only three remaining in the competition, I located a player in the process of re-loading his hopper with pellets. I jumped out screaming (a mixture of excitement and drama) but as I went for the kill my gun jammed. I was defenceless and as I turned to retreat in search of cover anywhere, I felt the barrage of pellets striking every part of my body. A multi-coloured explosion. Game over.

In later years, the age restriction was lifted allowing students fourteen and over to participate. It became one of the most popular activities of the day. With Ray always including me as a staff member I enjoyed many years as a would-be Rambo prowling the woods at Basset's Pole, a major paintballing venue with a variety of battlefields from trench warfare to inflatables.

On one occasion I gathered my small platoon behind a hedgerow of branches with the instruction that on my call we should all get over the small hedge and charge the opposition who were unaware of our presence on their left flank. I gave the call and immediately stepped onto the hedge which was not as sturdy as it appeared and collapsed face down. My platoon followed the instruction to the letter with several using me as a human bridge cutting through the hedge to advance and wipe out the opposition. Feeling slightly humiliated not to mention being trampled on, I stood up without thought, when a pellet exploded on my chest, its yellow fluid trickling down my sternum. Game over, again!

I did, however, break the rules on a couple of occasions over the years. Whilst walking to the start positions the participants are told not to fire their guns. Temptation was sometimes too great, particularly when the lad who had been a pain in the arse all year was walking ahead. Retribution was the shot at his buttocks from close range which would give him not only a quick jolt but would satisfy a handful of colleagues back at school who had prayed daily for such a moment.

On the day after the event at school, participants would compare their wounds, often the shape of a target. Following a shower my wife noticed two decorating my Gluteus Maximus and one year Raymond had a perfect ring in the middle of his forehead where the snood had risen and not offered much protection. They were the trophies of war. What I did notice repeatedly was the levels of perspiration during the whole day. If this was Staffordshire on a cloudy day, what must it have been like in the jungles of South-East Asia with the heat and humidity?

With the numbers of students opting to take Physical Education at GCSE level increasing and the introduction of the subject at Advanced level there was a need to think beyond the classroom. Any event or exhibition which could enhance their understanding or knowledge or help the staff in their delivery was explored. Cost was never a factor.

Convenience was never a factor. This was their time and their moment. For some students it will be a day away from school but for many there will be aspects of the day which will engage them, enlighten them and energise them. For a few it will provide life-changing direction.

A sports science exhibition in Leeds provided some excellent opportunities for the students to participate in experiments and activities. One activity provided able-bodied students with an opportunity to race over a 'virtual' 100-metres in a wheelchair. I decided to race against Danny, a year-ten student. With my sights firmly set on a sub fourteen second performance (the world record at the time was two seconds faster) I got off to a flyer. Just before the fifty-metre mark I began to feel "the burn". My arms started to feel like jelly. They appeared to be in slow motion for the second part of the race, with Danny breezing past me at the finish. I was knackered. My time of twenty seconds manged to secure a place in the top ten on the day (just!), but it made both me and the many students who engaged in the activity realise how much upper-body strength is needed by para performers.

A chance read of an article in the Guardian newspaper in early 2002 ignited my interest in another exhibition, one steeped in controversy. Gunther Von Hagen, a German scientist had opened his Body Worlds exhibition at a gallery in London's East End. Through a process called plastination he was able to preserve organs from donated bodies by replacing water cells with plastic material. A comment from a Tory MP at the time that the exhibition would *"only appeal to ghoulish groups in our society"* and to question *"what possible benefit can a normal person get from looking at dead bodies"* only fuelled my desire to visit the Brick Lane exhibition at the earliest opportunity with a group of students.

Within a few weeks, forty-five students and a couple of staff travelled to London to view the twenty-five corpses and more than one-hundred and seventy body parts. From the moment of entry, I realised that for many this would be one of the most influential and impactful events of their young lives. It unlocked the mystery of the human body, so often in the past confined to a limited audience. Now, in this former brewery the general public could see for themselves the structure of man, the mechanics of movement and the network of vessels.

It was no ordinary exhibition. It was a celebration of human life in its most artistic form.

There was the triumphant male holding aloft his entire skin surface like a trophy, which of course it was, to reveal all the muscles and bones beneath. A twenty-five-year-old athlete, a perfect physical specimen dribbling a basketball with every complex muscle in his legs taught and displayed, and the skinned male sat at a table playing chess with his cranium split open to reveal the brain, contemplating the next move.

The exhibits of body parts provided unique comparisons between normal organs and those effected by life-style actions. There was the healthy lung with a soft grey colour and the black, brittle and smaller sample impacted by smoking. Both my children who visited the exhibition were impressed enough to never smoke. Ironically, the former brewery also had on display swollen livers, a consequence of alcoholism and arteries impeded by cholesterol. It provided students with an opportunity to re-evaluate their lifestyle with a visual demonstration of the consequences.

There was also a section in a separate enclosure where the most controversial exhibit was staged, that of a bisected women who was eight-months pregnant with her womb opened to reveal the foetus. Resting on a chaise longue it exhibited both beauty and tragedy. It was one of the most powerful images I have ever recorded. This enclosure also contained exhibits of foetus at different stages of development from six weeks onwards some with genetic disorders.

The whole exhibition was an educational journey the likes of which I had never experienced. The supporting information at every display was uncomplicated and clear, with in many cases a brief summary of the individuals. It was artistic, it was exciting, it was a whole new world.

My final memory was of an exhibit of a complete skeleton, sliced thinly in a vertical manner and displayed as we would hang clothes in a wardrobe. It demonstrated amazingly how every section of our unique frame protected the organs within.

On leaving the exhibition I gathered several students together for a photograph at which point Professor Von Hagens, donning a black fedora approached to inform me that photography was not permitted. Unfortunately, he was three hours too late, with many of the images shared with students during the ensuing years before a second visit to

Manchester some five years later.

Since that time in 2002, more than 47 million people have visited exhibitions throughout the world. Many of the students on that trip were grateful of having the opportunity to witness not only the exhibition and its content but for being one of the first schools brave enough to take the step forward and challenge controversy.

# Chapter Thirty

Despite the increasing success of the school in football and hockey, the department was under continual scrutiny by Freddie. I felt sorry for the other members because they did not deserve to be included in his obsessive quest. The request for detailed schemes of work and lesson plans, the compulsory attendance at meetings, increased reporting demands and the insistence that we remain for the full duration of every Parent's Evening regardless of the number of appointments. Very often on such occasions a fixture would end at 5.30 p.m., followed by a quick shower, change and into the hall for 6.00 p.m.

There was no concession, only pressure. We needed more time. The school was competing in many different sports throughout the year and with success came greater participation. There were local, county and national competitions. More meetings and more paperwork made significant demands on time, but the students were our priority. They came first. I would face the flack on behalf of the department. How many teachers would arrange to take their students to County trials on a Friday night, having delivered a full timetable during the week, had three after school fixtures and a Parent's Evening? It wasn't an isolated occurrence and yet when members of the department requested time away from school, usually a single day, to represent the County or the Midlands in their given sport it was denied.

During this time my mother, in her mid-seventies, lived alone in Manchester at our family home surrounded by people she had known for many years. She lived independently and was highly active within the community - raising money for a local school. However, a severe and almost fatal house fire caused by a burning cigarette resulted in her being hospitalised for several weeks, during which time she was assessed as having the early onset of dementia. The hospital would not allow her to leave until a place was established at a care home.

My mother moved to a wonderful old house on the edge of Rugeley about six miles from our family home, where she was well-cared for.

With its huge garden she was able to potter around and enjoy the outdoor space for a couple of years before her condition worsened needing her to receive more specialist care.

There was a home within walking distance of our house offering the care, but it was fully occupied and her name was placed on a waiting list. A few months later having arrived home after school I received a phone call informing me that a place had become available for my mother. I was delighted but could not confirm acceptance before gaining the approval of the social service manager in Manchester who were the funding agency. The home gave me a three-hour window to confirm.

The manager in Manchester had been made aware of the situation and had provided a direct number for me to contact him. The number was in my diary at school. I returned to school and to the staff work room where I had been prior to leaving school. The plastic box with my diary and other teaching materials was missing. The assistant caretaker could not explain where it had gone. I looked in my office and in other areas of the staff room without any luck. There were other boxes evident but not mine.

I requested more time from the care home, but sadly the place was designated to another person. The following morning the assistant caretaker called me over and informed me that the caretaker had been told by Freddie to lock the box away to "teach me lesson". Apparently, I was "personalising the space" in the work room and preventing others from access. There were six spaces in total on the long work surface concerned and four computers and a large round table to seat six on the other side. I was unsure of the logic.

I was furious and burst into his office without knocking. For once I raised my voice informing him that his actions had cost my mother a place of care which she needed. He tried to justify his actions by commenting that my leaving the yellow plastic box in the work room was intimidating to other staff who may want to use that space. Pathetic.

The following day he did offer a brief apology, but the damage had been done. I waited a further six months before a place several miles away became available where she would spend the remaining year of her life, receiving the care she deserved.

He continued to make my life more difficult than needed. He

instructed the IT technician to track my internet activities, and he often appeared in the work room when I was using the computer. It was laughable that so much energy and time was unnecessarily being expended on the exercise. It culminated in one of the most distasteful and disturbing actions of my teaching career. It brought home the folly of my leaving the Union where protection against any accusation, harassment or intimidation, exists for every member.

The two deputy head-teachers arrived in my office on a Thursday afternoon and requisitioned my laptop, all my files, books and video tapes. Apparently, an anonymous call had been made to the headteacher stating that I was hording pornographic material. They removed everything from the office to be reviewed. My only thought was that some of the video tapes had been sent to me by a former student who was a handball fanatic who would record World Championship games and send them to me. Of the dozen or so tapes I had only ever viewed three or four, so was reliant on Joe's impeccable character that the tapes featured handball only.

On Monday morning, following what must have been a fantastic weekend for Max and Paddy, the articles were returned and dumped in a pile on my office floor. That apparently was their instruction. There was no attempt to re-instate the files; that, I was told, was my responsibility.

In the grand scheme of things, I did not hold anyone responsible other than Freddie who acted like the Godfather surrounding himself with people who would not question his actions, deliberately targeting teachers for whom he had a dislike with unrealistic demands, hurtful comments and little empathy.

Nineteen years after he first took office, the man who had introduced several positive changes to the school but who had bullied and intimated several staff and who had tried his very best to remove me from my post with harassment, lack of encouragement or recognition retired, disappearing through the gates, down a lonely street into the sunset. I smiled for a moment and then without further thought, I returned to my day job, working with eight-hundred children not fighting against one adult.

# Chapter Thirty-One

Sometimes you just know. You look and you listen. Call it a gut reaction or whatever, but it is the feeling, that unexplainable feeling which drives your judgement.

For many years working with the Bunac organisation there were several occasions when a candidate walked into the room and within minutes you sense they were special. Was it the tone of their voice or their body language? Was it their personality or a combination of all three?

Knowledge and ability are of course necessary, but people working with young people need people skills. Children respond best to those adults who excite and encourage them, who value their actions or ideas, who engage and enjoy being with them. Enthusiasm is paramount.

In June 2003, interviews took place for a male member of staff to join the department. There had been three applicants, all in their final weeks at university. I along with the deputy head conducted the interviews, which were reduced to two on the day.

The first applicant was greatly confident and sociable and responded to all questions quickly and fully. His questions to me seemed to relate more to social aspects of school life. The second applicant seemed slightly nervous and reserved. His responses were measured and concise and his questions related to roles and responsibilities.

On the way back to the staff room he commented that he was desperate to get the job. It was not emotional blackmail, it was a genuine statement. I said nothing.

I returned to the Deputy's office. He was impressed by the first applicant and thought he would be a good fit for the school. I disagreed. He was overconfident and his responses lack substance. They were too quick and almost rehearsed; he was a talker not a doer. He would spend more time in the staff room than in the sports hall.

The second applicant was not as outgoing but had a nervous energy. In his quiet desperation I could see a determination to succeed. In my opinion this was someone who did not have all the answers, who was prepared not only to teach but also to learn. Phil was appointed and it was one of the best decisions of my life. He contributed not only to many extra-curricular clubs, but to the expansion of the physical education curriculum. It was a golden time within the department.

With the support of the PTA several table tennis tables were purchased. These provided opportunities not only during lesson time but also during lunch breaks and after school for students to be purposefully engaged in activity. Phil and I would often join groups for a quick game, with students often keen to challenge us. A coach was employed for one evening a week and very soon individuals improved dramatically to become leading players within the region, with some joining adult league teams.

A Zumba instructor was introduced to engage the more disenfranchised girls and this proved a major success even though it was short lived with the instructor accepting full-time employment out of the area. Nevertheless, it was ten weeks which allowed some students to reset and renew their involvement in physical activity.

The focus of the department remained team sports. The girls continually achieved success in hockey, with Mel the driving force and the boys maintained their position of strength in every age group in football and cross country. Following a few quiet years, handball began to emerge as a significant sport within the school again with opportunities to participate in regular district tournaments which I organised at Norton Canes high school during the winter term for every age group.

The new head teacher was an avid Evertonian with a firm belief in the value of sport. He sanctioned a trip to Spain for the school team to take part in a junior international handball tournament. The timing was perfect being in the final week of the school year causing little disruption within the school.

Along with my eldest son Paul, then a six former at the school, and an old friend Keith Kelly as kitman, we departed from Birmingham airport for Alicante in the middle of July for one week. The team of twelve fourteen-year-old boys were to be housed in a large school where several classrooms had been converted into dormitories for the many teams taking part, both male and female. It was not an unusual arrangement on mainland Europe.

The playing courts, canteen and an outdoor swimming area or a short walk away. Within a twenty- minute bus ride the beaches of Alicante provided rest and relaxation. It was perfect.

The lads only won one game, but they were competitive and performed well. They became extremely popular with some of the female teams, particularly a group from Sweden. There were several social events organised throughout the week but there was also much to do within the school campus with tennis, volleyball, football and table tennis available. With both security and many coaches present it was a safe haven for all players.

On the final night following the presentations, teams returned to the school where groups socialised in several different areas with music, chat and laughter. The "oldies" retired to bed well before the music stopped. I did get up in the early hours to visit the toilet noticing that several of our beds were empty. I was a little concerned until I stepped out along the balcony to find the main concourse was littered with twenty or so bodies, both male and female, all huddled together, covered in blankets, sleeping bags and laying on pillows. It looked as though they had been thrown into a pile but all of them were blissfully asleep.

The boys all said their brief goodbyes the following morning before leaving for Alicante airport which was about fifteen minutes away for our Ryanair flight back to Birmingham at 11.10 a.m. All the players were wearing their red tracksuit tops which enabled easy identification. By 10.00 a.m., we had checked through into the departure lounge which had only two gates, A and B. The whole lounge was probably just a little larger than our school hall. Stefan, my youngest son, asked for some money for a burger and all players were told to be at gate A for 10.45 a.m. to board the flight.

At 10.45 a.m., there were only ten players at the gate. I searched the three shops, the VIP room and the toilets for my son and another player, Matthew, without success. I checked the seating areas looking for any sign of the bright red tracksuit. Surely they had not gone out of the area? Security was asked to try and locate them on CCTV, again without any luck. The gate was now closing and I had to tell the group to board the flight whilst I tried to locate the two missing players. The crew quickly removed my checked-in bag. I stood at the gate with my bag in one hand and a recently purchased Daily Mirror in the other.

For a third time, I began to walk around the seating area which snaked around the room. There were people sat on the laptops, people reading and some curled up asleep. I was mystified and confused. Then I gave a quick double-take as I glanced at a curled-up figure, asleep, wearing an olive-green T-shirt, with black hair and tanned skin. A typical Spanish boy? No. This was my son, Stefan.

Playing out a scene made famous by Basil Fawlty and his broken-down car, I began lashing Stefan not with twigs but with the rolled-up newspaper, much to the alarm of those sitting nearby.

"Wake up, wake up," I said through gritted teeth. "You need to wave goodbye to the Lads." He quickly rejoined the world of the living at which point I directed his attention to the airplane that was in the process of rising into the clear blue sky. Our intended flight home.

I located the other player asleep in a window well wearing a white T-shirt. It transpired that both were tired from their previous night's socialising and decided to use their tracksuit tops as a pillow, folding them in such a way that only the grey lining was visible.

We had to leave the departure lounge and book another flight leaving later in the afternoon. I notified the school about the incident, but more concerning was the phone call to my wife Diane to explain that having lost our youngest son I had now managed to locate him. However, our new flight was to East Midlands Airport and we would need a lift. The verbal battering didn't last as long as I expected and she agreed to meet me at Arrivals, by which time I knew she would greet me with a shake of the head and a smile.

When the main group arrived at Birmingham Airport the school minibus was waiting for them as arranged. The driver a teacher at the school asked where I was.

"He is still in Spain looking for a couple of the lads," someone called out.

The driver apparently smiled and shook his head.

"That old chestnut. He's inside waiting for his bag and you want me to drive off for a laugh."

Paul then made him aware of the situation, but he still failed to believe him. After fifteen minutes waiting time he finally departed, unsure and confused.

Three days after our return and the last day of the school year a friend called me and advised that I look at the front page of the Express and Star regional evening newspaper. The article in question had a headline:

*"Teacher leaves children in Spain"*

The article was factually incorrect, but even more alarming was that the reporter had made no effort to contact me for information.

That same summer my wife and I, accompanied by Stefan, returned to Spain for a holiday. Those travelling through the airport must have thought it strange to see a father holding the hand of his fourteen-year-old son until they were safely through to boarding.

The following year we again returned to the competition, minus Paul who had other commitments. Sadly, it did not end well. On the Sunday morning, we played a game close to the main court and the players decided to stay to watch some Senior Games. Keith and I decided to walk back to the school via the Catholic Church to find out the times of Mass later in the day.

When we arrived at the school a police car pulled up to the gates and a couple of our team emerged. The officer explained that some local youths had made an unprovoked attack as they were leaving the court area, witnessed by many, before running off. The boys informed me that there were several youths gathered at the court, and they seemed to target Johno, one of our stronger players. When they attacked him by the food area several of our players rushed in to help and the attackers eventually moved away. Luckily, no one was injured, with one of the organising committee present to witness the incident assuring me that there was no blame attached to our group.

For the next day I remained vigilant, insisting that the whole group moves together. The evening activity in the main square was a Mr and Mrs Torrellano event. We had entered Nick, a colourful character in many ways with his Hawaiian shirts and ginger hair sure to catch the eye of the judges.

With the competition about to start one of the players informed me that the older youth leaning against the wall about twenty yards behind me, holding a drink, was the gang leader who had initiated the attack the previous day. He was a few years older than our boys. I took out my Nikon camera and asked Keith to pose for a photograph, as I surreptitiously 'zoomed in' on the leader. Click. Photograph of the main culprit accomplished.

Several minutes into the start of the event I noticed a large group of boys gathering at one end of the square. I quickly got a message to our players to leave using the main road at the opposite end to the gang of youths and return to school which was about five minutes away. I told Keith to wait for Nick.

Turning into the wasteland which was in front of the school we were confronted by the group of charging youths' intent on causing harm. I managed to hold back a few allowing some of the players to get inside safely, others managed to avoid them and reach safety. However, one boy Alex, was being kicked by a couple of thugs. I raced over and charged into one knocking him over and the other youth ran away. The two security guards were useless and offered no help other than to phone for an ambulance and the police.

The police arrived quickly but the group had dispersed. A couple of police officers asked questions and I informed them that I had a photograph of the gang leader. Some adults had gathered outside the gate and one, aged about twenty, stepped forward to ask for my camera - suggesting that he may know the individual. I passed him the camera at which point the officer grabbed his arm firmly and ordered him to leave and return the camera. The officer acted quickly because he feared that the guy intended to erase the image. He viewed the photograph which revealed some distinctive facial markings, and then left. Alex was admitted to hospital with a suspected fractured rib where he stayed for three days before being released with severe bruising. Nick was runner up in the competition.

The following evening, a smirking gang leader arrived at the school to watch some of the games. His demeanour quickly changed when three police officers arrived, placed him forcibly against the wall before putting handcuffs on him and pushing him into their vehicle.

The next time I saw him was at the police station the following day when I was asked to identify him. His overnight stay had obviously been very unpleasant and he seemed in some pain as he sat on a chair whimpering, a far cry from the bravado of the previous evening.

Several months later I was informed that he was sentenced in a Spanish court for organising the attacks. Despite many invitations we never returned to compete in Torrellano again.

# Chapter Thirty-Two

My three children all attended the school I worked at. We lived in the catchment area and not only was it convenient, but the school had a strong reputation, academically, pastorally and in sport. The positives outweighed the negatives, but it did create an unusual challenge for all parties.

They had access to all the facilities at the school whilst waiting for my meetings to finish and in some cases additional help to complete their homework. The Bank of Dad was never far away should they wish to supplement their intake of food, and they were always included in appropriate external visits.

The downside was the expectation placed on them by some staff which was unrealistic. They set a high benchmark for both attainment and behaviour. They were well above average academically. However, they were normal children and sometimes they would misbehave. What I did notice was they performed best for teachers with character and personality.

There were a couple of staff who would approach me with a complaint during the school day. It was not a concern, but a complaint and it was during my working day. They would express disappointment at their behaviour or commitment to a task. All I asked was for consistency, to treat them as they would any other student, make an entry in the student daybook so that when at home (in parent mode) my wife and I could discuss it with them in a domestic setting. Surprisingly, they rarely responded to my request to enter a comment.

In later years all three selected to pursue courses in Physical Education both at GCSE and Advanced level. Being one of their tutors there was added pressure and scrutiny regarding marks attained during the course by each. The additional guidance they received was offset by the more rigorous assessment. Nowhere was this more evident with my son Paul.

He was a very committed student who submitted some quality work. He was on course for the highest grade at Advance level. The course included some practical assessments and an examination. The practical assessments not only included personal performance but also evidence of knowledge of performance, the strengths and weaknesses of an athlete and guidance on necessary improvements.

Several schools combined for the assessment day at a local comprehensive school where football, netball and badminton were being staged. Football provided the greatest number of candidates with a cross-section of performers. On this cohort's assessment day, the senior advisor for OCR in the region was in attendance in addition to the usual moderator. During the dozen years involved with and in some cases organising assessments it was the only time he ever attended.

His main concern appeared to be the analysis and assessment task. Students were asked to choose a player taking part in the football match and to analyses their strengths and weaknesses. They were then expected to deliver guidance to the player, both technically and tactically in the presence of an allocated teacher who would then provide an appropriate mark. My son was allocated to the senior advisor and the moderator.

My candidate had completed his assessment within five minutes and was delivering his findings. He had selected, as many did, a friend from his school, producing an analysis which had been scripted days before and was based on prior knowledge rather than the evidence of the day. A quick glance over to Paul revealed that he was still making notes and had yet to start his delivery.

During conversations with him regarding football I had always stressed that coaching follows observation. That players need time and opportunity before any accurate and appropriate comment can be made regarding their ability. Having chosen a random player, he spent almost fifteen minutes analysing the performance on the day.

On completion of his delivery the moderators both walked over to me with the Senior advisor stating that Paul had "swallowed the book" and his analysis and guidance was the most comprehensive he had encountered in years. They suggested the mark given by the school could have been higher.

A few months later the examination schedule began. The second paper for Physical Education was scheduled for 1.30 p.m. on a Friday afternoon, lasting three hours. Due to there being less than twenty candidates the examination secretary for the school decided to change the time and location at the very last minute. The group were moved from the normal examination centre to a small classroom and the examination start time changed to 1.00 p.m.

Not only was the room cramped but there was no signage in preparation for the examination. The external invigilator (non-teacher) distributed the papers without any additional instruction or reference to protocols and started the examination at 1.00 p.m.

Approximately five minutes into the session, Paul's phone rang. He did not answer the call but did give the phone to the invigilator. Several other candidates reacted by either turning off their phone or offering it to the invigilator.

At the end of the day, I was called to the new headteacher's office and told that the incident had to be reported to OCR, the examination body, for transparency reasons. He believed due to the fact it was at the very beginning of the examination with no candidate in the process of completing an answer there would be no repercussion. I understood his rationale and the need to follow the set protocols.

The two dates that impact most on any child in the United Kingdom are the results day for A level examinations and then traditionally a week later GCSE. For some it can have a serious impact on their well-being and effect long term plans. For others it is the gateway to a new and exciting challenge.

Paul's results were good and as expected except for Physical Education. In view of the incident the board had eradicated 80% of the marks from the second paper which reduced his grade from A to D. I was advised to appeal against the decision even though he had received an unconditional offer from the University in Manchester

Following a review of the OCR procedures which clearly stated that all appeals will be judged on their individual circumstances I submitted an appeal against their decision. A date was set and I was asked to travel to Cambridge to meet the panel.

In stating my case I informed the panel of the change of venue and time. I also indicated that the main hall had multiple signs regarding phones, electronic equipment and regulations with several boxes placed at the entrance to accommodate their temporary disposal. In the alternative venue there were no signs and no receptacles. This was an oversight by the school.

The phone did ring five-minutes into the examination, before any candidate began to write and was removed from a pocket and handed to the invigilator. The phone itself could not have provided any aid to the candidate as the examination at other centres in the area was not due to start for twenty-five minutes. The call, we later discovered, was from the England Handball coach informing him of his selection for the Under-23 team. Bittersweet.

Despite the production of work completed and comments made by the moderator; the panel ruled against me. They felt there had to be greater reasons for the school to submit the incident for consideration. All was not what it seemed, despite the written submissions of the invigilator and the head of sixth form.

They stated the headteacher had the capacity to deal with the incident internally but had chosen not to. I assured them that he was only following the existing protocols and being new to the school was concerned that all issues be dealt with in a consistent and transparent manner.

It would appear, very much in keeping with the student and his scripted conclusion, written days before the presented evidence, the Board too had made its decision long before I entered the field of play.

The situation had little impact on Paul's future. He completed a year at university before being selected to be part of the Great Britain handball squad, based in Denmark in preparation for the London Olympics.

There was no animosity towards Michael, the new headteacher. He did what he felt was the right thing to do at the time. The response by the Board would no doubt influence future actions.

He was a very keen sportsman with an interest in rugby, cricket and football. We would often enjoy long conversations about football and sport in general. He had an open-door policy and was not in the least intimidating. He would listen and respond when necessary.

The communication to staff also became more regular and diverse. Notices about events and awards were regularly shared on the Staffroom notice board. It appeared that since his appointment the amount of information made available to staff had increased considerably.

One such notice would lead to one of the great experiences of my life. The Goldsmiths Company invited teachers with over ten years' experience to apply for an annual award to venture on the "Trip of a Lifetime." It was an annual award which had existed for many years but for which information had never previously been made available to the staff at the school.

The conditions were simple. The trip should last between twenty-one and fifty-five days and be a solo venture. It must occur primarily during school-time, with part of the £5,000 award given to the school for supply teacher costs. The venture should be educational and have some impact on future teaching. The recipient must produce a photographic account of the complete trip for the Trustees.

Rose, who at the time was the School Sports Coordinator attached to the Department, informed me that she had successfully applied for the award several years earlier, travelling to New Zealand. Michael granted me approval to apply and offered his support and the awards office confirmed there was no age restriction.

There were two adventures which would provide challenge and enrichment. The first was to travel down the Andes from north to south eventually ending the journey in Santiago, Chile. After several considerations, namely a language barrier and safety of a lone traveller, I opted for the second option to travel across the United States from the Atlantic to the Pacific Ocean whilst also following the trail of Butch Cassidy and living the life of a cowboy. Some people would comment, no doubt, that I had lived the latter all my life!

During my many years of working in the United States my travels had been restricted by time to the east or west coast. I knew that there was another America out there. I wanted a piece of that America.

In March 2008, I received a letter informing me that I had been short listed and to attend an interview with the Trustees at Goldsmiths' Hall in London. The hall situated in the City of London and built in 1835 was magnificent, with some of its areas used to portray Buckingham Palace in films. The room hosting the interviews was equally impressive with its high ornate ceilings and huge table around which gathered the Trustees. Lord Sutherland welcomed me and introduced me to the members of the panel, one of whom was a current headteacher. Apparently, a supporting letter from Michael was both complimentary and informative, with Lord Sutherland describing it as an exceptional reference for a job rather than a supporting letter for an award.

I explained to the panel that having travelled a hundred miles inland to work in the summer camps I noticed a change not only in the landscape but the people. They seemed to move to a different drum. It was just the tip of an iceberg. US 50 extending from Ocean City in the east to Carson City in the west would provide the ideal pathway to explore the nation.

The secretary to the Trustees, Warren Benbow then asked about my desire to follow the trail of Butch Cassidy and live on a ranch. The panel were amazed when I informed them that Butch Cassidy was actually born as Robert LeRoy Parker and his grandfather was from Accrington, just north of my birthplace Manchester. He changed his name to Cassidy after the foreman who first introduced him to rustling. I also informed them that Wyatt Earp was a descendant from the Earp family in Walsall. I was surrounded by cowboy folklore.

Four weeks later I received a letter granting the award. I was numb with excitement. The dream was now a reality. The rolling tide of traffic on the M6 would be replaced for the summer by US 50, often referred to as the "Loneliest Road in America".

# Chapter Thirty-Three

On the 27th of June 2008, I stepped off the plane at Washington's Dulles Airport in the United States. It would be another two hours waiting on line for immigration clearance before I could pick up my rucksack, sleeping bag and tent which had by now been deposited in a large pile in a far corner of baggage collection along with other bags, boxes and a variety of marked musical instruments belonging to a large group of travelling Budhists who were slowly trickling through the limited entry booths. Picking up my rental car was considerably easier. The small red Datsun was fitted with a sat NAV which I renamed Joan. During the next twenty-eight days we would have many disagreements as to which way I should travel.

The first dilemma was in the direction of travel. I had not realised that the Atlantic Ocean was four hours' drive east - which was the opposite direction to where I intended to go. However, my plan was to the travel from the Atlantic Ocean to the Pacific and there could be no shortcuts. I stayed overnight in Ocean City, Maryland before taking a dip in the freezing Atlantic. The journey began the minute I saw the sign above the highway indicating the start of US 50 with Sacramento, California 3,020 miles in the distance.

It was a clear and sunny day with partial cloud, and I was making good time keeping to the maximum speed limit as I crossed Chesapeake Bay. The Eagles version of a Jackson Browne song *"Take it Easy"* was playing on the radio and it suddenly re-set my whole thinking. Why am I in such a hurry? With no responsibility and a generous amount of time to reach San Francisco I could indeed take it easy.

The journey across the Bay was so relaxing with various sailing craft enjoying the day. The music was good, and the presenter had a good sense of humour. He referred to the episode of the Sopranos aired the evening before on the Arts Channel. The channel prohibits any profanity, and the dialogue was dubbed with the word "fuck" being replaced by "forget" with conversations often including the phrase "forget you". In doing so, the whole cast, he observed, appeared to display the early onset of Alzheimer's.

The early evening was spent in Arlington Cemetery situated on a hillside overlooking Washington DC. It was an amazing celebration of life through death with total tranquillity and a brief historical guide through the conflicts and challenges that have confronted the country during the past three-hundred years. There was the small white Christian cross which marked the gravesite of Robert Kennedy, powerful in its simplicity with words from two of his most famous speeches engraved on the flat stone. The shrine to his more famous brother was more elaborate.

Moving west along US 50 the following morning I decided to pull into the town of Parkersburg. I parked the car as two nurses were passing. I asked them about the town to which they replied:

"The only thing we have here honey is the jail and the historic square. Take your pick," at which they smiled with the "have a nice day" expression to which I was now warming.

The historic Julia-Ann square had thirty-four houses as its focus. Built after the civil war by cash rich oil barons each house was totally different than the next, the most imposing of which is 1209 Ann Street, the Van Winkle-Wix house built in 1836 with imposing turrets and spires. It appeared to have been built with movies in mind. Many of the residents had gone to great lengths to maintain the original features of each home.

Having taken photographs of several buildings, Mae a resident in her late sixties sitting on her porch, enquired about the purpose of my interest. When I told her about my trip, she invited me into her home to look around. The rooms were exquisitely decorated with furniture from another era, some with a distinct colonial feel. The house appeared to have been unchanged for the past hundred years with Its story immaculately preserved. A widow of five years, the family she raised there had moved out of state long ago east and west. She offered me a cold drink as I gazed at the large garden at the rear of the house with its array of ornamental plants, flowers and bushes. It could easily have been the subject of a pictorial feature in a magazine, and it was all her own work.

This was the America I was searching for - the warm-hearted and sociable, the kind and the caring. People in control of the pace of their lives, with time to stop, share and embrace the things that matter.

The onward journey to Cincinnati started well with skies broken by sunshine. However, within a couple of hours the weather changed dramatically. I was driving into a storm. I was on a two-lane highway with conditions deteriorating rapidly into those of a cyclone. I could not see ten yards ahead of me with a continual wave of water battering the windscreen. The wipers were useless.

I had to reduce my speed dramatically relying on the visual display of the satellite navigation system to inform me of bends in the road. There were no exits, and I was surrounded by tons of shining metal all intent on informing me of their presence with a klaxon not out of place on the Titanic. They were all travelling at twice my speed and I was convinced it was just a matter of time before one of them would hit the rear of my car, terminating my existence in some remote place in Ohio. It was the most frightening hour of my life. When I finally arrived at the hotel I could not let go of the steering wheel, my fingers seemed to be locked.

I checked in, just managing to hold a pen to sign the register. The three-hour journey had taken nearly four and a half hours. Across from the hotel on the other side of a huge carpark was a Wal Mart and several stores. I had barely left reception when I was approached by a lady in her thirties offering to satisfy my every need. Unfortunately, she did not appear to be from Meals on Wheels so I thanked her kindly, declined the offer and headed over to the All You Can Eat Chinese Buffet.

The restaurant had many options, and the food looked tasty. I did, however, become aware of the blight that threatens the overall health of many Americans, the All You Can Eat Buffet. I had soup to start and a main meal of rice and chicken with some additional prawns. I was asked a couple of times if the food was okay. When I requested the bill, the manager asked if there was an issue with the food. I noticed that tables near to me had several empty plates piled high and they were still eating. It was an occurrence I would observe several times during the trip. Man versus food.

I left two plates and a tip for a bemused manager and entered the Wal Mart store where the second threat to welfare hit me at the entrance, a gun sales counter. In the United Kingdom very often the first product you encounter in a supermarket are flowers. Sadly, various handguns and rifles available for purchase by anyone over the age of eighteen had replaced roses and lilies.

I spent a couple of days in Cincinnati before moving west. The storms had left a mark on St. Louis where the Mississippi had broken its banks and flooded many areas. It did not, however, prevent me from sitting in a carriage the size of a small toilet with three strangers whilst slowly ascending the Gateway Arch. Clad in stainless steel the structure is 630 feet high with a narrow viewing area at its summit some five minutes (seemed much longer) after departure. The views were spectacular.

There was time to visit Blueberry Hill, the legendary music club, for a burger. Opened in 1972, the club featured a jukebox that attracted visitors from across America with its constantly changing selection of music, with the owner professing to have 30,000 records. In the course of time, 'live' music became a feature, with Chuck Berry appearing every month in the Duck Room from 1996 for the next sixteen years.

I could not leave the city without visiting the historic town of St. Charles. Situated on the banks of the Missouri river it was the starting point for the expedition by Lewis and Clark to discover a routeway to the Pacific Ocean. The group of forty began their journey which would last for two years in May 1804, travelling through unchartered areas. What made the journey remarkable was for almost 1,500 miles, until they reached the Continental Divide near the Lemhi Pass, the expedition moved against the flow of the Missouri river. With its old streets and dedicated museum, it provided not only some fascinating information but one of the best lemonades I have ever tasted.

The advantage of being a solo traveller is the ability to change course without having to consult any other party. On the way to St. Louis, I had decided to drive south to Marion to attend a minor league baseball game which the whole town seemed to attend with many activities to keep younger children engaged both before and during the game. The drive through Missouri had provided a unique experience. For approximately five miles the road was made up of steep rises and falls in what appeared to be the longest roller-coaster in the world. It is the only State in America which does not number their highways, instead they have letters. The DD highway had obviously been named by someone with a sense of humour.

I also left US 50 in Kansas to travel south to Emporia, a small University town which was the home of the Teacher's National Hall of Fame. Each year five teachers from across America are inducted into the Hall of Fame, presented with a scroll and a thousand dollars to be given to a student of their choice to advance their education. Built in 1992, it provides permanent recognition of the work of teachers, something sadly lacking in England.

Following a quick visit to Wichita, the birthplace of William Bonney and the Museum of the Wild West an appetiser for my ongoing travels I moved on to Greensburg a town which, a year earlier had been devastated by a tornado. The 1.7 mile-wide, path of destruction had reduced 95% of the town to rubble, with only one of its eight churches remaining. People had travelled from across the country to help with the recovery process. Many of the residents were now living in trailers on temporary sites but remained optimistic and extremely grateful for the help they had received. The most alarming feature was the makeshift local hospital which was a series of battle-field tents previously used in areas of conflict thousands of miles from Kansas.

Back on US 50, the highway runs alongside the rail track for much of the journey through Kansas separated only by the telegraph wires aptly described in the Dire Straits song Telegraph Road. This is bible belt country with the radio saturated with sermons. The only respite is the Bob Seegar CD which I purchased at Wal Mart which was on continual play until reaching Dodge City.

Dodge City celebrates its unique place in American history with the cast iron statue of ten cowboys on horseback which greet travellers arriving in the city. The statue of Wyatt Earp celebrates its most famous resident who during his time had a close allegiance with Batt Masterson and Doc Holliday. It is also the home of Boot Hill cemetery, the burial place of thirty-nine unfortunate souls who had crossed the law. Each has a wooden tombstone with my favourite being for Edward Hurley who was shot on 17th January 1873 with the inscription:

*"He drank too much and loved unwisely."*

The ongoing journey was long and uninteresting with flat roads, the constant whistle of the wind and tumbleweed. I decided to change course and head south into Colorado and across desolate Indian Reservation land towards Durango.

On route I decided to stop at the Great Sand Dunes National Park. With snow-capped mountains in the distance the thirty square miles of the park is one huge sandbox, a freak of nature with its highest point being 750 feet high. I was informed that it normally takes an hour to reach the summit which I thought at the time was over exaggerated.

Forty minutes into the climb on the unforgiving soft sand and only three quarters of the way up the dune I decided to rest with sweat tricking from my head and down my back. With temperatures in the seventies even at 8,000 feet above sea level I was knackered. I lay down and rested my head on the small rucksack with the warm sun on my face and closed my eyes. With thoughts of ending the task and returning to the canteen below running through my mind, I was suddenly disturbed by the noise of a small group nearby. I sat up. At first, I thought it was a mirage. It was indeed a small group, seven male dwarfs (I kid you not) running past my wilting body in search of the summit. Talking and seemingly full of energy, taking significantly more steps than I would need to reach the distant peak. It was time to stop being Snow White, drink some water and join the parade.

The views from the summit were amazing, with people in the distance appearing to be ants weaving their way through the sand. The descent was much quicker made up of giant strides and intermittent leaps into the soft surface. It brought out the child in me, throwing my small rucksack way ahead as I tumbled and rolled, unnoticed and free.

By late afternoon I reached Durango, the first stage of my Rocky Mountain expedition where I would visit the many places from Telluride to Thermopolis made famous by the outlaw Butch Cassidy.

# Chapter Thirty-Four

The United Campsite just on the outskirts of Durango is a smart and well-cared for site which slopes gently down to a river. The site is dissected by the Durango-to-Silverton narrow gauge railway line, which carries passengers on a picturesque ride through the Rockies.

The receptionist was very friendly and welcoming and once establishing that it was my first visit to Durango insisted that I visit Mesa Verde and various other local sites of interest of which he assured me there were many. Then he leaned across the desk and whispered:

"I apologise but I have had to put you next to the Navajo family," whilst circling an area down the hill near the river on a map of the camp which he then handed to me.

For the next four nights, which included Independence Day, home would be the soft patch of grass next to a couple of tents belonging to "The Navajo family." A dozen yards to my right was a large modern canvas structure with windows, separate bedrooms and a dining area furnished with a table, chairs and a small barbeque. My two-man tent purchased from Decathlon and my fold-up chair seemed a poor statement. It did not take long for the residents on the rich side of town to approach me as I sat in my chair enjoying the sunshine and a bottle of beer. The woman in her late forties introduced herself as a teacher from Ohio and I explained briefly that I had ended my school year early having been granted an opportunity to explore America and experience its people, places and culture. She then warned me to be very careful about the Navajo family, adding that they were from the reservation. I made some small talk and thanked her. I never spoke to her again. The America I was searching for was only a few feet away.

I made it my mission to talk to Ella and Charlie Big Thumb who were on a two-week vacation with their son Carlton and his three children aged between six and ten years. Ella was warm and sociable ever ready to make conversation. She explained that this was their annual holiday from their home at Window Rock, the Navajo reservation in Arizona.

We would engage in conversation every morning and in the early evening. She provided a fascinating insight into the life of a Native American. Carlton's wife an Iroquois Indian had died a few years earlier and he, like many of the younger generation, was forced to travel hundreds of miles from the reservation to earn money in construction to support the family. The older generation remain at home with little but the barren land to keep them occupied.

She talked with pride about the history and culture and how in 1864 the US government in a land grab, forced 9,000 Navajo men, women and children to leave their ancient home with a 300-mile journey into New Mexico. Known as The Long Walk, it claimed many lives and it was nearly a hundred years before they were eventually returned to their spiritual home.

One of the most widely spoken Native American languages it is often referred to as an "unwritten language." Ella informed me of the Navajo Code Talkers who were enrolled by the US army during the Pacific War. At a time when the Japanese were able to intercept communications on a regular basis the introduction of the Navajo language with its complex grammar and syntax was indecipherable to anyone without knowledge of the strange and complicated dialects. The war in the Pacific turned dramatically as a result.

Thirty-five miles west of Durango is the Mesa Verde National Park, where a thousand years earlier ancient Pueblo Indians had built homes into the rock face of the canyon. In one specific tower the windows were positioned in such a way as to indicate the season using the light from the sun.

The males would often climb to the top of the Canyon to tend their crops or hunt for food. They were essentially farmers, not warriors.

With any death, the body would be wrapped tightly in a thick blanket along with possessions and rolled into the canyon below. The whole place was an amazing testament to the skill of the Pueblo nation.

My stay in Durango was short and enjoyable. I thanked Ella and Charlie for their hospitality and headed north through the Rockies stopping at Silverton for a Sarsaparilla, the drink of cowboys at Natalia's. It is the starting point of the Billion Dollar Highway so named because of the precious metals mined in the area. It passes through some of

America's most scenic landscape on its route to Telluride and the start of the Butch Cassidy story.

Telluride is now a famous ski-resort but retains much of its authenticity with old wooden buildings, including the scene of Butch's first robbery. The San Miguel Valley Bank, now converted into a cycle shop, was relieved of $21,000 during the escapade on 24th June 1889. The former jailhouse was now a public library and one of the oldest Post Offices in the country was situated on the outskirts at Placerville.

My ongoing journey northwards through the Rockies towards US 50 was not without a concern. It was late afternoon, and I began to feel quite nauseous and light-headed. I pulled into a supermarket and walked a short distance for some fresh air still feeling unwell. I had discovered at Cincinnati that my mobile coverage was for the UK only. I was able to call England but not anywhere in the USA. In the event of an emergency, I may as well have carried a pigeon on my travels.

A short distance along the road was a motel, which I checked into, closed all the curtains and in the darkness of the room slept for thirteen hours. The following day, feeling fine I checked out, with the receptionist suggesting that I had experienced altitude sickness. I was apprehensive as the next part of the journey would take me high into the Rockies.

At Monarch Pass, with an elevation of 11,312 feet, I sat at what would be the first of many Continental Divides. These are the high points where water either flows east to the Atlantic or west to the Pacific. The cable car tested my recovery by taking me to 12,000 feet with no further effect.

It would soon be time to leave US 50 again and head north on US 24 towards historic Leadville and the Rocky Mountain National Park, passing places such as Robber's Roost, where the clue was in the name.

Leadville, the highest city in the United States at 10,000 feet above sea level has a history which epitomises the phrase the Wild West. The wealth of the town was built on its vast silver mines, once the largest and richest in the world. By 1880 there were over 15,000 people living in the city, with more than sixty saloons and brothels catering for the mining community. It was lawless, with shootings common place.

The Tabor Opera House, a three-storey building opened in 1879 still stands in the same pristine condition as when Oscar Wilde delivered a lecture on The Decorative Arts to 888 people on a Thursday evening in

1882. After the performance he was taken to the Silver Dollar Saloon directly across the street. In his recollections of the visit, Wilde said:

"Here I saw the only rational method of art criticism I have ever come across. Over the piano was printed a notice: *Please do not shoot the pianist. He is doing his best.*

The Silver Dollar saloon was my first place of call with its swing doors still in operation. The place appears to have retained all its features from when it first opened in 1879 and in some places the dust! I ordered a large beer only to be told by the bar tender, a woman sporting a black-eye, that draft beer was not available because of the air pressure. When she opened the bottle, it foamed like a magnum of champagne leaving a trail of ale along the highly polished bar which curved round towards a quiet room at the rear featuring a visual history of the wild west.

There were photographs of Wild Bill Hickok, Annie Oakley, Batt Masterson, William Bonney and Mart Duggan, a fearless gunfighter who was appointed marshal in 1878 to bring law and order to the town. Ten years later he too was shot and killed. The Saloon had played host to the Hole in the Wall gang and Doc Holliday, the legendary gambler and friend of Wyatt Earp who was involved (with the Earp brothers) at the famous gunfight at the OK Corral. The table at which he played, and allegedly shot a cheat remains set in place.

Leadville, with a population of less than 3,000 was still ambitious. A year previous they had hosted the first Independence Film Festival, with a second organised in September. There was also a marathon race planned and various other attractions for tourists.

It would have been discourteous not to have a second and third beer and allow my imagination to dance with joy in the back room with its history and resident ghost.

The drive along Trail Ridge Road through the Rocky Mountain National Park was only thirty-five miles long but took nearly four hours to complete. Around every corner was a view to die for with snow-capped mountains and flower-filled meadows. I sat in snow in the middle of July.

On one occasion I sat on a wall watching a herd of mule deer crossing the road casually several yards away. I was suddenly made aware of movement from behind me with six large Elk ambling in my direction without a care in the world. This was their land. We were guests. They crossed the road and climbed to the ridge on the other side and as some of the herd disappeared from view the two largest members as if by design or expectation turned and stood motionless and proud against a sky-blue backdrop punctured by snow-capped peaks as if making a statement to their transfixed audience below.

On leaving the park I headed north through Laramie towards Grand Teton National Park a journey of four hundred miles across the Great Divide a desolate area where oil drilling appeared to be the only activity. I stopped at Grandma's Café, the only place for food for forty miles.

I ordered the "no frills" turkey sandwich, which was huge, thanked Grandma (evidently not a person to cross according to a couple of oil workers) and left a tip.

My only other stop was at Fort Washakie on the Wind River Reservation, home of the Shoshone Tribe. Chief Washakie was one of the most revered figures in Native American culture. He was a great warrior who defended his tribe against enemies but encouraged dialogue with "the white men." His contribution to peace was recognised in Washington and when he died at the age of one hundred, he became the only Native American to be given a full military funeral.

It was also the burial place of Sacaweja, famed for her contribution to the Lewis-Clark expedition where she acted as interpreter and peacemaker with the many tribes they confronted in their search for a passage to the Pacific.

The two-hour drive to the Grand Tetons National Park was a mixture of forest and plains made memorable by the spectacle of a herd of wild horses with a mixture of colours, running free across the arid land.

The Tetons were named by French trappers (Trois Tetons), and it is easy to appreciate their humour with the translation being three breasts. They can indeed be seen from over forty miles away as they draw you towards their magnificent landscape. It would be my home for three days before making a short journey to Yellowstone.

On the second day I decided to go into Jackson Hole. On route I noticed that many vehicles had stopped at the side of the road. Out of curiosity I pulled over. In the adjacent field were two sibling Grizzly Bears grazing. It provided a great opportunity for a photograph and video as bears are rarely seen.

On cue for my video the bears began to move towards the road, slowly at first and then a little quicker at which point a Ranger screamed at me to get back into my vehicle. I ran the short distance, clambered into the driver's seat seconds before the two bears reached the road where they eventually crossed into the wooded area on the other side. The irate Ranger walked slowly over to my car to inform me that the bears can run at speeds of forty miles per hour over short distances, and though they have pepper spray to protect the public from harm they are reluctant to use it because in his words "they live here, you don't." A fair comment. I pulled away slightly embarrassed but more knowledgeable.

The scenery within the park was breath-taking with the snow-covered peaks overseeing Jackson Lake with its crystal-clear water providing a mirror image of the world above. The mountain trails, waterfalls and gushing rivers provided a sensory explosion for all those on the narrow paths. Each morning, I would take my fold-away chair to the shoreline at Coulter Bay and sit in the silence for a while, at peace with the world as the rising sun, warm, gentle and dependable slowly appeared over the distant forest.

It was soon time to move on from the serenity and majesty of the Grand Tetons one-hundred and sixty miles northwards to Yellowstone National Park, one of God's gifts to mankind.

The park covers a total area of 3,400 square miles with many of its roads only open for part of the year. On arrival I was provided with the safety leaflet advising travellers to use defined trails only and ways to keep safe from wildlife, particularly bears. It contained information for the storage or disposal of food near your tent, reminding everyone that bears have an acute sense of smell and are attracted by unusual odours. I was also informed to be extra vigilant as there had been reports over the past few days of a bear in the vicinity of my designated camping area. Not an issue as I did not carry food, but then when unpacking my sleeping bag, I noted that the contents of my aftershave had leaked considerably into the soft feather down. The inside of my tent was transformed into a giant testing station for Chanel and for the next two nights a place of paranoia where every movement outside was depicted as an inquisitive bear searching for a snack rather than a sniff.

Yellowstone is alive with colour and activity. From bubbling pools of blue, yellow and all shades in between to streams of water heated from thermal springs and magnificent waterfalls. At every turn there is a thing of beauty. It was impossible to drive any distance through the park without stopping seemingly every few minutes to take in the surroundings. Ole Faithful provided its extensive audience with its regular display, gushing water almost a hundred feet into the air. Nearby rocks leading into Firehole River were streaked with gold and copper as the steaming water ran down them.

I decided to make the sixty-mile trip north to Mammoth Hot Springs, close to the Montana Border, which is an area of crystalised rock. During the journey (which took nearly three hours) I saw three buffalo walking in line on the opposite side of the road in the traffic. They would occasionally pass a stationary vehicle and walk along the centre line for a while brushing into the occasional wing mirror but oblivious to the human population in awe of these magnificent beasts. They were in no hurry, and neither were the vehicles. A little further along the route I came across Hayden Valley where I saw a herd of buffalo in their hundreds grazing on the land below.

Mammoth Hot Springs did not disappoint. Though not an extensive area it provided a landscape like no other, a different world, a different planet. With large, rounded mounds of white rock infused with browns and golds and steam gently rising from the crystal white surface below. There were stagnant pools with decayed trees standing guard as they had done for years.

Sadly, my time in Yellowstone was over but not before I had seen the sunrise at 5.30 a.m. over Yellowstone Lake with the rising steam from hidden thermal springs adding to the already imposing view.

It was now time to live the life of a cowboy.

# Chapter Thirty-Five

Twenty-six miles east from Yellowstone Park lies the Bill Cody Ranch. Once home to the legendary figure known as Buffalo Bill it still retained its links with the frontier lifestyle. The basic log cabins are close to the corrals with horses of every description. There are some separate areas where a horse is broken to be eventually ridden by guests across the wide and varied expanse of Wyoming.

This would be my home for the next seven days, five of which would be spent riding, something which I had not done for many years. Check in made it very clear that breakfast would be 7.00 a.m. with the trailers and horses ready to move out at 8.00 a.m.

The first day involved a three-hour trek through some woodland and raised grassland on a grey called Spur. He was exceedingly kind and just lolled along without any drama. This apparently was one of the horses used for riders with limited experience. The small group of riders stopped for lunch by the side of a fast-flowing stream with ice cold water. Josh our leader cooked burgers on a hastily built campfire. He also informed us that the horses would alert the group if there were any cougars in the vicinity of the camp.

I must admit after day one I was sore. I seemed to stay in the deep bath for a while in the hope for a miracle cure. Wishful thinking. Following a hearty evening meal (steak of course) and a quick visit to see the horses I retired. Knackered but happy.

The following day my aches and pains had subsided somewhat, and I was upgraded to Tornado, a chestnut with a really kind head. He would be my four-legged friend for the rest of my stay. He was a little bit of a character, occasionally catching me out with a trot, particularly up inclines, and there were many. With the paths only a few feet wide and a drop of two hundred feet into the stream below I had to trust Tornado and he didn't let me down. Foot perfect. When we reached the summit the views across Wyoming towards Montana were breathtaking. Tornado took me to the very edge, standing totally still and allowing me time to not only see but to consume and digest a panorama that would last a lifetime. Now I really did feel like Clint Eastwood.

By day five, with some tuition from Howdy who was an expert roper, I was able to consistently rope the mechanical calf from six metres. He assured me that a five- month stay would enable me to progress to the real thing.

Twenty-five miles east of the ranch is the town of Cody where the pace of life is slow. The people are welcoming and friendly and most of the menfolk wear rodeo style hats. It is rightly billed as the Rodeo centre of America.

Originally the home of Buffalo Bill, famous throughout the world for his Wild West Show. Though never actually staged in Cody, the town became recognised for its nightly rodeo established in 1938. Open from 1st June to 31st August it is the only one of its kind in America.

The event started at 7.00 p.m., with the National Anthem and praise for all members past and present of the armed forces, something which is quite common at mass events in the United States. For the next few hours, the entertainment was captivating – bucking broncos, bull riding, horsemanship, team roping and so much more. The youngest competitor was twelve years of age. At one stage a raging bull was seen attempting to climb out of its pen, trying desperately to remove the hat off a nearby spectator with his horns.

At the interval, the commentator asked young members of the 3,000 plus crowd to gather in the arena. The guy sat next to me who had explained some of the nuances of the whole event during the evening casually informed me that the next event was an example of "Wyoming Day Care." Approximately a hundred children from age five to twelve gathered in the centre of the arena as three calves with red ribbons on their tails were let loose. The task was simple, pull off a ribbon and run to centre to get a prize. It was mayhem with many of the kids clearly enjoying the challenge of chasing the tails. Some ended up in the dirt and a lucky couple ended up with the ribbon. The whole show lasted about ten minutes with many of the participants exhausted but happy.

Closer to the centre of the town is the Buffalo Bill Historical Centre (now known as the Buffalo Bill Centre of the West). It takes you to the very heart of the history of the Wild West, bringing to life such characters as Buffalo Bill, Annie Oakley and Sitting Bull. Part of the complex included a museum that celebrates the life and traditions of the Plain Indians from the past two hundred years and the Whitney western art museum where the works of several renowned artists including Frederic Remington are displayed. They all captured the times and none more so than William Tyler Ranney's Burial on the Prairie which chronicles the tragic aspects of western migration with a young grieving family standing by a small grave, a sad reminder of the many children who died during the period.

A mile west close to the rodeo is Old Trail Town. Buildings and horse drawn carriages of historical significance to Wyoming have been gathered and relocated, positioned in the style of an old town pre-1900. Amongst the collection of the buildings is the Coffin School named after Alfred Nower who tragically died in the building from gangrene as a result of an accident whilst cutting logs.

There are twenty-six buildings all of which provide a fascinating insight into life at the time. Two however, provide important elements to the pilgrimage which started in Telluride, Colorado.

The River's Saloon was retrieved from the mouth of the Wood River. Its clientele of prospectors and outlaws included Butch Cassidy, Harry Longabaugh (the Sundance Kid) and Black Jack Ketchum, with its colourful past evidenced by the bullet holes in the door.

The second building, a two-room log cabin, was that used by Butch Cassidy and the Wild Bunch at the Hole in the Wall area, a remote and almost inaccessible pass in the Big Horn Mountains. For several minutes I sat in the chairs once used by the infamous outlaw to plan a series of train and bank robberies. Surrounded by photographs and artifacts the rebel inside was ignited in an escape from reality.

Following five days in the saddle it was time to move south to Thermopolis a town long associated with the outlaws but more importantly with thermal baths which the public could enjoy. At one hundred degrees Fahrenheit, the hot baths provided significant relief for my aching body and a break from the ongoing journey to Cheyenne.

The only further stop was at a geological oddity known as Hell's Half Acre. The deep ravine is packed with caves and unusual rock formations that protrude like teeth from its base. The name derives from its use by the native Indian population who would drive herds of Buffalo to their death providing food and hide for the harsh winter months. Standing on the edge of the ravine was one of the most uncomfortable moments of my life. I felt uneasy. I could sense death. It seemed to hang in the air. Time to move on.

My two-night stay in Cheyenne coincided with Frontier Days, a major exhibition of everything about the culture of the Wild West from food to clothing, saddles to guns and of course one of the biggest rodeos in the United States, followed each evening with a concert by a leading Country act. The event which takes place the final ten days of July attracts people from across America and beyond.

The grounds outside the arena are packed with horse drawn Wagons and exhibitors demonstrating their skills with fabric, metal, clay and wood. There was, of course various chuck wagons serving some of the tastiest barbeque available.

Lance Grabowski was different than the rest. He had a range of animal skins and furs on display. A mountain man for over forty years, living alone he survived through his hunting skills. In one year, during a two-week period, he collected 125 pelts, mainly fox and racoon, for sale to the masses living on the East coast. Now accepting commissioned work only (usually from Hollywood studios) he still resides for much of the year in his mountain retreat.

The rodeo event began at 1.00 p.m. and concluded at 5.00 p.m. It was on a different level to the local nightly event at Cody, with prize money of a million dollars available. There were all the traditional events, saddle and bareback riding, team roping, steer wrestling and barrel racing but also a couple of events which made me smile. The first featured a dozen foals who had been separated from their mothers. They were gathered at the far end of the stadium and about 150 yards at the other end were their mothers. Once the gate was opened for the foals it was a race to see which one located his mother first. Some wandered around lost for a short time before picking up the scent and running towards their waiting food supply.

The final event involved fifteen teams of three cowboys. One had the responsibility to rope a horse, the second to put a saddle on him and the third to ride one lap around the outside of the stadium. It seemed easy having seen many of the cowboys in operation. That was until they brought into the arena fifteen wild horses. The fifteen minutes that followed provided intense amusement with rope men being dragged through the dirt by horses, one even being kicked in the teeth. Saddle men jumping around to catch ejected tack or avoid a rampant horse whilst his partner frantically held on for dear life. Eventually three teams were able to complete the task which had considerable prizemoney for the winner plus an appearance on television. Once completed the crowd vacated the stadium which was then prepared for an evening concert featuring Rascal Flatts, a major Country act.

Some migrated to the square in the centre of town with multi-coloured statues of a cowboy boot on every corner and a stage for performers. One particular corner was the domain of the Harley-Davison owners, with their mechanical chrome stallions gleaming in the evening sun, standing proudly in line, unmoved by the attention of the passing stream of people.

With a beer I sat and watched as the square began to populate. Within several minutes I noticed a significant dynamic emerge. In the manner that oil separates from water the cowboys who had participated in the rodeo, many still in their muddied Levi's, separated from their families. Together the cowboys gathered in small groups, no doubt discussing the day's action, whilst their wives or partners were confined to the "outer circle" designated to look after the children. After an hour or so they eventually merged as the evening entertainment kicked in and family life resumed.

Cheyenne in the last days of July is alive with activity and music and Frontier Days serves an abundance of culture and entertainment in equal measure. I could easily have stayed for more but sadly it was time to move on south to rejoin US 50. The loneliest road in America was calling out to me.

# Chapter Thirty-Six

Westbound US 50 was pleasant and uneventful with the road passing through mountain valleys and past hidden small towns until eventually reaching the Colorado National Monument on the western edge of the state. Established by presidential acclimation the area is home to some of the most memorable landscape of the American West. Rim Rock Drive is twenty-three miles of twisting road rising through the sandstone and granite pillars to what was a high desert plateau. Along the route it provides amazing views of the differing rock formations including the Kissing Couple and the Coke Ovens, a series of rocks standing 6,000 feet high, which looked remarkably similar to the bottle ovens familiar to all who live in Stoke-on-Trent.

A couple of hours later, having crossed into Utah, and over the Colorado River, I checked into the Lazy Lizard hostel in Moab. The hostel had various choices from single rooms to mixed dormitories. For six dollars a night, including clean sheets I opted for the male dormitory which had one other resident, Joe from Oklahoma who had cycled over a thousand miles to reach the town.

The town is small but attracts visitors from all over the world due to its proximity to the Arches National Park and its terrain for mountain-bikers. Having settled into my "home" for the next two nights I wandered down Main Street in search of food, particularly Pizza. The first restaurant I found advised me to wait in the adjoining bar until a table became available. I ordered a large beer. Within minutes, the waitress called me into the seating area, and I walked over carrying my beer, at which point I was apprehended by a member of staff and informed that I was not allowed to carry the beer personally. Only a member of staff was authorised to carry or serve alcohol. Utah was a dry state with strict rules on the sale and consumption of alcohol.

The pizza was exceptionally good, and the beer was wet. Further down the street I could hear live music which has always been a magnet. In a small bar a troubadour delivered some American classics from Dylan to John Prine and following my request, Jerry Jeff Walker's classic Mr. Bojangles. Once he realised I was from England, he even threw in a Beatles number. His name was Jack (short for Jackson), and I bought him a beer during his break. He informed me that several years earlier he had spent a whole summer in Europe busking, mainly in Germany and England. I told him of my Manchester roots and my love of street musicians, at which point the perception that some Americans have surfaced again in his question.

"Do you know Bill in Blackpool? I busked with him a for a couple of weeks back then. Nice guy"

There is a belief, that on our small island everybody knows everybody else. Mention your hometown and there is an expectation that if they have met someone who originates from within a thirty-mile radius you would know of them. To not know a native of Manchester would be pure ignorance. He seemed disappointed with my response.

Early the following morning I travelled the short distance to The Arches National Park where temperatures often reached 110 degrees by midday. The visit was amazing with some of the world's most iconic rock formations including the Double Arch, Window Rock and the magnificent Landscape Arch with a span over eighty-eight metres examples of the artistic quality of the wind and sun. Incredibly nothing is done to protect the formations with nature allowed to take its course and a few weeks later the twenty-two metre wide wall arch, which had existed since before the pyramids were built, collapsed. In time, new structures will appear to fascinate a new generation of visitors.

Whilst at the Park I met Jess, Fred and Ronnie, three retired men in their late fifties who on their Harley Davison motorcycles, made annual trips to various destinations in the United States. This year they would enter the Glacier National Park and parts of Canada before returning to life in Arkansas, 8,000 miles later. With saddle-bags and boots they were the Twenty-first century cowboys.

The four-hour drive to Delta along US 50 had only one point of interest. A pull-in area to the side of the highway which provided a magnificent view across the rugged landscape of mesas, caves and canyons. The large information board described it as "Outlaw Country" stating that amongst others Elza Lay, Flat Nose George, Kid Curry and the infamous Butch Cassidy and the Wild Bunch had evaded the law here at different times. How the area was even navigable with a horse was beyond belief.

It was ironic that a few feet away from the boards was a large white cross dedicated to patrolman Dennis Lund who was shot and killed whilst pursuing a stolen car on this stretch of the highway in 1993. Outlaw country indeed.

I stopped for lunch in Delta and stocked up on water and fuel in readiness for the six-hundred mile journey along the loneliest stretch of road in America. The first part of the journey was easy, across flat and arid land. There were occasional small buildings scattered on hillsides, the timber frames showing signs of age with some having been replaced by trailers. Many of them had a small coral or barn with horses. This was remote living.

About sixty minutes into the drive, having not seen another vehicle for at least thirty minutes I decided to get out of the car to take a photograph of the straight highway gently disappearing into the distant horizon with heat rising from its surface. I was into my third or fourth shot when the wind slammed shut my car door. Following another couple of shots I returned to the car, whose engine was still running, to discover that not only had the door slammed shut but the locking mechanism had also dropped down. I was locked out of the car.

For a few minutes I tried shaking the door, hoping to release the mechanism, but to no avail. I tried the rear door but that too was locked. My phone was on the passenger seat, not that it would have been any use, having to phone England to get emergency help in Utah. Maybe the boot would be open, and I could climb over the back seat? No chance.

Maybe if I waited another motorist may drive by and be able to help? The option to smash the driver's side window and complete the rest of journey to San Franscico and pay the penalty charge on arrival at the drop off centre was a last resort.

Twenty minutes seemed to be forever as I sat and waited with still no site of a vehicle and sweat dripping down my neck and shoulders. I noticed several buzzards circling high in the sky no doubt contemplating a possible meal without wheels. Finally, I walked around to the passenger side to look for a rock. It was then that I noticed to my surprise and absolute delight, the passenger door was unlocked which was a complete freak occurrence.

When filling the car with fuel in Delta (my only fear was an empty tank), I had paid in the shop and returned to the car with water in hand and being on auto-pilot got into the right side (passenger) of the car as I would have done in England, before stepping out and casually transferring across to the other side, under the watchful eye of the attendant who was obviously questioning my faculties and ability to drive.

I did not stop again until I reached the Border Line Motel and gas station. Despite being one building the motel was partly in Utah and partly in Nevada. Payment for gas and food stuffs were paid for in the Utah section and everything else in Nevada. The distinguishing feature was the Nevada zone was equipped with tables for dining and a wall lined with fruit machines. Alcohol was available to buy and consume.

I had a coffee and some cake before striking up a conversation with a guy called Gary who had lived in the area for nearly forty years. He explained that the large hotels and casinos in Las Vegas were attempting to buy ranches in the area, not for farming but to pump water from the artesian wells below the surface to the gaming capitol who currently had to buy their water from neighbouring Colorado. The diversion of the water would impact on the whole of the farming community in northern Nevada eventually turning the area into a wasteland with no farming and no employment.

My overnight stay was planned for Ely a small town on US 50. When I approached the outskirts of the town, I noticed scrub land on the left side of the road which appeared to have a community of trailers of different ages and condition placed at a variety of angles. The land had obviously not been levelled or cleared. From my travels I knew that this was Reservation land. Across the bridge was a different town, with clean and preserved buildings and sidewalks.

By complete chance the evening of my stay in Ely coincided with a Pow Wow taking place a few miles north of the town. The gathering between the Shoshone and Paiute tribes aims to celebrate Native American culture through music, dance and pastimes, passing down their traditions and beliefs to a new generation. More than four-hundred people gathered for what was an uplifting experience with the whole ceremony opened by an emotional address from a female elder wearing traditional costume. It was not necessary to understand the language, her voice carried a spiritual message which resonated with all present, a call for respect, tolerance and peace for all nations. The period of silence at the end was to remember all who had departed this life.

All members of the tribes were dressed in colourful costumes, adorned with feathers and ornate head-dresses as they danced to the chants and the beat of the drums. For each there was a sense of pride on their faces and in their stature. There were small groups taking council from the elders and babes in arms, whilst young children played pitch and toss. The whole experience was a joy to the senses.

Before leaving Ely, I collected a small passport type document from the information centre. This was a promotion by Nevada to encourage people to make the historic trip along US 50 from Ely to Carson City, three-hundred miles through salt flats, desert and ghost towns. A journey through an essential part of American history. At various places during the journey the document would be stamped before finally surrendering it at the Capitol building in Carson City to confirm that I had indeed completed the journey along the Loneliest Road in America.

The town of Eureka is eighty miles west of Ely. Allegedly named after a miner's exclamation when he discovered silver ore, it once had a population of over 10,000 when lead was a major mineral mined around the town. It still retains an Opera House (similar to Leadville), a Court House and the historic Jackson House Hotel.

A kind volunteer at the Sentinal museum explained the history of the area as she walked me through various items of interest from early printing presses to mining and farm equipment. Numerous photographs testified to the expanse of this once booming town whose population had now sadly dwindled to less than seven-hundred.

I did go into the General Stores on Main Street, a small white building with the only internal light being from the two windows and one hanging light. The storekeeper was an elderly woman sat behind a counter which separated a storeroom with various items of equipment from the food and drink displayed on the shelves. Most of the food was canned, with some seemingly from a previous century. Out of courtesy I bought some candy and a drink from the small fridge, the only obvious appliance before venturing across the road for some food.

The drive from Eureka to Austin is desolate with little evidence of life in between each town as you cross the Great Basin rising from flat open space into the mountainous terrain of Austin, another ghost town which clings on desperately to life with US 50 its lifeline. With four churches, including a Catholic church, a few small shops, an International Serbian bar (no kidding) and a gas station serving the two-hundred plus residents there was a high dependency on the passing trade, with the next town Fallon almost one-hundred and twenty miles away.

An hour down the road stands Old Middlegate Station established in 1860 for the Pony Express and the Overland Trail Stagecoach. To describe it as a bar is an injustice. The old wooden building with its sheltered porch and abandoned horse drawn trailer and wagon wheels is more of a refuge and iconic building located "in the middle of nowhere".

The bar inside is warm and welcoming with many original features. Russell the owner was very sociable, explaining that they visited Fallon seventy miles away once a fortnight for supplies, so they had to be organised. There were no deliveries. When asked about customers and how the bar was viable, he explained that there were still men living in the surrounding hills prospecting for gold and silver. They may not appear for months on end, or even years. However, when they did strike lucky, they descend on the Station to party for several days, staying in the adjoining motel rooms which have been added close by, before travelling to Fallon with their find.

Russell had taken over the bar on this day twenty-three years earlier in 1985 at which time he encouraged visitors not to leave a tip but stick dollar bills on the ceiling so that when they return, they would already have a drink paid for. I bought him a drink and stuck a dollar bill on the ceiling with Pop/Manchester clearly inscribed in black felt-tip pen.

Further down the road I came across the famous "Shoe Tree" on US 50. The story behind the tree which is adorned with shoes hanging from its branches is that a married couple on their way to Fallon had an argument and in frustration the man threw a shoe into the tree which stuck in the branches. On reaching Fallon, the couple resolved the argument and made up, but the wife insisted that they drive back to the tree and throw the remaining shoe to join the other as shoes belong together, just as husbands and wives do. Since that time, throwing your shoes into the tree is supposed to bring you luck in marriage.

I was compelled to contribute to the story of the tree and removed my now very worn Ted Baker boat shoes, tied them together and flung them high into the branches. Sadly, the exercise is not that easy. I made several unsuccessful attempts throwing and retrieving my shoes in a manner of someone possessed, before they eventually hung from the branches close to some walking boots and several pairs of training shoes. A little bit of Britain hanging in the desert sun.

I drove on to Fallon, passing the two-mile long Sand Mountain with its huge singing sand dunes that whistle and boom as the wind passes over them to my right and a little further on my left an extensive area of pure white salt flats. Fallon in comparison had little of interest so I continued my journey to Carson City, passing the unmistakeable sign which indicated the direction of Denis Hoff's infamous Moonlight Bunny Ranch, where prospectors and cowboys alike were sure to be kept warm on a cold night.

Within thirty minutes I had checked into my hotel in Carson City, showered and changed ready for a visit to the steak restaurant across the road followed by a brief encounter with the roulette wheel in the adjoining casino.

Carson City is a beautiful town with some fine historical buildings, including the Capitol Building. It is named after the legendary frontiersman and scout Kit Carson and was a major station for the Pony Express service on the route from its westernmost destination Sacramento, California. Following a walking tour of the city and a visit to authenticate my passport at the Capitol Building where I received the final of five stamps, a certificate, key ring and pin badge confirming that I had completed the journey, I left for the short drive along US 50 towards Lake Tahoe.

For three nights I camped on the South shore of the stunning Lake with its backdrop of mountains and pine trees. The approach to the camp site again provided the interesting division between states with Bally's Casino proudly standing on the corner where a set of traffic signals indicated the divide between Nevada and California.

The peace and calm of the lake plus the warm weather was a welcome relief from my travels. It allowed me time to reflect on the places I had been and the sights I had seen; on the people I had met from various sections of American society and their willingness to engage in conversation. During the thirty-nine days I had been challenged and at times scared, but I had also been enthralled and excited navigating areas which had only ever been a place on a map or a location on a film.

Before leaving the campsite early in the morning I dismantled my tent and gathered together the more useful equipment I had used for the past thirty-nine days, placing them outside the dormant tent of a single parent mother nearby who was at the start of a ten-day vacation with three young children cramped into a small tent.

Then all that was left was a final journey for the cowboy from Manchester. With my Wrangler boots and rodeo hat I headed through Gold Rush country and on to San Francisco. My heart, however, had already been lost, far away in the Rocky Mountains.

# Chapter Thirty-Seven

The department had functioned well during my time away in North America. Phil had enjoyed the extra responsibility, and the examination results had been excellent. It was time, however, to return to the real world.

Though there were good athletes in each year group, there was a particularly strong group of fourteen-year-olds who were very keen on handball. They had a combination of technical ability, speed and strength. They had the potential to set the bar for following years. All they needed was a push.

Ryan was one of the most gifted performers I worked with over the years. He was a strong soccer player and a capable athlete. In handball he was outstanding. He was a committed and reliable student but could at times be frustrating. He would sometimes seek to perform the spectacular, be it the shot at goal from the half-way line in football (he did eventually score one from many attempts) or the improvised finish in handball. He did not do ordinary.

Shemik was smaller but more agile and was very direct. A talented table-tennis player he was effective in both attacking and defensive phases of play with his quickness of thought and action. Together they were almost unstoppable, eventually becoming National Schools' Under-15 Champions and National Under-16 County Champions. Their finest hour, however, was when they defeated NEM Hawks from Manchester, one of handballs top clubs, to become England Handball Association Under-18 champions. The success had a significant impact on not only the boys in the years below but also the girls, who included the game as part of the Key Stage 3 curriculum.

By this time, the school lunch breaks were being reduced almost annually, eventually reaching a cap at thirty-five minutes. The opportunity to run practices during the break had diminished and changes had to be made. On three days from January to April, I would present street-handball for differing years. Players turned up, trainers on, ties off and joined in a game. Games would often start as 3 v 3 but as more players arrived the game would eventually become 7 v 7. Later arrivals would form a new team ready to compete. It was quick to organise and effectively engaged students. A couple of girls asked about a handball team and I suggested that they should join in with the street handball, expecting the suggestion to be dismissed. When mentoring coaches in both handball and football I would always remind them to expect the unexpected. Performers have a habit of surprising you.

Eight girls appeared on a regular basis to take part. They were integrated with the boys and at first would receive the occasional pass only. The girls were not perturbed and were persistent, as their abilities improved so did their inclusion.

I was impressed with their enthusiasm and commitment so arranged some after-school sessions. They were very coachable and responded well. I organised a couple of games which they seemed to enjoy. The following year, the team of eight girls represented Staffordshire in the National Under-16 County competition held at Wellington in Somerset. The girls were amazing, winning all their games to become champions, defeating teams from handball hotbeds such as Cheshire and London. It was time to get a little more serious with the girls.

Maria Moore, who had herself played in the girl's team which had won the National Championships in 1986 and was now a local physical education teacher agreed to coach the team. We entered the girls into the Under-18 National League, only the second female team ever to represent the club, but times were changing.

For the next two seasons they finished runners-up in the league and reached two cup finals. Their momentum created a significant swell in the years below them at the school where a group of girls, several from St. Luke's Primary School, were beating teams readily. They became National Schools Under-13 champions and then the following two years won the Under-15 championship without losing a game. They were a joy to work with, each having different qualities. Liv was technically and tactically one of the best junior players of the decade and Athalia was quick, agile with a terrific shot. Supported by Hannah, with abundant stamina, Annie an intelligent and strong defender and Megan a fearless keeper they became National Club Under-18 and Under-19 League Champions.

Their final game together was at the Copper Box, built for London 2012, against Great Britain Under-19. In a fast and furious game, the girls from Cannock stormed to a 40-29 victory, testimony to the amazing work that Maria had done over the years. Sadly, despite her team having been undefeated for two years she was not awarded the Female Coach of the Year by the England Handball Association. An abject failure of the officers of the Association to recognise not only commitment, but the personal qualities that enabled her to support and guide every player on their journey to an unmatched threshold.

Within months of my return Phil was offered a head of department role at a school closer to his home in a socially deprived area. Though he was a major asset and a valued friend I suggested he consider a move to enhance his career development. The challenges were immense, but he had the quality and commitment to succeed. Replacing one of the best teachers I have worked with was never going to be easy. Ten years later he returned to the area to become headteacher at a leading academy.

Just before the end of the school year the headteacher asked for a meeting. He proposed that a new post Director of Sport be created leaving an opening for a younger Head of Department to steer the highly successful vocation courses created by Phil. My brief would be to promote the school to a wider audience and using my contacts establish fixtures against some of the leading public schools. I was also expected to explore possible grant-aid opportunities for facility development. I would still have a full teaching timetable.

With the support of Steve Biggins, a long-time friend and director of football at Shrewsbury School, I was able to arrange fixtures against some of the established private schools in the area for a Wednesday afternoon. There was first XI, second XI and in some cases an Under-14 game. I was encouraged to play games away from Cannock, firstly to make it easier for schools to accept but also to provide the students with a different experience. Their response at all games was a tremendous reflection on the character of the players and the good name of the school. Every school was keen to include the fixture on their list going forward.

The second part of my role was more intriguing and a challenge. It was an opportunity for me to secure improved facilities for the school which would endure long after my departure.

Many years earlier I had directed Peter Bateson, the then headteacher, to accept the offer made by a local farmer to sell some land to the school for additional playing fields. The parcel of land, approximately 4.5 acres, was purchased by the school for £5,000. A dozen years later, a major housing company offered £2.5 million for the land on which they planned to build ninety-five houses and though the school accepted the offer, with a caveat of alternative facilities being built on land near to the school, the local council refused the planning application.

The original proposal was for a large tarmac area and an adjoining grass area which was only used in summer for softball due to its tendency to retain water for much of the year, to be converted into an all-weather playing area. I felt it was time to revisit the plans.

During the early part of this century the number of football pitches around the area had been drastically reduced. Football pitches associated with works teams such as GKN, GEC and Lucas had been sold for commercial use or housing. Often in such cases there was financial compensation, to ensure that the local community would not be deprived of sporting and recreational facilities. The Section 106 agreement stipulated that any such facility be constructed within 1.5 miles of the existing playing field to ensure a minimum of inconvenience and ease of access.

The sale of Cannock Youth Centre and the Mid Cannock Social club for the construction of a large supermarket, removed two of the best football pitches in the district. Over half-a-million pounds was given to the local council by the developers to spend on a project to replace them within five years. For four years there appeared to be stagnation, so I decided to apply for that money to provide an all-weather football pitch at Cardinal Griffin which would serve the wider community of Cannock Chase. Despite frequent meetings I was informed that the money was to be allocated to another project in the district. The project had started sometime earlier but had stopped for various reasons and had no definite competition date. It was incidentally, never completed.

A good friend and a former parent reminded me of a smaller pot of money that the council had received for the loss of a football pitch at Lucas Lighting in Bridgetown. Initially, the council had designated the money for the improvement of a local park and pathway, but it did not include a football pitch. With the support of Staffordshire Football Association, I eventually managed to convince Mike Edmonds, the Director of Leisure at the council, to support our project.

Over the next eight months regular meetings between the school, the Football Foundation and Cannock Council resulted in an outline plan for a full-size artificial turf football pitch to be constructed at Cardinal Griffin on the site proposed twenty years earlier. If approved by the local planning committee it would be the first project undertaken on the Football Foundation Framework, a scheme to help with the provision of more facilities for more teams.

The outline plans were submitted to the council, but a vocal group of local residents opposed the development. Years earlier the science department had established a small pond in an area adjacent to the existing playground to examine pond life. However, in recent years it had been severely neglected being reduced to a small pool of water with rubble and debris being its main components. There had been, however, in the past, sightings of frogs in the area. The group insisted that the development would threaten the natural habitat of the frogs, and a suitable alternative would need to be constructed and monitored over a period of time.

Ecology experts were engaged to supervise the building of a new pond in an area of meadowland a hundred yards from the site and to ensure the safe transfer of frogs to their new home, which was equipped with polythene walls to prevent the frogs from climbing out and returning to the former area. The site would be monitored by the Ecologist for a period of six weeks to confirm that the frogs had remained in the constructed pond.

Vandals destroyed the surrounding fence of the pond within the first two weeks and deposited a shopping trolley and various other items into the pond damaging the walls which allowed some frogs to return to the original habitat. Once repaired and cleared the frogs were returned and the six weeks of monitoring was restarted. Following further damage and the need to re-start the period again, I asked for a wider perimeter fence to be constructed within the existing vegetation. I then displayed two signs:

*"DANGER – Toxicodendron radican has been detected in this area and is highly dangerous. Contact may cause serious inflammation and damage to the skin. Please keep out."*

This proved beyond doubt that those responsible for vandalism could read, with the pond remaining intact which allowed the monitoring to be completed. A further resident asked for a bat survey to be conducted, which further delayed the application as these can only be administered at specific times of the year. The survey produced a negative response, confirming that the area was not in any flight path or close to any established roosts.

I then appeared before the planning committee to appeal against the original rejection, having satisfied all the conservation concerns. Sadly, one of the group opposing the plans was a former chairman of the school's Parent Teacher's Association who assured me that the development was a great idea, but not on his doorstep. There was a suggestion that the noise from the proposed facility would impact on Bluebell Wood, an ancient area near to the school. This was dismissed by the Committee when I informed them that for the past thirty years groups of students from the school had passed through the wood as part of the cross-country element of the curriculum without any impact.

One councillor insisted that noise and light pollution from the floodlights would impact on the lives of all residents within four-hundred metres of the development. Some of the committee seemed to nod in approval, until a long-standing councillor, who up until that point had remained silent, stood to remind the Planning group that they had previously allowed floodlights to be erected at the council owned Cannock Stadium which were actually less than twenty-five meters from his bedroom window. This seemed to seal the deal, and the plans were approved with the provision that an acoustic fence be erected to deflect any noise away from those living in the more affluent area of the district.

The Football Foundation framework provided a list of approved contractors which following review, was reduced to three who were all supplied with the project specifications. A meeting with all representatives from each funding agency and the contractors was arranged and following long discussions two remained. Each provided a sample of their carpet. They were both luxurious and would provide a fantastic playing surface. It was my decision to make.

"I would like to see a development where the carpet has been laid before I make a decision," I said, which seemed to surprise a number of those present. To me it seemed logical. I wanted to feel it beneath my feet, play on it and fall on it.

The first contractor informed me that there was no development in the United Kingdom with the specified carpet. To his knowledge the nearest was in Milan at the San Siro. The remaining contractor had a facility in the final week of completion near Glasgow.

Within twenty-four hours I received a call informing me that a flight to Amsterdam had been arranged for early Tuesday morning to assess the facilities at Ajax Academy which had two pitches with the specific carpet. The whole complex was fantastic with one of the pitches having cork infill instead of rubber. This I was assured by the director did not impact on performance, but players commented that it did not smell in warm weather. I changed my footwear and with the aid of a match ball ran, changed direction, passed and hit shots from the ground and in the air. I was like a kid a Christmas.

I also met with some of the staff and discussed the Ajax approach to gifted and talented young players, for which they were renowned. Young players would spend several afternoons and evenings per week at the centre combining football training with academic studies. The Academy placed a high priority on the latter. They would eat the correct foods to help with their development before being transported back at their homes later in the evening.

I was also taken for dinner at the Amsterdam Arena (now the Johan Cruyff Arena) the home of Ajax Football Club and had a tour of AZ Alkmaar's ground. Interestingly both grounds had banks of ultra-violet lights to help cultivate the grass as the level of sunlight during the football season was not sufficient.

The flight to Glasgow was booked for three days later. The new facility which was to be the home of a Second Division team, looked glorious in the mid-morning sunshine. I performed my usual routine with a ball on the pristine surface. It was kind to the body and significantly seemed easy to play on. From twenty-five yards I was able to hit the crossbar on three from five attempts. This was a dream surface.

Eventually Greenfields, the company with the development north of the border, were awarded the contract and they agreed to improve the access road to the facility at no additional charge.

There was, however, a further issue. The delays and charges caused by various objections and appeals had impacted on the overall cost of the facility. There was now a significant shortfall, and a make-or-break meeting was arranged, attended by the CEO of the Football Foundation. Both the council and the Foundation had provided grants to their limit. Other avenues were discussed with little ground gained and time running out for the project to be completed in the financial year. The CEO asked me to talk to the meeting about the development. For several minutes I explained not only the impact that it would have on the current players in the district but on the much younger generation who would have an opportunity to develop skills in a safe and appropriate environment. How the facility would be administered to facilitate juniors only in the early evening slots, with opportunities for girls, female teams and veterans all with an accessible price point which would enable the facility to generate a significant ring-fenced annual profit to be used to replace the carpet after ten years of use.

The CEO seemed impressed that all the administration for the facility would be in house. That attempts would be made to engage the whole football community. I sensed that he wanted to get the project over the line. I informed him of the shortfall amount after which he declared that the Foundation would meet the new demand to ensure that the process began as soon as possible. He then presented me with a cheque for the school which included the additional £69,000 shortfall and wished me luck.

The facility was completed in May 2012 and officially opened by Dean Smith, then the Walsall FC team manager, with a game between Chase Veterans and a Midlands ex- Professional players' team which included Dean Smith, Steve Biggins, Des Little, Richard Forsyth, Stevie Taylor and Des Davies. We named the facility the Liam Keeling Arena after a talented young footballer from the school who sadly died through meningitis at the age of thirteen.

With all the wheels now in motion, the headteacher arranged a meeting to discuss the project and establish if I would be willing to consider retirement at the end of the school year in July but remain as a consultant during the build of the pitch. Following a discussion with the Union, I accepted the offer with the provision that I be appointed as the Facility Manager going forward to ensure that the promises I made to the CEO and the Football Foundation would be implemented.

In July 2011, I formally retired from education after thirty-nine years. Throughout that time the daily contact with children had helped me grow as a person. The challenges, the unlimited banter and laughter, the enthusiasm and the support had not only been enriching but provided the motivation to continue with optimism and enterprise to ensure that everyone had the opportunity to engage in sport and in some cases travel outside the immediate area.

I have been fortunate to work with some outstanding professionals whose imagination, innovation and commitment was impressive and whose personal qualities were inspirational.

It was a time populated with characters, young and old, many who are still close friends. I have witnessed some grow from teenagers into parents and grandparents. I have celebrated with them at numerous weddings, birthdays and social events, where new stories always emerge, and old ones are re-cycled.

Recollections from a time long gone. Recognition that many of the lessons for life take place beyond four walls.

# Acknowledgements

My thanks go to all the young people I had the pleasure to work with
in both Staffordshire and at Camp Towanda in America many of whom
have become lifelong friends irrespective of distance. Their contribution
to my story is unquestionable.

To inspirational colleagues who embraced their opportunity to enrich
the lives of those in their care, swimming against a tide of bureaucracy
with unbelievable energy. They did make a difference.

To Glyn Harding for first inviting me into the world of professional
football and who for many years provided opportunities for many of my
students to extend their education at the University of Worcester.

Special thanks to Andy Lovell whose continual encouragement and
guidance has been invaluable in getting my story down on paper.

Finally, to my wife Diane and three children Verity, Paul and Stefan,
whose unconditional love and support has been the very foundation
upon which my life has been built.

Pop

2025

www.ingramcontent.com/pod-product-compliance
Lightning Source LLC
Chambersburg PA
CBHW022004080426
42733CB00007B/468